458-4574

Economic Education

ECONOMICS INFORMATION GUIDE SERIES

Series Editor: Robert W. Haseltine, Associate Professor of Economics, State University College of Arts and Science at Geneseo, Geneseo, New York

Also in this series:

AMERICAN ECONOMIC HISTORY—*Edited by William K. Hutchinson**

ECONOMIC DEVELOPMENT—*Edited by Thomas A. Bieler**

EAST ASIAN ECONOMIES—*Edited by Molly K.S.C. Lee**

ECONOMIC HISTORY OF CANADA—*Edited by Trevor J.O. Dick*

ECONOMICS OF EDUCATION—*Edited by William Ganley**

ECONOMICS OF MINORITIES—*Edited by Kenneth L. Gagala*

HEALTH AND MEDICAL ECONOMICS—*Edited by Ted J. Ackroyd*

HISTORY OF ECONOMIC ANALYSIS—*Edited by William K. Hutchinson*

INTERNATIONAL TRADE—*Edited by Ahmed M. El-Dersh**

LABOR ECONOMICS—*Edited by Ross E. Azevedo*

MATHEMATICAL ECONOMICS AND OPERATIONS RESEARCH—*Edited by Joseph Zaremba**

MONEY, BANKING, AND MACROECONOMICS—*Edited by James M. Rock*

PUBLIC POLICY—*Edited by Michael Joshua**

REGIONAL ECONOMICS—*Edited by Jean Shackleford**

RUSSIAN ECONOMIC HISTORY—*Edited by Daniel R. Kazmer and Vera Kazmer*

SOVIET-TYPE ECONOMIC SYSTEMS—*Edited by Z. Edward O'Relley**

STATISTICS AND ECONOMETRICS—*Edited by Joseph Zaremba**

TRANSPORTATION ECONOMICS—*Edited by James P. Rakowski*

URBAN ECONOMICS—*Edited by Jean Shackleford**

*in preparation

The above series is part of the

GALE INFORMATION GUIDE LIBRARY

The Library consists of a number of separate series of guides covering major areas in the social sciences, humanities, and current affairs.

General Editor: Paul Wasserman, Professor and former Dean, School of Library and Information Services, University of Maryland

Managing Editor: Denise Allard Adzigian, Gale Research Company

Economic Education

A GUIDE TO INFORMATION SOURCES

Volume 6 in the Economics Information Guide Series

Catherine A. Hughes

Librarian
Holcomb Center for Learning and Professional Development
State University College of Arts and Science at Geneseo
Geneseo, New York

Gale Research Company
Book Tower, Detroit, Michigan 48226

Library of Congress Cataloging in Publication Data

Hughes, Catherine A
  Economic education.

  (Economics information guide series ; v. 6) (Gale
information guide library)
  Includes indexes.
  1. Economics—Bibliography. 2. Economics—Study
and teaching (Secondary)—Bibliography. 3. Economics—
Study and teaching (Elementary)—Bibliography. I. Title.
Z7164.E2H8   [H62]   016.33   73-17576
ISBN 0-8103-1290-5

VITA

Catherine A. Hughes is the librarian of the Holcomb Center for Learning and Professional Development, State University College of Arts and Science, Geneseo, New York. She received her M.S. from the University of Syracuse.

CONTENTS

INTRODUCTION

In a recent article in the NEW YORK TIMES MAGAZINE, Leonard [S.] Silk referred to economics as a "discipline that nobody loves and many actively despise." This may be true, but surely there has never been a time when people have been so aware of this study. News magazines have added economics departments, television stations have economic commentators, newspaper headlines are frequently concerned with unemployment, inflation, fiscal policy, and tax relief. The president's economic advisors are important public figures. Books about banks are on the best-seller lists. Television programs are devoted to the state of the economy. People may despise economics but they are talking about economics, they are reading about economics, and they are viewing television programs about economics. The current period of economic unrest has done much to develop curiosity and concern about economics. Everyone needs to be more knowledgeable in this area.

In a book published in 1914, John Haynes insisted that "the elements of economics must be taught in some form in both high and elementary schools." It has taken us a long time to get to that point. In the early 1900s, many of the larger high schools were offering introductory courses in economics, most of them running half a year. Through the years the interest in the teaching of economics has risen and fallen. Economic education increased after World War I and after 1929. In 1947, only 2.7 percent of the high school students in this country had taken economics courses. The figure had risen to 5 percent in 1951.

The Joint Council on Economic Education was founded in 1949. Its single goal was to "reduce economic illiteracy by improving the quality and the quantity of economics taught in our schools and colleges--by trained teachers using effective teaching materials."

This council was founded because of the need expressed by leading educators from across the country at a 1948 New York University workshop on economic education. The Committee for Economic Development and the Ford Foundation's Fund for Adult Education supported the development of the joint council. This is an independent, nonprofit, nonpartisan, educational organization. The American Economic Association and American Association of Colleges for Teacher Education are officially affiliated with the Joint Council on Economic Education as are the professional groups within the National Education Association involved in economic education. A network of affiliated councils functioning at the state level and Centers for Economic Education on college and university campuses have been organized to expand and improve economic education.

In 1960 the American Economic Association appointed a National Task Force on Economic Education to find out what economic training was needed to equip high school graduates for good citizenship. The economic programs in our schools today have developed as a direct result of the findings in this report. The economic education movement to effect change in the teaching of social studies and to develop economically literate citizens has been spearheaded by the Joint Council on Economic Education and its affiliated councils and university centers. Reforms started in the high schools and then moved to the elementary grades. Among the greatest successes of the economic education movement is the development of materials and the evaluation of materials for the teaching of economics.

The materials in this guide represent a cross section of the books and media that are available to the teacher of economics. Material for preschool children through high school; books, pamphlets, charts, tapes, games, transparencies, films, filmstrips, pictures, and kits are included. The range is great. There are free ten-page pamphlets and expensive kits containing all of the equipment needed to teach a total elementary program. Materials have been developed by commercial companies, school systems, college workshops, and industrial organizations.

In this bibliography all materials have a grade level indicated: primary (Prim), elementary (Elem), junior high school (JH), and high school (HS).

A list of periodicals that contribute to the field of economic understanding or the teaching of economics is included. There is also a list of pamphlet series that have proved useful to teachers. These materials are frequently very inexpensive and can supply information on current issues. Periodical and pamphlet materials provide excellent information for supplementing text book teachings.

The following terms and organizations are frequently mentioned in this bibliography:

Committee for Economic Development (CED)

> The Committee for Economic Development is an independent research and educational organization. It conducts research and formulates recommendations in four areas: (1) the national economy, (2) the international economy, (3) education and urban development, and (4) the management of federal, state, and local governments.

Educational Resources Information Center (ERIC)

Educational Resources Information Center is a national information system designed to meet needs of the educational community by disseminating significant educational research and resources that are not available through major publishing channels. The function of this center is to acquire, select, index, and abstract documents and journal articles in particular subject areas.

Gross National Product (GNP)

Gross national product is the value of our total production of goods and services.

International Bank for Reconstruction and Development

The bank, popularly called the World Bank, was created by the United Nations Monetary and Financial Conference in 1944. There are more than one hundred member nations. It provides long term loans to members for the replacement of goods destroyed by war and to supply the needs of underdeveloped areas of the world. Loans are made to members who cannot obtain money from other sources at reasonable terms to assist them in developing their national economies.

Joint Council on Economic Education

The Joint Council on Economic Education is an independent, non-profit, nonpartisan, educational organization. The American Economic Association and American Association of Colleges for Teacher Education are officially affiliated with the Joint Council as are the professional groups within the National Education Association involved in economic education. A network of affiliated councils functioning at the state level and centers for economic education on college and university campuses have been organized to expand and improve economic education.

Chapter 1
AGRICULTURE

Ames, Gerald, and Wyler, Rose. FOOD AND LIFE. Creative Life Series.
Mankato, Minn.: Creative Education, 1966. 144 p. Illus. Elem.

This simply written and fully illustrated book covers all aspects
of the subject of food: the role of food in growth and nutrition;
history of food from hunters and gatherers and domestication of
herds to the development of great food species; the treasures of
the soil and the need for conservation; and the hungry world and
man's responsibility to man through research and education.

Cochrane, Willard W. THE WORLD FOOD PROBLEM: A GUARDED-
LY OPTIMISTIC VIEW. New York: Crowell, 1969. 331 p. HS.

This book analyzes the relationship of food production to consumption in both developed and underdeveloped countries. The
author concludes, from the data presented, that the future ratio
of food produced per capita can be kept near the present level
if technical skill and personal determination remain strong.

Committee for Economic Development. AN ADAPTIVE PROGRAM FOR
AGRICULTURE. New York: 1965. 74 p. HS.

A program for agricultural adjustment is proposed within the
framework of the free market. The "adaptive program" focuses
on the role of government in encouraging the movement of labor
and capital out of agriculture along with appropriate cushioning
effects upon people and property. The roots of the farm problem
are explored along with an appraisal of the measures taken.

_____. A NEW UNITED STATES FARM POLICY FOR CHANGING WORLD
FOOD NEEDS: A STATEMENT ON NATIONAL POLICY BY THE RESEARCH
AND POLICY COMMITTEE. New York: 1974. 66 p. HS.

Food shortages of 1974 have caused the committee to look at the
relationships of the United States with the world food market.
The productivity of the United States is of crucial importance to

1

the world at large. The part that the government should play in achieving maximum food production is discussed.

Dumont, Rene, and Rosier, Bernard. THE HUNGRY FUTURE. New York: Praeger, 1969. 271 p. HS.

The authors predict that 1980 will be a point of no return in food production, and advocate world coordinated trade, the extensive application of technically advanced agricultural methods, intensified use of fertilizers, land reform, the development of new sources of nutrition, and population control.

Freeman, Orville. WORLD WITHOUT HUNGER. New York: Praeger, 1968. 190 p. HS.

The author outlines the history of U.S. food relief to foreign countries from World War I to 1966; traces the history of the Food for Peace Act of the U.S. technical assistance in agriculture, and of American private and voluntary projects to help agriculture abroad. He has serious concern over the world food crisis but is encouraged that underdeveloped countries are being given technical aid by the advanced countries and that they are starting to help themselves.

Lewis, Alfred. NEW WORLD OF FOOD. New York: Dodd, Mead and Co., 1968. 79 p. Elem.

The future of the world depends in part on the abundance of food. This book discusses the progress man has made in the production of food through plant breeding, insect control, animal care, and improved methods of harvesting, storing, freezing, and packaging. The author calls attention to possibilities for increasing food production by developing and using new products from the seas.

Raskin, Edith. WORLD FOOD. New York: McGraw-Hill, 1971. 160 p. Elem.

The author discusses the ways man has improved his food supply by improving crop yield and livestock quality as well as by utilizing diverse food sources. Man's food supply has increased many times due to the breeding and genetic selection of animals and plants.

U.S. Department of Agriculture. THE FARMER'S WORLD: THE YEARBOOK OF AGRICULTURE. Washington, D.C.: 1964. 592 p. Distributed by Government Printing Office. HS.

This book reveals the vital stake everybody in the United States has in a healthy export trade for American agriculture, not only because farmers have so much to sell and because the livelihood of so many Americans besides farmers depend on it, but also because the world so greatly needs what we can offer.

_____. A PLACE TO LIVE: THE YEARBOOK OF AGRICULTURE 1963. Washington, D.C.: 1963. 584 p. Distributed by Government Printing Office. HS.

This book was written to inform all Americans about the effects of urbanization and industrialization on rural America and the need for plans and action so that people will have a proper place to live. It describes many natural and social changes that have occurred as a result of growing cities and gives suggestions for action to guide these changes.

U.S. Department of Agriculture, Farmers Cooperative Service. OPPORTUN-ITIES IN THE CO-OP BUSINESS WORLD: A LEADER'S PROGRAM FOR YOUTH. Washington, D.C.: 1969. 14 p. HS.

This program, on cooperatives in the American private enterprise system, is designed for youth as a study of local business organi-zations and operations or to further career interests in distribution, finance, law, or other areas as they pertain to local business opera-tion, including cooperatives.

MEDIA

AGRICULTURE AND INDUSTRY. Mahwah, N.J.: ERS Audio-Visual Division. 8 filmstrips. Color. Prim.

A wide variety of products, resources, and services used by the community are described. Titles are as follows: "Modern Agri-culture"; "Vegetables and Fruits"; "Dairy and Beef Cattle"; "Cotton and Wool Fibers"; "Modern Industry"; "Manufacturing Clothing"; "Manufacturing Trucks"; "Building Houses."

AGRICULTURE IN WEST AFRICA. Subsahara Africa Series. Santa Ana, Calif.: International Communication Films, 1968. Filmloop. Color. JH, HS.

The irrigation and harvesting of crops and livestock herding in both wet and dry areas are shown.

ALASKA'S MODERN AGRICULTURE. Los Angeles: Bailey Films, 1960. Film. 15 mins. Sound. Color. Study guide. JH.

The historical development of farming in Alaska is traced, con-trasting the struggles of early settlers with Alaska today. Con-servation and development of resources for recreation, transpor-tation, education, and the interdependence of the people are depicted.

Agriculture

CENTRAL FARMING REGION: FOOD FOR THE NATION. New York: McGraw-Hill, 1963. Film. 14 mins. Sound. Color. JH.

This film discusses the climate, drainage, and soil of the central farming region of the United States, pointing out the different kinds of farming and focusing on the changes in farm life since the region was first settled, stressing the role of highways.

THE CORN BELT. Bloomington, Ind.: Audio-Visual Center, 1961. Film. 17 mins. Sound. Color. Elem.

Dairy, feeder-cattle, and cash grain farming throughout the country are shown. Emphasis is placed on the interrelationships between corn farming, transportation, and rural and city life.

THE COTTON BELT: YESTERDAY AND TODAY. Bloomington, Ind.: Audio-Visual Center, 1961. Film. 17 mins. Sound. Color. Elem.

The story is told of the changes that have taken place in the southern states where cotton is grown and once was king. Now there is a greater diversity of crops and there are changes in man's physical and cultural environment.

THE COTTON FARMER. Chicago: Encyclopaedia Britannica, 1963. Film. 15 mins. Sound. Color. HS.

The film shows the advantages gained and the problems brought about by technological improvements in the production of cotton. Costs were cut and output increased but it was not always possible to sell the increased output.

COTTON IN TODAY'S WORLD. Chicago: Coronet Instructional Films, 1961. Film. 11 mins. Sound. Color. JH.

The evolution of cotton technology from the invention of the cotton gin to contemporary times is traced. The consequences of technological change are described.

CREDIT WHERE CREDIT IS DUE. Washington, D.C.: Farm Credit Administration, 1960. Film. 28 mins. Sound. Color. HS.

The film points out how the industrialization of American agriculture came about because credit was made available to the farmers. The American farmer has become among the most productive in the world because of the mechanization of the productive processes.

THE DAIRY. Santa Ana, Calif.: International Communication Films, 1965. Filmloop. 3 mins. Color. Elem.

In this single concept film milk is traced from the dairy farm to the consumer. The various processes in production from feeding cattle to bottling milk are followed closely.

DAIRY BELT. Bloomington, Ind.: Audio-Visual Center, 1962. Film. 16 mins. Sound. Color. Elem.

The region containing half of the milk cows in the United States is identified and described. Similarities and differences in production and marketing patterns are discussed. Two dairy farms, one in southeastern Wisconsin and one in central New York State, are compared.

FARM AND LABOR MOVEMENTS. Washington, D.C.: Civic Education Service. 18 transparencies. Color. Teacher's guide. HS.

Included are transparencies on: migration to cities, the Grange, overpopulation, machinery, scientific agriculture, working conditions, immigration, social legislation, and growth of labor unions.

FOOD AROUND THE WORLD. Chicago: Coronet Instructional Films, 1966. Film. 11 mins. Sound. Color. Teacher's guide. Prim, Elem.

Using examples from six continents, this film shows that local conditions of land and climate will determine the kinds of food people eat. The basic similarities in human needs are emphasized.

FOOD OF SOUTHEAST ASIA. Los Angeles, Calif.: Film Associates, 1966. Film. 18 mins. Sound. Color. Elem, JH, HS.

This film shows how the main foods of Southeast Asia (fish, rice, and vegetables) are produced and how they reach the consumer. It follows the activities of a fisherman, a rice grower, and a vegetable farmer.

FOODS WE EAT. Chicago: Singer/SVE, 1971. 6 filmstrips. Sound. Color. Elem.

This series attempts to acquaint children with how we get our major food resources and how they are produced or made available to the consumer. Titles are as follows: "How We Get Bread"; "How We Get Milk"; "How We Get Meat"; "How We Get Poultry and Eggs"; "How We get Fruits"; "How We Get Vegetables."

GROWTH OF FARMING IN AMERICA, 1865-1900. Chicago: Coronet Instructional Films, 1967. Film. 14 mins. Sound. B&W. HS.

The period from 1865 to 1900 was one of transition for the American farmer. The shift from small local opportunities to large national ones came about during this time. Economic difficulties brought about by rising farm costs, increasing transportation costs, unavailability of credit, and fluctuating prices led the farmers to seek political solutions through the Grangers, Populists, and the Free Silver advocates.

HARD TIMES IN THE COUNTRY. Bloomington, Ind.: National Educational Television, 1970. Film. 59 mins. Sound. B&W. HS.

This film describes the economic dilemmas facing many American farmers. Technology tends to favor large corporate farms over smaller family operated units. The farmers frequently sell their output to oligopolistic buyers and buy their inputs from oligopolistic sellers.

HOW FARMING HAS CHANGED. Chicago: Denoyer-Geppert Audio Visuals. Filmstrip. Color. Teacher's guide. JH.

The development of American agriculture from the age of the one-family farm to modern agribusiness is traced. The changes in farming, wrought by industrialization, and the impact these changes have had on the country as a whole are discussed.

MIGRANT WORKER. Pleasantville, N.Y.: Guidance Associates. 2 filmstrips: 10 and 12 mins. ea. Sound. HS.

These filmstrips were created exclusively from interviews and photos taken on location in Florida. They examine the life styles, working conditions, wages, housing, education, nutrition, racial attitudes, relations with townspeople, employers, and unions.

NEW SOUTH: ECONOMIC OVERVIEW. Wilton, Conn.: Current Affairs Films, 1964. Filmstrip. 42 frames. B&W. HS.

Changes in the southern economy, brought about by current technology are described. New uses of natural resources, the influx of industry, and improved agricultural methods now characterize the south.

OUR FOOD SURPLUS--A MIXED BLESSING. Wilton, Conn.: Current Affairs Films, 1964. Filmstrip. 42 frames. B&W. HS.

The application of science and technology has resulted in greatly increased productivity of the American farmers. In spite of this farm incomes remain very low. Government agricultural programs have not been successful in alleviating this problem.

SMALL FARM. New York: Sterling Education Films, 1967. Film. 11 mins. Sound. Color. Prim.

The film describes the operation of a strawberry farm and depicts all the decisions that must be made by the farmer from producing the crop to marketing it for ultimate consumption.

Chapter 2

BUSINESS AND INDUSTRY

Andreano, Ralph [L.]. NO JOY IN MUDVILLE: THE DILEMMA OF MAJOR LEAGUE BASEBALL. Cambridge, Mass.: Schenkman, 1965. 191 p. HS.

This is an analysis by an economist of big league baseball's condition. Included are commentaries on history of the game, development of baseball in Japan, the possibility of international competition, and the subject of baseball as big business.

AUTOMATION, CAPITAL EQUIPMENT AND ECONOMIC PROGRESS. Exploring Basic Economics Series. New York: Good Reading Rack Service, 1964. 14 p. HS.

A brief consideration of the productivity of capital equipment and how more capital produces more jobs. It indicates how automation can lead to greater productivity provided we use our knowledge effectively.

Buckingham, Walter. AUTOMATION: ITS IMPACT ON BUSINESS AND PEOPLE. Bergenfield, N.J.: New American Library, 1963. 169 p. HS.

This author reviews the fundamental principles and history of automation and its impact on industrial organization, unemployment, prices, economic stability, and economic growth. The book is written in nontechnical language.

Buehr, Walter. MEAT FROM RANCH TO TABLE. New York: Morrow, 1956. 95 p. Illus. Elem.

A survey of the American meat-packing industry, covering the raising of animals, their slaughter, and processing.

Bullock, Paul. STANDARDS OF WAGE DETERMINATION. Los Angeles: Institute of Industrial Relations, University of California, 1960. 99 p. HS.

The standards used to determine wages are described. These standards are as follows: cost of living, ability to pay, productivity,

family budgets, purchasing power, and technical and miscellaneous
factors. The usefulness, advantages, and limitations of these wage
determiners are analyzed.

Chamber of Commerce of the United States of America. BUSINESS UPS AND
DOWNS. Washington, D.C.: 1966. 32 p. HS.

This pamphlet answers questions such as what causes fluctuations
in business, how a sharp change in business can be predicted,
and how runaway booms and disrupting recessions can be prevented.

_____. NATIONAL INCOME. Understanding Economics Series, no. 5.
Washington, D.C.: 1967. 30 p. HS.

Economic accounting methods can be used to show the overall
results of such market actions as total production, income, and
consumption. It is explained how progress can be measured sta-
tistically, and how we can determine the direction in which the
economy is moving.

Chamberlain, John. THE ENTERPRISING AMERICANS: A BUSINESS HISTORY
OF THE UNITED STATES. New York: Harper & Row, 1963. 282 p. HS.

The author describes the growth of American business, from its
mercantile beginnings in New England and along the Delaware
and James River valleys to the great trade and industrial com-
plexes which span the free world today.

Chandler, Alfred D., Jr., ed. GIANT ENTERPRISE: FORD, GENERAL
MOTORS, AND THE AUTOMOBILE INDUSTRY. New York: Harcourt, Brace,
& World, 1964. 241 p. HS.

This is a collection of readings which analyze the impact of the
automobile industry on our economy.

CHILDCRAFT: HOW WE GET THINGS. Childcraft How and Why Library,
vol. 7. Chicago: Field Enterprises Educational Corp., 1972. 368 p. Elem.

The story of how more than 500 items of daily use are made,
distributed, sold, and used is told in this volume. Money, chew-
ing gum, foam rubber, and buttermilk are among the myriad commercial goods explained here. There is a special section on
"What's economics?"

Chilton, Shirley, et al. HOW PEOPLE LEARNED TO MOVE ABOUT.
Chicago: Children's Press, 1970. 54 p. Illus. Prim.

A description of the development of methods of transportation
from early times to space exploration and the effect of transportation on trade and cultural exchange.

_____. HOW THINGS WE USE ARE MADE. Chicago: Children's Press, 1970. 48 p. Illus. Prim.

This is an explanation of our free enterprise system: how a company starts, develops a product, and makes a profit for its stockholders.

_____. WHERE THINGS WE USE COME FROM. Chicago: Children's Press, 1970. 48 p. Illus. Prim.

Everyday products are traced from the retail distributors to the manufacturers to their natural sources. A description of surplus, scarcity, and the importance of conservation of natural resources is included.

Cochran, Thomas C. BASIC HISTORY OF AMERICAN BUSINESS. 2d ed. Princeton, N.J.: Van Nostrand Co., 1968. 191 p. HS.

This book focuses on the ideas, customs, and organizations which helped develop business from colonial times to the 1950s. The author discusses big business as affected by management, government, and society.

Dorfman, Robert. THE PRICE SYSTEM. Modern Economic Series. Englewood Cliffs, N.J.: Prentice-Hall, 1964. 152 p. HS.

The importance of prices in a modern economy is explained. The effect of business decisions on prices is considered.

Dutton, William S. ADVENTURE IN BIG BUSINESS: A STIRRING ACCOUNT OF AMERICA'S INDUSTRIAL GIANTS, HOW THEY GREW, HOW THEY AFFECT YOUR LIFE. New York: Winston, 1958. 118 p. Illus. Elem.

Described are the development of big business in America since 1900, the men who are associated with its growth, and the resulting advantages and disadvantages to American society.

Engle, Elizabeth W. KEYS FOR BUSINESS FORECASTING. 3d ed. Richmond, Va.: Federal Reserve Bank, 1969. 32 p. HS.

This booklet is directed at improving public understanding of the nature and significance of the statistical ingredients that go into professional analysis of business prospects. It describes in terms as nontechnical as possible the techniques that provide much of the basis for professional forecasts.

Federal Reserve Bank of Philadelphia. AUTOMATION. Philadelphia: 1964. 10 p. HS.

This introduction to the subject of automation defines the terms and shows how a society becomes more productive through automation. The pamphlet shows that historically automation decreases want and in the long run has not increased unemployment.

Gery, Frank, and Wagner, Lewis E. INCOME, EMPLOYMENT, AND PRICES. Primer of Economics Series, no. 4. Iowa City: Bureau of Business and Economic Research, State University of Iowa, 1972. 48 p. HS.

This monograph aims to help the understanding of basic economic relationships underlying prosperity and depression. It gives a framework for interpreting business fluctuations. Charts and illustrations are included.

Industrial Relations Center. PROFITS--SPARKPLUG OF THE ECONOMY. Basic Economic Series. Chicago: University of Chicago, 1965. 29 p. JH.

A simple objective explanation of the role of profits. It includes (1) problems of defining and measuring profit, (2) kinds of risk, (3) taxation, (4) role of incentive, (5) size of profit in the economy, and (6) the question of fairness of profit rates.

Kaplan, Abraham, and Prehen, Edward C. THE PROFIT SYSTEM. Economic Issues in American Democracy. Bedford Hills, N.Y.: Teaching Resources Films, 1972. 46 p. HS.

A thorough look at the subject of profits under the topics: the role of profits in economic development, the nature of profits, the structure of American business enterprise, evaluation of the profit system, analysis of the role of profits in free enterprise economies and in the Socialist economies of Eastern Europe.

Keyserling, Leon H. WAGES, PRICES AND PROFITS: PHASE II GUIDE-LINES VS. APPROPRIATE POLICIES. Washington, D.C.: Conference on Economic Progress, 1971. 88 p. HS.

The author discusses national goals and policies, the prevalent confusion about national goals and means, long neglect of basic goals or purposes, persistent economic imbalances, and cumulative evidence of the wage and salary lag.

National Council for the Social Studies. PRODUCTIVITY AND AUTOMA-TION. Washington, D.C.: National Education Association, 1966. 180 p. HS.

Designed for high school seniors, this is an analysis and description of productivity and automation. Concepts of productivity, GNP, growth, and technology are defined. There is a discussion of work as a social activity, work incentives, automation, and profit-sharing plans.

Paradis, Adrian A. BULLS AND THE BEARS: HOW THE STOCK EXCHANGE WORKS. New York: Hawthorn Books, 1967. 94 p. Elem.

Beginning with one man's idea for a new product, the author shows how a business may grow to a publicly owned corporation with stock in the hands of many shareholders. There are also chapters on the history of Wall Street and other stock exchanges, the working of a stock broker's office, and how to read a stock market report.

_____. BUSINESS IN ACTION. New York: Julian Messner, 1962. 191 p. Illus. Elem.

The American system of free enterprise is explained. The trends and problems of this system are described and the roles of government, labor, farming, and industry are discussed.

Philipson, Morris, ed. AUTOMATION: IMPLICATIONS FOR THE FUTURE. New York: Random House, 1962. 456 p. HS.

A varied collection of writings by nineteen authors, such as Arthur Goldberg, Peter Drucker, and Walter Reuther. Among these essays students will be able to find interesting discussions of the impact of automation on industry, labor, government, the social sciences, education, and leisure.

RESEARCH AND DEVELOPMENT--INVESTMENT IN THE FUTURE. New York: Good Reading Rack Services, 1967. 14 p. HS.

The role of research and development in the American economy is discussed. The benefits that consumers, employees, and stockholders can enjoy as a result of research and development is explained, but a note of caution is also sounded that research and development used unwisely could be unprofitable.

Ross, Myron H. INCOME: ANALYSIS AND POLICY. 2d ed. New York: McGraw-Hill, 1969. 477 p. HS.

Topics discussed are: definition of income, determination of the level of income and employment, cycles, growth and price level, public policy, distribution of income, international economic problems.

Shippen, Katherine B. MIRACLE IN MOTION: THE STORY OF AMERICA'S INDUSTRY. New York: Harper & Row, 1955. 150 p. Elem.

This is the story of three centuries of American industry--from colonial days to the present, from America's early days as an agricultural country until it emerged as the most powerful industrial country in the world. The author describes not only steps taken by government to curb monopolies but also the organization of labor to safeguard its rights.

Theobald, Robert. FREEMEN AND FREE MARKETS. Garden City, N.Y.: Doubleday, 1965. 173 p. HS.

The author contends that a guaranteed annual income is the only way to prevent the emergence of a technologically dehumanized consumer society.

_____, ed. THE GUARANTEED INCOME: NEXT STEP IN ECONOMIC EVOLUTION? Garden City, N.Y.: Doubleday, 1966. 237 p. HS.

Ten leading social scientists discuss the various implications of one of the most spectacular proposals to preserve our free enterprise system--the guaranteed income which is an extension of our present income-tax exemption in which each citizen would be guaranteed a basic income sufficient to live on.

Towle, Joseph W., ed. ETHICS AND STANDARDS IN AMERICAN BUSINESS. Boston: Houghton Mifflin, 1964. 315 p. HS.

This book is intended as a supplementary textbook for courses in management, public relations, government, and business. It deals with ethical problems in business administration.

U.S. Department of Commerce. DO YOU KNOW YOUR ECONOMIC ABC'S? Rev. ed. Do You Know Your Economic ABC's?, no. 1. Washington, D.C.: 1967. 46 p. Distributed by Government Printing Office. HS.

A simplified explanation of gross national product and how it mirrors our economy. It aims to make the lay reader aware of GNP and learn how it ties into his personal accounts and the welfare of the country.

_____. PROFITS AND THE AMERICAN ECONOMY. Do You Know Your Economic ABC's?, no. 3. Washington, D.C.: 1965. 48 p. Distributed by Government Printing Office. HS.

This is a simple explanation of profit and how it stimulates economic growth. The role of the profit incentive in the workings of our capitalistic system, the allocation of resources, price and its relation to competition, and the consumer as the balance wheel between supply and demand are discussed.

_____. SCIENCE AND TECHNOLOGY FOR MANKIND'S PROGRESS. Washington, D.C.: 1966. 46 p. Distributed by Government Printing Office. HS.

A simplified explanation of science and technology and how they

are applied to further economic growth. The role of research
and development and the results of inventions and innovations are
discussed.

Wagner, Lewis E. MEASURING THE PERFORMANCE OF THE ECONOMY.
Rev. ed. Iowa City: Bureau of Business and Economic Research, State University of Iowa, 1971. 43 p. HS.

This monograph explains how to measure changes in the operation
of the economy. The nature of commodity and money flows,
GNP, and the national income are discussed. Charts and illustrations are included.

Weiss, Leonard W. CASE STUDIES IN AMERICAN INDUSTRY. 2d ed.
Introduction to Economics Series. New York: John Wiley & Sons, 1971.
381 p. HS.

This book considers economic concepts and public policy in the
market place. Agricultural policy, regulation, antitrust cartels,
and trade union policy are all covered.

MEDIA

AGE OF SPECIALIZATION. New York: McGraw-Hill, 1957. Film.
15 mins. Sound. B&W. JH.

Changes that have taken place in agriculture and industry in the
first half of the twentieth century are described. The results of
rapid changes in technology are examined.

ALL THE FISH IN THE SEA. New York: United Nations Television, 1973.
Film. 30 mins. Sound. Color. JH, HS.

The dramatic emergence of Peru as the leading fishery nation of
the world has brought considerable economic benefit to the country. The discovery of vast shoals of fish in the Pacific Ocean
off the coast of Peru has led to the development of a large industry that processes fish meal for use as cattle feed and fertilizer;
however, the exploitation of this resource has brought a menace:
a whole species of fish is in danger of extinction because of
overfishing; further, none of the protein being won from the sea
is being used to improve the diet of the people of South America
who need it badly. The film shows how market demand in one
country can damage the environment thousands of miles away.

AMERICAN BUSINESS--ORIGIN AND GROWTH. South Holland, Ill.:
H. Wilson Corp., 1974. 4 filmstrips. Sound. Color. Elem.

These filmstrips tell the development of the Yankee peddler, the
general store, chain stores, A&P Tea Co., mail-order houses, and
the beginning of modern department stores. Authentic historical
background provides good basic information.

AMERICAN INDUSTRY: FROM ARTISAN TO AUTOMATION. Our National
Heritage Series. New York: McGraw-Hill, 1962. Filmstrip. 40 frames.
Color. JH.

Old handicraft skills are depicted as they are still practiced in
Williamsburg and Sturbridge. The growth of large-scale industry
and the role of American inventors in our country's development
are explored.

AUTOMATION: PROMISE OR THREAT? Pleasantville, N.Y.: Guidance
Associates. Filmstrip. 20 mins. Sound. HS.

Effects of automation on industry, labor, education, and medicine
are explored. Management consultant John Diebold examines the
social, economic, and geopolitical implications.

AUTOMATION: THE NEXT REVOLUTION. New York: McGraw-Hill, 1963.
Film. 20 mins. Sound. B&W. HS.

The film describes the development of automation and discusses
the need to develop socially beneficial adaptations to rapidly
changing labor-displacing technology. Automation is depicted as
a major source of social dislocation in the years ahead.

BUSINESS CYCLES AND FISCAL POLICY. New York: McGraw-Hill, 1950.
Filmstrip. 36 frames. B&W. HS.

Business fluctuations are described and the causes and possible
cures for economic stability are discussed.

BUSINESS ORGANIZATION. Chicago: Coronet Instructional Films. 6 filmstrips. Sound. HS.

Different levels of business organization and the division of responsibility among various departments are described. Interrelationships between different departments are stressed. Types of ownership, management, production, marketing, and accounting services
are discussed.

BUSINESS ORGANIZATION. Glenview, Ill.: Educational Projections Corp.
4 filmstrips. Color. Elem.

The organization of business, its operation, and its role in the
economy are explained in this series. Titles are as follows:
"We Learn about Business"; "How Business Works"; "Rules for
Business"; "Business is Important."

CITIES AND COMMERCE. Chicago: Singer/SVE, 1963. Filmstrip. 55 frames. Color. Elem.

The characteristics of several midwestern cities are depicted by showing their people, industries, and commerce. The importance of water transportation, power, raw materials, and commerce are described.

CITIES AND COMMERCE: WHERE WE GET OUR GOODS AND SERVICES. New York: McGraw-Hill. Film. 8 mins. Color. Elem.

Goods and services used regularly by a family are identified. Some of these services such as mail, gas, and electricity are delivered to their home, but they must shop for others such as food.

CITIES AND MANUFACTURING: WHERE WE MAKE THINGS. New York: McGraw-Hill, 1967. Film. 9 mins. Sound. Color. Teacher's guide. Prim.

The manufacturing and factory production of goods is shown. The division of labor, assembly-line production, and standardization of parts are discussed.

CITIES AND SHOPPING: WHERE WE GET OUR FOOD. New York: McGraw-Hill, 1967. Film. 9 mins. Sound. Color. Teacher's guide. Prim.

How people in the city obtain food, food processing and manufacturing, wholesaling, use of computers in filling orders, refrigeration, jobs in a supermarket, and the meaning of profit in business are explained.

CLOTHING: A PAIR OF BLUE JEANS. New York: Learning Corp. of America, 1974. Film. 15 mins. Sound. Color. Elem.

The film describes the process of clothing production, from harvesting the raw material to the marketing of the product. At each stage the viewers can see how raw goods, labor, marketing, advertising, and profit all affect the final price.

COMPETITION IN BUSINESS. Chicago: Coronet Instructional Films, 1962. Film. 14 mins. Sound. Color. JH, HS.

The pressures on a business by close competitors and potential rivals are discussed to illustrate how competition affects business behavior.

CONTROLLING THE BUSINESS CYCLE. Economics of Our Times Series. New York: McGraw-Hill, 1962. Filmstrip. 36 frames. Color. HS.

This filmstrip correlates with the text, ECONOMICS FOR OUR TIMES, by Augustus H. Smith. It describes a typical business cycle. Accelerator and multiplier analyses are introduced to explain cumulative movements. There is a discussion of built-in stabilizers and of contracyclical fiscal policy. (See Smith, Augustus H. ECONOMICS FOR OUR TIMES. Chapter 10.)

COTTON CLOTHING FROM FIELD TO YOU. Lakeland, Fla.: Imperial Film Co., 1968. 6 filmstrips. Color. Elem.

These filmstrips explain the long and complex process of producing cotton clothes. Many different skills and workers are involved. Basic information about how a segment of our economy operates is provided as well as information on a wide range of careers associated with the manufacture of cotton clothing. Titles: "Cotton Growing and Ginning"; "Cotton Spinning and Weaving"; "Designing Cloth for Clothes"; "Silk-screen Printing"; "The Garment Factory"; "The Retail Store."

DISTRIBUTION OF INCOME. World of Economics Series. New York: McGraw-Hill, 1963. Filmstrip. 34 frames. Color. HS.

This filmstrip correlates with THE WORLD OF ECONOMICS, by Leonard [S.] Silk. The significance of profits in the American economy is emphasized. Efforts of government to reduce gross inequities in the distribution of income are described. (See Silk, Leonard [S.]. THE WORLD OF ECONOMICS. Chapter 10.)

ECONOMICS: NEWSPAPER BOY. Santa Monica, Calif.: BFA Educational Media. Film. 10 mins. Color. Elem.

A newspaper boy is a businessman. He sells a product, provides a service, and makes a profit. With no narration except to pose questions at the beginning, the film allows the viewer to identify these basic economic concepts as they appear in this familiar situation.

ECONOMICS OF BUSINESS. Bedford Hills, N.Y.: Teaching Resources Films in cooperation with Joint Council on Economic Education, 1973. 2 filmstrips. Sound. Color. Teacher's guide. HS.

These filmstrips show that regardless of size the basic function of all business is the same: the bringing together of raw materials, labor, plant, and equipment to produce a product. The conflict between the business goal of profit and the public interest is examined and the regulations the government provides to protect the public are reviewed.

ENERGY FOR THE CITY. Cambridge, Mass.: Ealing Corp., 1969. Film-loop. 4 mins. Color. Elem. JH, HS.

This loop pictures the arrival of bulk fuel by sea, rail, road, or pipeline to be used directly or converted into electricity or gas, which is then distributed to many different industrial and domestic users.

FACTORIES AND THEIR WORKERS. Glenview, Ill.: Educational Projections Corp. 3 filmstrips. Color. Elem.

This series presents a brief history of manufacturing and describes types of work available in factories including assembly line production. Titles: "We Learn How Things Are Made"; "We Visit a Clothing Factory"; "Factory Workers."

THE FINANCIAL MARKETPLACE. Jamaica, N.Y.: Eye Gate House. 6 filmstrips. Sound. JH, HS.

This series is designed: to introduce the student to the various financial institutions in our economy; to show the student the different forms a business may take; and to give an understanding of the different methods a business may use to raise and apply capital. Titles are: "Institutions We Deal With"; "The Different Forms of Business"; "Going into Business"; "What is the Stock Market"; "How Does the Stock Market Work"; "What It Means to You."

FOOD: THE STORY OF A PEANUT BUTTER SANDWICH. New York: Learning Corp. of America, 1974. Film. 15 mins. Sound. Color. JH.

This film starts with a sandwich-making party and traces the peanut butter through its production from harvesting and processing the peanuts to the time when the jars of peanut butter arrive on the retailers' shelves.

FOOD IN THE CITY. A Child's Life in the Big City. Irvington-on-Hudson, N.Y.: Hudson Photographic Industries, 1968. Filmstrip. 42 frames. Sound. Color. Teacher's guide. Prim.

The importance of the distribution and preparation of food and the many types of foods and markets that are found in the city are explained. Street vendors, supermarkets, shops catering to ethnic groups, and food processing plants are pictured.

FUELS AND AUTOMOBILE PRODUCTION. Glenview, Ill.: Educational Projections Corp. 2 filmstrips. Color. Prim.

A guide at a science museum explains exhibits and tells about different types of fuel. A worker in an automobile factory shows the process of producing an automobile. Titles: "We Learn about Fuels"; "Automobile Workers."

GOING PLACES. Searcy, Ark.: National Education Program, 1960. Film.
10 mins. Sound. Color. Elem.

A boy starts a soap business that grows into a flourishing success.
The film details the problems and opportunities that are faced by
the firm in its search for profits.

GROSS NATIONAL PRODUCT. New York: McGraw-Hill, 1970. Film.
10 mins. Color. HS.

This film teaches how the gross national product is computed and
describes the various uses made of this computation. It emphasizes that the GNP does not measure the quality of life.

GROWTH OF BIG BUSINESS IN AMERICA, 1865-1900. Chicago: Coronet
Instructional Films, 1967. Film. 16 mins. Sound. B&W. JH, HS.

The growth of big business in the United States in the railroad,
steel, and oil industries is described. As a result of the growth of
these businesses during the period from 1865 to 1900, Congress
passed antitrust laws.

HOW CLOTHING IS MADE. Los Angeles: Film Associates, 1965. Film.
14 mins. Sound. Color. Study guide. Prim.

The steps used in mass production of men's shirts is followed from
the preliminary design to the display of the article in a department store, with emphasis on the specialized role of each machine
and operator.

JAPAN: MIRACLE IN ASIA. Chicago: Encyclopaedia Britannica Films, 1963.
Film. 30 mins. Sound. Color. Elem. JH.

This film explains how Japan's rapid industrial growth has influenced the way of life in the country and has affected the international political and economic position of the country.

MICHAEL'S MOON STORE. New York: AVI Associates, 1970. Filmstrip.
52 frames. Sound. Color. Teacher's guide. Prim.

The risks involved in starting a business are explained. Factors
of production are discussed.

THE MODERN CORPORATION. Los Angeles: Sutherland Educational Films,
1966. Film. 28 mins. Sound. Color. HS.

The film shows how a single proprietorship becomes a corporation.
It describes the principal effects of competition and monopoly.

MONEY TALKS: GOALS AND GROWTH. New York: Carousel Films, 1962. Film. 30 mins. B&W. HS.

The meaning and measurement of the gross national product are described. The importance of full employment is explained and ways of achieving this economic goal are suggested.

MOVING GOODS IN THE COMMUNITY. Chicago: Coronet Instructional Films, 1970. Film. 11 mins. Color. Teacher's guide. Prim.

The importance of different kinds of transportation in bringing the goods we need to our homes is shown. Trains, airplanes, ships, and trucks are all needed to move goods from factories to warehouses, to stores and to homes.

PROFIT AND COST EQUILIBRIUM. New York: McGraw-Hill, 1950. Filmstrip. 44 frames. B&W. HS.

This filmstrip describes the things that will shape a firm's decisions in establishing prices. The desire for profit, competition for materials, and market for goods are considered.

PROGRESS IN MIDDLE AMERICA. Santa Ana, Calif.: International Communication Films, 1965. Filmloop. 4 mins. Color. Elem, JH, HS.

The changes made in the economy of middle class Americans due to many development projects are discussed. The effects of electricity, technology, and modern architecture are clearly shown. Questions concerning the meaning of progress are raised.

THE PUBLIC MARKET. Seattle, Wash.: King Screen Productions. Film. Color. Prim.

The public market offers a vital and dynamic cross-section of American life today. This film shows the activity. Early arriving farmers bring their fresh fruits and vegetables from country to city. Spice merchants and junk dealers open their shops in the early morning quiet. Displays are arranged. By noon, the marketplace is crowded, people crowd in to look and to buy.

A RETAILER VISITS THE MARKET. New York: Fairchild, 1973. 36 slides, 2"x2". Color. Script. HS.

This set of slides follows the activities of a small retailer as she visits various wholesalers while on a buying trip in New York City. It examines the nature of a small retail store as well as the large merchandise producers.

THE SECURITIES INDUSTRY. San Bernardino, Calif.: Creative Studies. 6 filmstrips. Sound. Color. JH.

Through the use of dialogue, the filmstrips describe the process whereby a broker/dealer assists an investor in obtaining information on selected securities traded over-the-counter. Also shown are the functions of the market and the influences that affect investment decisions. Titles are: "How a Trade is Made"; "The Exchanges: Past, Present and Future"; "Evolution of a Corporation"; "Securities Markets"; "The Specialist"; "History of the American Stock Exchange."

THE SOUTHEAST: CHALLENGE AND CHANGE. Lawrence, Kans.: Centron, 1965. Film. 14 mins. Sound. Color. Teacher's guide. Elem.

Economic and social developments in the southern states are surveyed. It is shown how the growth of industry and commerce added to a changing agricultural economy has helped to make the South a land of challenge and change.

THE STORY OF THE WHOLESALE MARKET. Los Angeles, Calif.: Churchill-Wexler Production Films, 1963. Film. 11 mins. Sound. Color. Elem.

The basic activities of one workday at the wholesale produce market is shown. The film pictures the unloading of the trucks, the sorting and display of the produce, the arrival of buyers, and the cleaning and closing of the market at the end of the day.

VILLAGE MARKETS IN EASTERN EUROPE. Santa Ana, Calif.: International Communication Films, 1966. Filmloop. 4 mins. Color. Study guide. Elem, JH, HS.

The activities which take place in rural markets in all parts of Eastern Europe are shown. Here private "free enterprise" trading takes place even under a Communist economic and political system.

WHERE DOES IT COME FROM. 2 groups. Lakeland, Fla.: Imperial Film Co., 1971, 1972. 4 filmstrips in each group. Sound. Color. Elem.

To discover where everyday products come from, these filmstrips trace the process of producing important consumer goods explaining the skills and technology required at each stage of the process. These filmstrips present a wide ranging survey of our industrial economy in action and help the student to understand better his own role in the economic system. Titles in Group I are: "Where Do We Get Our Lumber?"; "Where Do We Get Our Milk?"; "Where Do We Get Our Paper?"; "Where Do We Get Our Bread?"; Titles in Group II are: "Where Do We Get Our Meat?"; "Where Do We Get Our Iron?"; "Where Do We Get Our Seafood?"

WHY COMMUNITIES TRADE GOODS. Los Angeles, Calif.: Churchill-Wexler Production Films, 1966. Film. 10 mins. Sound. Color. Study guide. Elem, JH.

Communities specializing in different types of production are described to illustrate the reasons for specialization and the advantages of exchange.

YOUR SHARE IN TOMORROW. New York: Modern Talking Picture Service, 1950. Film. 25 mins. Sound. Color. HS.

The growth of the American economy and the New York Stock Exchange along parallel paths is described. The use of public savings to make capital funds available to corporations is explained.

Chapter 3

CONSUMER

Bohlman, H.W., and Bohlman, E.M. INSURING YOUR LIFE, INCOME AND PROPERTY. Accent/Consumer Education. Chicago: Follett, 1968. 48 p. HS.

> This pamphlet discusses different types of insurance, the kinds of protection they offer, and government regulation of insurance.

_____. INVESTING YOUR SAVINGS. Accent/Consumer Education. Chicago: Follett, 1968. 48 p. HS.

> Rules for effective investing are discussed, including the question of where to put savings, such as the following: life insurance, government savings bonds, real estate, and stocks and bonds. The reader is encouraged to select investments that are best for him.

_____. KNOWING HOW TO BUDGET AND BUY. Accent/Consumer Education. Chicago: Follett, 1968. 48 p. HS.

> This is concerned with the following: how people spend their income, budgeting, knowing how to buy, saving for future purchases, fluctuating prices and the effect on your budget, agencies that help consumers, and how the government protects consumers.

_____. UNDERSTANDING CONSUMER CREDIT. Accent/Consumer Education. Chicago: Follett, 1968. 48 p. HS.

> This pamphlet offers an explanation of credit and some cautions about credit and credit buying. It also discusses borrowing and the cost of borrowing, types of buying, borrowing with collateral, and government regulations of consumer credit.

CONSUMER'S HANDBOOK: 100 WAYS TO GET MORE VALUE FOR YOUR DOLLARS. Princeton, N.J.: Dow Jones Books, 1969. 163 p. HS.

A collection of articles from the NATIONAL OBSERVER on a
broad range of marketplace activities. It will help both teachers
and students to become discriminating shoppers and should be a
valuable supplementary text.

Credit Unions National Association. USING CREDIT WISELY. Madison,
Wis.: 1971. 31 p. HS.

This pamphlet was prepared to assist teachers in the teaching of
credit in consumer economics. It discusses the responsibility of
the consumer, truth in lending, and different ways of borrowing.

DeCamp, Catherine Crook. THE MONEY TREE: A NEW GUIDE TO SUC-
CESSFUL PERSONAL FINANCE. Bergenfield, N.J.: New American Library,
1972. 352 p. HS.

This is a book of practical economics. It offers sound advice on
understanding and coping with current economic trends from the
credit revolution to preparing income tax forms.

DIRECTORY: STATE, COUNTY, AND CITY GOVERNMENT CONSUMER
OFFICES. Washington, D.C.: Government Printing Office, 1974. 44 p.
HS.

Here is a listing of consumer offices by state. Each listing includes the addresses, phone numbers, and names of responsible officials in each office. A special section provides information on
consumer offices with toll-free phone numbers, the types of calls
accepted, and hours of operation. The directory was developed
for consumers, businessmen, and consumer organizations in order
to provide a basic source of information on government involvement in consumer protection.

Foster, G. Allen. ADVERTISING: ANCIENT MARKET PLACE TO TELEVI-
SION. New York: Criterion Books, 1967. 224 p. HS.

The importance of illustrative matter in influencing the tastes and
economy of the American public is shown.

Graham, Ada. THE GREAT AMERICAN SHOPPING CART: HOW AMERICA
GETS ITS FOOD TODAY. New York: Simon & Schuster, 1969. 94 p.
Illus. Map. Elem.

This book describes the extraordinary changes in America's largest
industry, food marketing, and how these changes have affected
the growing, harvesting, packaging, preserving, and selling of
food, and the speed with which items now become available to
the consumer.

GUIDE TO FEDERAL CONSUMER SERVICES. Washington, D.C.: Government
Printing Office, 1971. 151 p. HS.

> This directory lists the consumer services of every federal agency
> or bureau that is either directly or indirectly concerned with con-
> sumer issues. You will learn what the National Park Service,
> Environmental Protection Agency, Veterans Administration, and
> more than seventy other agencies and bureaus are doing for you,
> how to obtain their services, and where to write for free infor-
> mation.

Hawver, Carl F. BASIC PRINCIPLES IN FAMILY MONEY AND CREDIT
MANAGEMENT. Rev. ed. Washington, D.C.: National Consumer Finance
Association, 1970. 12 p. HS.

> Basic information about consumer finance and its role in family
> money management is contained in this pamphlet, which was de-
> signed for student use as background reading for consumer credit
> teaching units.

IT'S YOUR CREDIT--MANAGE IT WISELY. Chicago: Household Finance
Corp., Money Management Institute, 1972. 43 p. HS.

> Consumer credit is an important financial tool in personal and
> family money management. Effectively used, consumer credit can
> help achieve some of our most important goals in life. Misused,
> it can create problems and lead to serious financial difficulties.

Klein, David, and May, Mary. SUPERSHOPPER: A GUIDE TO SPENDING
AND SAVING. New York: Praeger, 1971. 175 p. HS.

> This book aims to turn the reader into a skillful shopper and to
> teach him to get good value for every dollar spent. There are
> suggestions on increasing one's income, saving money, buying by
> mail, warranties and guarantees, buying items by special purchase
> or below wholesale cost, and comparing prices.

McClellan, Grant S., ed. THE CONSUMING PUBLIC. Reference Shelf,
vol. 40, no. 3. Bronx, N.Y.: H.W. Wilson, 1968. 219 p. HS.

> This volume deals with consumer problems and protection in
> America, from the standpoints of government, business, and con-
> sumer organizations. It is arranged topically under the following
> headings: "The Citizen as Consumer"; "The Role of Government
> as Protector"; "Business and Consumer Protection"; "Consumer
> Concerns"; "The Consumer Interest Movement."

National Commission on Economics and the Consumer. ECONOMICS AND
THE CONSUMER. New York: Joint Council on Economic Education, 1966.
40 p. HS.

This easy-to-understand document details the principles of economics through the experience of the student and his family.
There is a discussion of the essential principles of economics that are needed to make wise decisions as consumers; understandings needed by the consumer as saver, investor, and borrower; the school's responsibilities; and opportunities for developing the required economic competence for success in tomorrow's job market.

National Foundation for Consumer Credit. USING OUR CREDIT INTELLI-GENTLY. 4th ed. Washington, D.C.: 1967. 54 p. HS.

This analysis of consumer credit defines and explains in detail the advantages and disadvantages of the numerous types of consumer credit readily available. Family budgeting and establishing and maintaining a good credit standing are discussed as an advantage to the individual and a significant contribution to the overall economy.

Rosenblum, Marc. ECONOMICS OF THE CONSUMER. Minneapolis: Lerner, 1970. 87 p. Elem.

The consumer's role in the free market economy of the United States is discussed with emphasis on the continuing need for consumer protection.

Rossomando, Frederic, and Szymaszik, Marilyn. SPENDING MONEY. New York: Franklin Watts, 1967. 47 p. Prim.

Designed for young readers, this basic text explains what a budget is and how families use it, and helps children understand how to spend money carefully.

Schoenfeld, David, and Natella, Arthur A. THE CONSUMER AND HIS DOL-LARS. 2d ed. Dobbs Ferry, N.Y.: Oceana, 1970. 365 p. HS.

The author aims to develop an awareness and an alertness to the importance of making wise consumer decisions, not only to lead to increased benefits to the individual, but to result in perpetuation and improvement of our nation's free enterprise system.

Trump, Fred. BUYER BEWARE. Nashville, Tenn.: Abingdon Press, 1965. 207 p. HS.

The author tells succinctly how to avoid being defrauded and where to turn for help. He exposes common confidence games and other ways the public has been defrauded: by fake guarantees, magazine salesmen using sob stories, homework schemes, home improvement rackets, health quackery, food fads, investment, real estate and insurance trickery, and the false lure of the vanity press in publishing.

Warmke, Roman F. CONSUMER ECONOMIC PROBLEMS. 8th ed. Cincinnati: South-Western, 1971. 665 p. HS.

The purpose of this book is to relate personal economic decision making to the total economy. It aims to make the reader understand how the economic system operates; economic principles that are essential for participation as a citizen and voter in resolving economic issues; the application of principles and procedures of business to personal and family problems relating to earning an income; and wise management of money and savings.

MEDIA

ADVERTISING AND THE CONSUMER. Wilton, Conn.: Current Affairs Films. Filmstrip. 65 frames. Sound. Color. Teacher's guide. HS.

This filmstrip shows how various media are used to influence the consumer, how advertising plays upon fears and desires. There is a discussion of the need for more regulation to counteract deceptive practices.

BE CREDIT WISE. Chicago: Household Finance Corp., 1970. Filmstrip. 87 frames. Sound. Color. Teacher's guide. JH, HS.

The filmstrip, which shows the economic aspects of personal finance, develops the importance of wise management of the use of credit.

BUYING THE BASICS: FOOD AND CLOTHING. Wilton, Conn.: Current Affairs Films. Filmstrip. 65 frames. Sound. Color. Teacher's guide. HS.

Advice is given on comparing prices, reading labels clearly, comparing brand names, recognizing deceptive practices, shopping the ads, and judging quality.

CLASSROOM MONEY MANAGEMENT KIT. Madison, Wis.: CUNA Mutual Insurance. Kit. 4 cassettes. Game. Booklets. Teacher's guide. HS.

This package on money management contains useful elements including interesting, informative tapes on the opportunities and pitfalls of credit. Booklets enable the student to begin realistic budgeting. The game is designed to give the players an experience in economic realities.

CONSUMER AND CREDIT. Wilton, Conn.: Current Affairs Films. Filmstrip. 65 frames. Sound. Color. Teacher's guide. HS.

Types of credit available, how credit is granted, how the consumer can judge what he will have to pay for, the legal protec-

tions available to the consumer, and legal recourses available to
creditors are discussed.

CONSUMER BE WARNED: FRAUDS AND DECEPTIONS. Wilton, Conn.:
Current Affairs Films. Filmstrip. 65 frames. Sound. Color. Teacher's
guide. HS.

The filmstrip shows how to recognize and avoid being duped by
various frauds and deceptions.

CONSUMER EDUCATION. New York: Miller Brody Productions. 6 filmstrips, 30 mins. ea. Sound. Color. JH.

This program is intended to reach young people at a time in their
lives when they are beginning to establish life-long buying habits.
Tomorrow's consumers need guidance in today's complex world of
business. The titles are as follows: "The Consumer and Credit";
"Buying the Basics, Food and Clothing"; "Wheels and Deals";
"Buying Cars and Motorcycles"; "Advertising and the Consumer";
"Consumer Be Warned"; "Frauds and Deceptions"; "Consumer Power
and Social Change."

CONSUMER EDUCATION. 2 pts. Hollywood, Calif.: AIMS Institutional
Media Service. 8 filmstrips, 15 mins. ea. Sound. Color. Teacher's
guide. HS.

This is an attempt to provide basic consumer information. The
viewer is made aware of psychological traps surrounding fads, contracts, credit, insurance, food, housing, furniture construction,
and automobiles. Part 1 is titled MONEY MANAGEMENT.
The titles in this part are: "Credit and Contracts"; "Food";
"Housing"; "Money and Management." The title of part 2 is
BUYING PROTECTION. The titles in this part are: "Clothing";
"Furniture and Appliances"; "Health and Life Insurance"; "Transportation."

CONSUMER EDUCATION FOR THE ELEMENTARY GRADES. Lawrence, Kans.:
Centron Educational Films, 1974. 3 filmstrips, average 112 frames ea. Sound.
Color. Teacher's guide. Elem.

These filmstrips help prepare elementary students for a lifetime of
enlightened consumership. They deal with such basic precepts as
wise buying and money management; analyzing goals in relation
to needs; setting limits in the financial resources available; developing a list of acceptable alternatives; evaluating goods; con-
sidering various methods of financing; critically analyzing standard merchandising and promotional techniques. Titles: "Choosing
What to Buy"; "Advertising and You"; "Consumership"; "Getting
More for Your Money."

CONSUMER GAME. Santa Monica, Calif.: Pyramid Films, 1973. Film. 20 mins. Color. HS.

This is a fast-moving, humorous presentation. Problems of young consumers are emphasized, and topics include the credit trap, false advertising and false packaging, and faulty guarantees.

CONSUMERISM: THE DANGERS OF AFFLUENCE. Holyoke, Mass.: Scott Education, 1972. Filmstrip. Sound. Color. HS.

Part 1 reviews the modern proliferation of goods and. services, and the federal regulations now in force. It emphasizes the need for consumer protection through education and law. Part 2 examines the pressures of advertising and the need for regulation in this area; the dangers posed by corporate giants; consumer credit and consumer frauds.

CONSUMERLAND: HOW HIGH THE MOUNTAIN? Niles, Ill.: Argus Communications. Filmstrip. 125 frames. Sound. Color. HS.

Cartoon illustrations take the viewer on an ironic tour of a fictitious country where citizens are guaranteed the right to life, poverty, and the pursuit of happiness by the Right to Bills Act and the Declaration of Dependence. It concludes with an open-ended question designed to make the viewer think about his own involvement in the consumer-syndrome.

CONSUMER POWER AND SOCIAL CHANGE. Wilton, Conn.: Current Affairs Films. Filmstrip. 65 frames. Sound. Color. Teacher's guide. HS.

This is a discussion concerning whose responsibility it is to see that consumer interests are protected. "Consumer power" is represented by government spokesmen, independent consumer groups, and organizations at the community and neighborhood level.

ECONOMICS: MONEY. Santa Monica, Calif.: BFA Educational Media. Film. 11 mins. Color. Elem.

Using children's spontaneous thoughts and feelings about money and what they would do with it, this film clarifies some basic economic questions: What is money? Why do we need it and how do we get it? What can we do with our money? The primary emphasis is on the values and choices involved in being the consumers of goods and services.

THE FINANCE COMPANY. Hollywood, Calif.: Bailey Films, 1968. Filmstrip. Sound. Color. HS.

Basic information about borrowing money from a finance company is illustrated through the case of a young girl applying for a loan

to buy a used car on time. The advantages and risks involved
are mentioned.

GETTING YOUR MONEY'S WORTH. Group 1. Chicago: Singer/SVE, 1974.
6 filmstrips, 17 mins. ea. Sound. Color. Teacher's guide. JH, HS.

Much useful information is given about consumer related economic
principles and practical money management. The aims are to
teach students basic consumer skills needed in today's complex
marketplace, and to show that intelligent consumer practices help
one get the most from his resources. Titles include: "Why You
Need Consumer Know-how"; "A Blueprint for Money Management";
"Buying Wisely, Making Credit Work for You"; "Saving to Reach
Your Goals"; "Let the Consumer Beware."

GOOD GOODIES. West Los Angeles, Calif.: Stephen Bosustow Productions,
1971. Film. 4 1/2 mins. Color. Elem.

This brief non-narrated animated film explores the value of advertising in a trade war between two groups of children, selling
goodies at competing stands.

HOW TO HAVE MORE MONEY AND END YOUR FINANCIAL WORRIES.
Cleveland: World Publishing Co., 1973. Cassette. 60 mins. Script. HS.

The principles and procedures of effective money management are
discussed. Indebtedness, balanced income and outgo, and budgeting income are considered.

JUSTICE IN THE MARKET PLACE. Washington, D.C.: Changing Times Education Service, 1974. 2 filmstrips, 109 frames ea. Sound. Color. Teacher's
guide. HS.

These filmstrips were designed to show the power of the consumer
and his right to be heard and to obtain redress of grievances.
Situations with which students can easily identify are presented
as open-ended inquiries. In part 1, "Complaining to the Source"
is about a defective car and complaints to the manufacturer,
while "Washday Blues" involves the Better Business Bureau as
well as the Major Appliance Consumer Action Panel in repairing
a faulty washing machine. In part 2, "Where to Now?" deals
with fraudulent advertising and "Your Day in Court" concerns
contracts regarding door-to-door salesmen and truth in lending.

LEARNING PACKAGE. Consumer Education Series. Baltimore: Media
Materials, 1976. 3 cassettes. Student booklets. Performance tasks. Teacher's
guide. Elem.

This series aims to familiarize students with the idea of proper budgeting, spending, and saving. The first part, "Budgeting and Saving Your Money," introduces the student to the concept of budgeting money. The general rules discussed allow for proper spending and saving. Activities emphasize filling out budget sheets, how to save, and how to plan for the future. The second part, "Shop Wisely--Understand Advertisements," makes students aware of proper and improper advertisements and teaches them how to identify each. Through activities, students learn to read and understand advertisements.

LET THE BUYER BEWARE. Jamaica, N.Y.: Eye Gate House, 1974. 6 filmstrips. Sound. Color. Elem, JH.

This series will provide the basic information which people require concerning consumer education. Terms and concepts are presented through examples and situations that become meaningful to the student. Titles: "Everything Is Not What It Appears to Be"; "Can You Believe Advertising?"; "Johnny Has One"; "Measures, Values and Bargains"; "Use, Quality and Service"; "Is It Safe?"

THE LITTLEST GIANT. Washington, D.C.: National Consumer Finance Association. Film. 14 mins. Color. HS.

The history of credit, the role of consumer credit, the economy, and the services of the consumer finance industry to the American family is explained. The importance of the consumer in our society is clearly illustrated.

MAKING ENDS MEET. Pleasantville, N.Y.: Guidance Associates. Filmstrip. 8 mins. Sound. HS.

A model family budget is structured, with emphasis on orderly allocations of money resources, the importance of staying within preset limits, and flexibility in viewing priorities, particularly in approaching luxury purchases.

MANAGING THE FAMILY'S AFFAIRS. Jamaica, N.Y.: Eye Gate House. 12 filmstrips. Sound. Color. HS.

Each filmstrip presents a direct experience with a situation and concrete solutions or methods of solution are suggested. The titles include: "Learning to Live Together"; "The New Home"; "The Budget Today and Tomorrow"; "Cash and Credit"; "How to Shop"; "Just Sign Here"; "As the Family Grows"; "The Family and Its Legal Rights"; "The Family and Its Legal Responsibilities"; "Protecting What the Family Has"; "The Family and the Community"; "Help! This Is an Emergency."

MODERN CONSUMER EDUCATION. New York: Grolier Educational Corp.

Kit. 39 teaching units. Filmstrips. Wall chart. Teacher's manual. Elem.

Topics included in this program are: food, clothing, shelter; cars; furniture and appliances; protecting family health and security; you and the law; ways to handle money; ways to shop.

MONEY AND CREDIT MANAGEMENT. Washington, D.C.: National Consumer Finance Association. 2 filmstrips. Sound. JH.

These two filmstrips, YOUR MONEY MATTERS and YOU TAKE THIS CREDIT, are designed to complement an introductory unit in consumer credit and money management.

MONEY HAS MEANING. Our Living American Economy. Tujunga, Calif.: Herbert M. Elkins Co., 1966. Filmstrip. 59 frames. Color. HS.

The principles of family budgeting and savings are presented.

MONEY MAKES CENTS. Our Living American Economy. Tujunga, Calif.: Herbert M. Elkins Co., 1966. Filmstrip. 46 frames. Color. HS.

The importance of saving money is stressed. Interest is introduced and budgeting a limited income is reviewed.

MONEY NEEDS MANAGING. Our Living American Economy. Tujunga, Calif.: Herbert M. Elkins Co., 1966. Filmstrip. 46 frames. Color. HS.

The possibility of better living through budgeting the family income is shown. Interest and borrowing are discussed.

MONEY WELL SPENT. Pleasantville, N.Y.: Guidance Associates. Filmstrip. 8 mins. Sound. HS.

The vastness of the American economy is described. The relationship between consumer and seller/advertiser is explained. Sales appeal based on insecurity and gullibility is considered and the importance of digging hard information from ads and labels is emphasized.

OUR CREDIT ECONOMY. 2 pts. Pleasantville, N.Y.: Guidance Associates, 1969. Filmstrip. 19 mins. Sound. Color. HS.

The filmstrip traces the history of the development of consumer credit and describes the economic roles of consumer credit. Among problem areas dealt with are interest, disadvantages of buying on credit, and the dangers of disclosures of personal data by credit bureaus.

OUR ROLE AS CONSUMERS. New York: Association Sterling Films, 1968. 56 frames. Color. Elem.

The effects of economics on the lives of two teenagers are illustrated through ordinary life situations. The fact that our consumer actions affect our lives and the lives of others is emphasized.

PAYING YOUR BILLS. New York: McGraw Popular Science, 1954. Filmstrip. Color. HS.

Useful pointers are given concerning the establishment of a credit rating, the use of a charge plate, methods of paying bills, and how long to keep paid bills and tax receipts.

THE PRICE IS RIGHT--OR IS IT? New York: Miller Brody Productions. 4 filmstrips. Sound. Color. Teacher's guide. Worksheets. Prim.

This consumer education program for primary grades stresses individual buying power and consumer protection and responsibility. Titles: "Let's Make a Deal"; "Get Your Money's Worth"; "Supersnooper"; "Big Sister and the Lemon."

PROBLEMS FOR YOUNG CONSUMERS. New York: Miller Brody Productions. 6 filmstrips. Color. Teacher's guide. Student worksheets. Elem.

These filmstrips present real consumer problems for children to face and solve. The problems include those which children are likely to encounter in their everyday lives, such as half-filled candy boxes (excessive packaging), or an advertisement that misleads and leaves the child disappointed and unhappy. Titles: "What Do You Pay?"; "The Big Sale"; "The Come-on"; "Buy Now, Pay Later"; "The Street Vendor"; "The False Package."

SAVING AND INVESTING. Washington, D.C.: Changing Times Educational Service, 1973. Kit. Booklets. Simulation game. Transparencies. Bulletin board kit. Teacher's guide. HS.

This kit is divided into four units of study. It provides the various materials needed in the study of savings and investments.

SAVINGS FOR SECURITY. Functional Living Series. Wichita, Kans.: Graphic Research. Filmstrip. Sound. Color. JH.

Ways in which a person can make his money earn more money are pointed out. Some of the ways suggested are bank savings accounts, savings and loan associations, credit unions, U.S. government bonds, stocks, and mutual funds.

SPEND, SPEND. Seattle, Wash.: King Screen Productions, 1974. Film. 11 mins. Sound. Color. Available from BFA Educational Media. Elem, JH.

This film concerns the experiences of a young boy who bought a

scale-model sports car which quickly fell apart. His friend advised
him to return the defective car to the producing company. The
incident brings into focus the need for high production standards,
a manufacturer's responsibility to the consumer, the need to buy
wisely, ways to protect consumers, and the waste that results
when poorly made items are marketed.

SPENDING YOUR FOOD DOLLARS. Chicago: Household Finance Corp.,
1972. Filmstrip. 77 frames. Color. HS.

Helpful information is provided on planning the use of food dollars
and on buying, storing, and preparing foods.

SPENDING YOUR MONEY. Managing Your Money Series. New York:
McGraw Popular Science, 1954. Filmstrip. Color. HS.

The principles and practices of planned spending are reviewed.
Intelligent buying, quantity buying, and purchasing by mail are
also covered.

WE WANT GOODS AND SERVICES. Pasadena, Calif.: Arthur Barr Productions, 1968. Film. 10 mins. Color. Prim.

The film shows that we are all consumers and that it takes many
producers to provide the goods and services we want. Distinctions
are made between producer's goods and consumer goods and between durable goods and nondurable goods.

WHAT CONSUMERS SHOULD KNOW ABOUT TRUTH IN LENDING. Washington, D.C.: National Consumer Finance Association. Filmstrip. Sound.
HS.

Developed to present the essentials of the truth in lending law,
this filmstrip explains the law in an easy-to-understand consumer-
oriented way.

WHEELS AND DEALS: BUYING CARS AND MOTORCYCLES. Wilton, Conn.:
Current Affairs Films. Filmstrip. 65 frames. Sound. Color. Teacher's
guide. HS.

This filmstrip advises the buyer on: picking a dealer, state requirements on title, registration, and insurance coverage, methods
available for financing, questions to ask regarding warranties and
service, how to judge the worth of extras and accessories, and
how to judge quality and condition.

WISE USE OF CREDIT. Washington, D.C.: National Consumer Finance Association. Film. 11 mins. Color. HS.

The film provides a basic understanding of consumer credit and introduces economic terms, types of credit, and cost factors. It illustrates guidelines to follow when using credit.

YOU AND MASS PRODUCTION. Chicago: Singer/SVE, 1974. 4 filmstrips, average 50 frames ea. Sound. Color. Guide. Prim.

Automation, the assembly line, and mass production are explained for primary children. Titles: "From One-by-One to Lots and Lots"; "Clarence the Car"; "Buttons! Buttons!"

YOU AND RECYCLING. Chicago: Singer/SVE, 1974. 4 filmstrips. Sound. Color. Guide. Prim, Elem.

The problem of disposing of items no longer wanted or useful is discussed. Titles: "The Magician"; "Kiwi and the Bottle"; "Water All Around Us"; "Trash Treasure Hunt."

YOUR MONEY AND YOU. Chicago: Household Finance Corp., 1972. Filmstrip. 72 frames. Color. HS.

An outline of five basic steps is presented as a suggestion in planning income to reach personal and family goals.

YOUR WARDROBE AND YOU. Chicago: Household Finance Corp., 1972. Filmstrip. 63 frames. Color. HS.

Suggestions for achieving a well-dressed appearance within your clothing budget are presented. Emphasis is placed on the importance of wardrobe planning, shopping, and care.

YOUR WORLD AND MONEY. Chicago: Household Finance Corp., 1972. Filmstrip. 59 frames. Color. HS.

Advice in personal finance is given to teenagers. Suggestions are given on how to set goals and how to direct spending.

YOU THE CONSUMER. Chicago: Singer/SVE, 1974. Filmstrips, average 50 frames ea. Sound. Color. Guide. Prim, Elem.

Animated characters examine why we buy; what we buy; how blue jeans, bubble gum, and comic books are produced; truth in advertising; and the complete process of production. Titles: "Where Does the Allowance Go?"; "Blue Jeans, Bubble Gum, and Comic Books"; "The Commercial"; "It All Works Together."

YOU THE SHOPPER. Chicago: Household Finance Corp., 1972. Filmstrip. 66 frames. Color. HS.

The shopper's roles as family purchasing agent, consumer, and citizen are explained.

YOUTHFUL CONSUMER. Hackensack, N.J.: Valient IMC., 1973. Filmstrip. Sound. HS.

This is an important appraisal of the buying habits and consumer patterns of the new generation of seventy-eight million Americans and the major impact they are making on consumerism in America.

Chapter 4
ECONOMIC GROWTH AND STABILITY

Bernstein, Peter L. THE PRICE OF PROSPERITY. New York: Random House, 1966. 140 p. HS.

> The author discusses the choice between government spending and private freedoms as the major issue for future public policy.

Committee for Economic Development. ECONOMIC GROWTH IN THE UNITED STATES: A STATEMENT BY THE RESEARCH AND POLICY COMMITTEE. Rev. ed. New York: 1969. 56 p. HS.

> The Committee for Economic Development is an independent research and educational organization. It conducts research and formulates recommendations in four areas: (1) the national economy, (2) the international economy, (3) education and urban development, and (4) the management of federal, state, and local government.

_____. FISCAL AND MONETARY POLICIES FOR STEADY ECONOMIC GROWTH. New York: 1969. 85 p. HS.

> The role of fiscal and monetary policies in achieving the basic economic objectives of high employment, price stability, economic growth, and equilibrium in the nation's international payments is re-examined.

Daugherty, Marion, and Leppert, Ellis C. UNDERSTANDING ECONOMIC GROWTH. Economic Series, no. 54. Minneapolis: Curriculum Resources, 1961. 119 p. HS.

> What economics and history can tell us about the causes of economic growth is considered. There is an explanation of what economic growth is, how it is measured, what our growth record is, and what economic growth has to do with our national goals.

ECONOMIC STABILIZATION POLICIES. Economic Topic Series. New York:

Joint Council on Economic Education, 1970. 23 p. HS.

Part 1 defines the problem of economic stabilization and explains the fiscal and monetary measures used to help control the traditional ups and downs in the economy. Also included is the current and more complex problem of creeping inflation. Part 2 reviews the successes and failures of policies since World War II and explains why institutional changes and built-in automatic safeguards make a 1929-sized crash unlikely. Part 3 outlines a number of stabilization issues that policy-making authorities faced at the end of the Vietnam War.

Federal Reserve Bank of Philadelphia. MYSTERY OF ECONOMIC GROWTH. Philadelphia: 1962. 12 p. HS.

This pamphlet distinguishes between "real" growth and money growth and traces the surges of economic growth in the American economy throughout its history. It gives explanations of the basic kinds of economic growth and ways of stimulating this growth in the economy.

Gill, Richard T. ECONOMIC DEVELOPMENT: PAST AND PRESENT. Modern Economic Series. Englewood Cliffs, N.J.: Prentice-Hall, 1964. 120 p. HS.

Factors responsible for rapid and persistent economic growth are related to the problems faced by the underdeveloped countries.

Lewis, Wilfred, Jr. POLICIES FOR ECONOMIC STABILITY. New York: Joint Council on Economic Education, 1969. 23 p. HS.

The original draft of this pamphlet was prepared as a basic discussion paper for a round table of economists. The final document includes revisions made by the participants and the JCEE committee for the project. It lays ground work for understanding of stabilization policies.

North, Douglas C., comp. ECONOMIC GROWTH OF THE UNITED STATES 1790-1860. New York: Harper & Row, 1968. 251 p. HS.

American economic history and economic growth are studied. The author gives credit for the U.S. economic development from 1790 to 1814 to external influences. The economic growth from 1815 to 1860 was brought about by the westward movement and the industrial development in the United States.

Rostow, Walt W. THE STAGES OF ECONOMIC GROWTH: A NONCOMMUNIST MANIFESTO. 2d ed. New York: Cambridge University Press, 1971. 253 p. HS.

Five basic stages of economic growth based on a dynamic theory of production are interpreted in terms of actual societies. Causes of economic growth are analyzed.

Slichter, Sumner H. ECONOMIC GROWTH IN THE UNITED STATES--ITS HISTORY, PROBLEMS AND PROSPECTS. New York: Free Press, 1966. 189 p. HS.

The five essays included concern the determinants of the growth of the American economy and the evolution of its economic institutions.

U.S. Department of Commerce. U.S. ECONOMIC GROWTH. Rev. ed. Washington, D.C.: Government Printing Office, 1969. 47 p. HS.

This booklet is a simple explanation of the input and output factors promoting economic growth. Our growth is traced through the steel, petroleum, electrical, and automobile industries. The growth record of the United States is compared with the records of sixteen other countries.

Wagner, Lewis E. INCOME, EMPLOYMENT AND PRICES. Primer of Economics Series, no. 4. Iowa City: Bureau of Business and Economic Research, State University of Iowa, 1960. 42 p. HS.

Macroeconomic analysis is the approach used in studying the problem of economic instability. Policies for economic stabilization are considered.

MEDIA

ADAM BUILDS A BANK. New York: AVI Associates, 1970. Filmstrip. 52 frames. Sound. Color. Teacher's guide. Prim.

The processes of spending, saving, and borrowing are described for very young students.

DOLLAR VICTORY. Chicago: International Film Bureau, 1970. Filmstrip. Sound. Color. Elem.

The services available from the community bank, such as checking accounts, loans, counselling services, and budget advice are revealed to a young man who is having financial problems.

ECONOMIC STABILITY: THE QUEST AND THE QUESTIONS. New York: American Bankers Association, 1969. Film. 22 mins. Color. HS.

The film describes the symptoms of economic instability and discusses the uses and limitations of monetary and fiscal policies as countercyclical devices. It challenges viewers to consider the consequences of choices among alternative courses of action.

ELEMENTARY JUNIOR HIGH SOCIAL STUDIES. New York: Western Publishing Co., 1965. 33 transparencies. Color. JH, HS.

Economic concepts including our rising standard of living, population movements, economic geography, conservation of natural resources, foundations of capitalism, factors of production, formation of capital, and nature of technology are presented.

NATIONAL INCOME. New York: McGraw-Hill, 1950. 2 filmstrips, 36 frames ea. B&W. HS.

The first filmstrip describes how gross national product, net national product, and national income are measured. The second explains the distinction between gross and net investment, and discusses capital formation.

PRODUCTIVITY: KEY TO AMERICA'S ECONOMIC GROWTH. Los Angeles: John Sutherland Productions, 1964. Film. 27 mins. Sound. Color. Teacher's guide. HS.

This film provides an overview of the American economy. A historical analysis of the record of productivity in America is presented. The relationship between productivity and the rising level of living of the American people is emphasized.

Chapter 5
ECONOMIC PROBLEMS

American Federationist. URBAN CRISIS: ANALYSIS AND ANSWER. Washington, D.C.: American Federation of Labor and Congress of Industrial Organizations, 1967. 16 p. HS.

> This pamphlet presents the AFL-CIO's analysis of the urban crisis and a program for action.

Ashell, Bernard. CAREERS IN URBAN AFFAIRS: SIX YOUNG PEOPLE TALK ABOUT THEIR PROFESSIONS IN THE INNER CITY. New York: Peter H. Wyden, 1970. 111 p. HS.

> In this book six urban specialists explain their jobs and discuss what they like and dislike about their work. Represented here are a school social worker, a community organizer, a public housing expert, two city planners, and an assistant to a mayor.

Bell, Carolyn Shaw. THE ECONOMICS OF THE GHETTO. New York: Pegasus, 1970. 266 p. HS.

> This study looks to the ghetto to find out how economics can improve the plight of the people in terms of factors like income, housing, employment, welfare programs, education, and the economy within the ghetto.

Birch, David L. THE ECONOMIC FUTURE OF CITY AND SUBURB. CED Supplementary Paper, no. 30. New York: Committee for Economic Development, 1970. 42 p. HS.

> The author describes the changes in central-city employment since World War II and population shifts that have resulted because of employment shifts. He attempts to assess the strengths of the trends affecting central-city development and the effects that several changes in policy and technology might have upon these trends.

Bish, Robert L., and Kirk, Robert J. ECONOMIC PRINCIPLES AND URBAN PROBLEMS. Englewood Cliffs, N.J.: Prentice-Hall, 1974. 199 p. HS.

This volume is designed to illustrate how market forces shape and influence our urban areas and how basic economic principles can be used to analyze and understand market forces, market failures, urban government organizations, and urban public policies.

Blaustein, Arthur, and Woock, Roger R., eds. MAN AGAINST POVERTY: WORLD WAR III. New York: Vintage Books, 1968. 456 p. HS.

Forty articles make up three sections of this book: "Beyond the Cold War," "Poverty in the U.S.," and "Poverty in the World." Each section discusses the problems, presents cases, and suggests solutions.

Breetveld, Jim. GETTING TO KNOW THE FAO: HOW U. N. CRUSADERS FIGHT WORLD HUNGER. New York: Coward-McCann, 1962. 64 p. Illus. Elem.

The author explains how experts of the Food and Agriculture Organization are fighting world hunger by teaching farmers how to produce more and better food.

Brown, Douglas M. INTRODUCTION TO URBAN ECONOMICS. New York: Academic Press, 1974. 301 p. HS.

This urban economics textbook claims to cover the field completely. It discusses the following topics: economic history of urban areas; economics of urban growth; intraurban location decisions; land use; housing; urban transportation; the role of urban governments; urban poverty; and the problems of urban governments.

CAN WE SAVE OUR CITIES? Public Affairs Pamphlets, no. 374. New York: Public Affairs Committee, 1966. 28 p. JH, HS.

Urban renewal programs are evaluated. Social and political implications and economic costs and benefits are discussed.

Chamber of Commerce of the United States of America. WORLD POPULATION: PROSPECTS AND PROBLEMS, A REPORT TO THE ECONOMIC POLICY COMMITTEE. Washington, D.C.: 1966. 24 p. HS.

It is hoped that the booklet will stimulate discussions of the crucially important population question. It presents the facts of the "population explosion," explores the relation between population growth and economic development, examines the prospects of curbing population growth, and discusses the policies of the United States with regard to population pressures.

Chinitz, Benjamin, ed. CITY AND SUBURB: THE ECONOMICS OF METROPOLITAN GROWTH. Englewood Cliffs, N.J.: Prentice-Hall, 1964. 181 p. HS.

This book discusses the development and growth of metropolitan areas in our country. It looks at these areas, discusses their problems, and suggests possible future developments.

Coles, Robert. STILL HUNGRY IN AMERICA. Cleveland: World, 1968. 115 p. HS.

This is a collection of eloquent photographs and accompanying commentary documenting the hunger and malnutrition still prevalent among many of the poor in the United States.

Committee for Economic Development. EDUCATION FOR THE URBAN DIS-ADVANTAGED FROM PRE-SCHOOL TO EMPLOYMENT, A STATEMENT ON NATIONAL POLICY. Washington, D.C.: 1971. 86 p. HS.

Although three urban disadvantaged groups receive particular attention in this book, the black minority, Mexican Americans, and the Puerto Ricans, the conclusions and recommendations apply to all urban poor. The role of educational institutions in carrying out their part in eliminating poverty in the United States and of opening up the doors of opportunity to those who have been denied an equitable share of society's rewards is discussed. Education's role in this enterprise is to be the instrument by which the disadvantaged enter the mainstream of American thought.

_____. FURTHER WEAPONS AGAINST INFLATION. Washington, D.C.: 1970. 96 p. HS.

The problem of reconciling high employment and price stability is examined. It points out that the present challenge for the U.S. economic policy is not only to check the on-going inflation but to achieve price stability as the economy returns to high employment. Measures to supplement general fiscal and monetary policies will be needed including the use of voluntary wage-price policies, as well as measures to change the structural and institutional environment in which demand policy operates.

_____. IMPROVING THE PUBLIC WELFARE SYSTEM: A STATEMENT ON NATIONAL POLICY. Washington, D.C.: 1970. 75 p. HS.

This statement analyzes the national problem of poverty and the role played by the present welfare system. It recommends major changes in both the rationale and the administration of the public assistance program, with a view to establishing need as the sole criterion for coverage. Proposals include the establishment of a federally financed, nationwide minimum level of income maintenance coupled with work incentives, and the development of a national program of day-care centers.

_____. RAISING LOW INCOME THROUGH IMPROVED EDUCATION: A STATEMENT ON NATIONAL POLICY BY THE RESEARCH AND POLICY COMMITTEE. New York: 1965. 51 p. HS.

This paper suggests ways to broaden the country's educational base in order to raise the productivity and incomes of many Americans now well below the national average. It offers recommendations on steps to be taken at federal, state, and local government levels and by business leadership.

_____. TRAINING AND JOBS FOR THE URBAN POOR. Washington, D.C.: 1970. 78 p. HS.

Ways of abating poverty that arises from low wages and chronic unemployment or underemployment are explored. Current manpower training and employment efforts by government and business are evaluated and recommendations for new government programs are made.

Davis, Kenneth S., ed. THE PARADOX OF POVERTY IN AMERICA. Reference Shelf, vol. 41, no. 2. Bronx, N.Y.: H.W. Wilson, 1969. 224 p. HS.

The articles included in this volume discuss the nature and extent of poverty in the United States; the experience of being poor; measures undertaken by government and private enterprise to eliminate poverty; and proposed new approaches to the question.

Downs, Anthony. WHO ARE THE URBAN POOR? Urban Study Series. New York: Committee for Economic Development, 1970. 64 p. HS.

This study clarifies the concept of poverty among individuals and families, presents estimates of the numbers in each group and suggests why they are poor.

ECO-CATASTROPHE. Edited by Ramparts Magazine. New York: Harper & Row, 1970. 158 p. HS.

These articles, on such subjects as population control, oil in Santa Barbara and Alaska, and radiation pollution, originally appeared in RAMPARTS MAGAZINE. Paul Ehrlich and Gene Marine are two of the contributors. They believe that we need a redistribution of existing real wealth and a reallocation of society's resources. Solutions are not posed. The aim is to arouse the readers.

ECONOMICS OF POLLUTION. Economic Topics Series. New York: Joint Council on Economic Education, 1969. 23 p. HS.

One of the reasons for the present concern regarding pollution of the environment lies in doubts about whether economic growth is possible without proportional increases in the pollution of air, land, and water. Part 1 examines the economic relationships that help to explain why pollution is a special problem of production and consumption. Part 2 surveys the difficulties of measuring and assigning costs. Part 3 analyzes measures to combat pollution.

ECONOMICS OF THE CITIES. Economic Topics Series. New York: Joint Council on Economic Education, 1968. 19 p. HS.

This monograph describes the economic aspects of the problems of our cities. It consists of three articles: the first deals with the origins of cities and the city as a device for reducing the costs of overcoming space; the second covers the economic advantages of the cities, why cities differ, and trends in urban development; the third is a summary of fiscal and transportation problems faced by the modern city.

Federal Reserve Bank of Philadelphia. INFLATION AND/OR UNEMPLOY-MENT. Series for Economic Education. Philadelphia: n.d. 12 p. HS.

A discussion of the problem of stabilizing prices while maintaining a high level of employment and the problems of holding both at a practical level.

_____. NEW POVERTY. Series for Economic Education. Philadelphia: 1964. 10 p. JH, HS.

A description and interpretation of the kinds of poverty which continue to exist in a generally prosperous economy. Antipoverty programs are discussed.

Fels, Rendigs, and Uhler, Robert G., eds. CASEBOOK OF ECONOMIC PROBLEMS AND POLICIES: PRACTICE IN THINKING. St. Paul, Minn.: West Publishing Co., 1974. 176 p. HS.

The cases in this book, designed to train students to apply economic principles to the kind of articles they will encounter throughout their lives in newspapers and magazines, provide training in analyzing economic issues.

Fielder, William, and Feeney, Georgiana. INQUIRING ABOUT CITIES: STUDIES IN GEOGRAPHY AND ECONOMICS. New York: Holt, Rinehart & Winston, 1972. 308 p. Elem.

This book attempts to explain the economic factors that contribute to the development of cities.

Fisher, Tadd. OUR OVERCROWDED WORLD. New York: Parents' Magazine Press, 1969. 256 p. JH.

This book deals with one of the world's most pressing problems. Facts are presented about the population explosion, and its implications for the whole world--the economically advanced as well as developing nations.

Frankel, Lillian. THIS CROWDED WORLD: AN INTRODUCTION TO THE STUDY OF POPULATION. Washington, D.C.: Population Reference Bureau, 1970. 60 p. Elem.

The "population explosion" with its serious consequences for rich as well as poor countries is described. Hunger, poverty, and the worsening state of our environment are emphasized. The author calls for new ways of thinking to solve these problems, pointing out that science cannot meet the challenge of balancing peoples' needs and available resources.

Gay, Kathlyn. WHERE THE PEOPLE ARE: CITIES AND THEIR FUTURE. New York: Delacorte, 1960. 148 p. Elem.

A look at the cities and the problems of pollution, conservation, housing, ghettoes, and transportation.

Gladwin, Thomas. POVERTY IN U.S.A. Boston: Little, Brown and Co., 1967. 182 p. HS.

This is an appraisal of the accomplishments of the "war on poverty" to date, with background on the New Deal programs and explanation of the interrelationships between antipoverty and civil rights goals. Some of the proposals which the author discusses favorably and convincingly are guaranteed income, major welfare reforms, educational reforms, and a better image for the neglected service occupations as a source for wide employment.

Goldman, Marshall I., ed. CONTROLLING POLLUTION: THE ECONOMICS OF A CLEANER AMERICA. Englewood Cliffs, N.J.: Prentice-Hall, 1967. 175 p. HS.

This volume contains a collection of writings dealing with economic aspects of water, air, and scenic pollution caused by the activities of producers and consumers, and the role of government in disputes over environmental quality.

Gordon, Margaret S., ed. POVERTY IN AMERICA. San Francisco: Chandler Publishing Co., 1965. 465 p. HS.

This is a collection of writings discussing the nature of poverty and the public policies which affect it, including income programs, education, welfare services, and urban renewal.

Harrington, Michael. THE OTHER AMERICA: POVERTY IN THE UNITED STATES. Rev. ed. New York: Macmillan, 1969. 191 p. HS.

This book is credited with sparking the "war on poverty." It identified two societies in the United States; one affluent and one underdeveloped, "a culture of poverty."

Helfman, Elizabeth S. THIS HUNGRY WORLD. New York: Lothrop, Lee and Shepard, 1970. 160 p. HS.

This book tells why two-thirds of the world's population is hungry and deals with the reasons for hunger in the United States. It describes modern scientific methods of farming, the opening of new lands for cultivation, and the developing of new food products by nutritionists. There are also reports on the work of United Nations agencies in fighting hunger throughout the world.

Hyde, Margaret O. THIS CROWDED PLANET. New York: McGraw-Hill, 1961. 159 p. Illus. Elem.

A study of the growth of population on this planet and of what is being done to provide food, shelter, space, and other resources for its billions of people.

THE INDIVIDUAL AND THE ECONOMY. Chicago: Industrial Relations Center, University of Chicago, 1965. 39 p. HS.

This booklet discusses the individual's search for security, the reasons for economic insecurity, and the private and government measures taken to combat insecurity. There are sections on poverty, on family income, and on the expense statement as a means of providing security through financial planning.

Joseph, Myron L., et al. ECONOMIC ANALYSIS AND POLICY: BACKGROUND READINGS FOR CURRENT ISSUES. 3d ed. Englewood Cliffs, N.J.: Prentice-Hall, 1971. 612 p. HS.

In this book there are ninety-two readings on economic problems which involve public policy issues. The intent is to give students vital problem-solving experiences with today's economic problems.

Keyserling, Leon H. GROWTH WITH LESS INFLATION OR MORE INFLATION WITHOUT GROWTH. Washington, D.C.: Conference on Economic Progress, 1970. 79 p. HS.

The author offers explanations as to why we experienced accelerating inflation, declining economic growth, recession, and rising unemployment from 1966 to 1970. He proposes programs to remedy the situation.

_____. PROGRESS OR POVERTY: U.S. AT THE CROSSROADS. Washington, D.C.: Conference on Economic Progress, 1964. HS.

Basic elements of the "war" against poverty are spelled out. The author describes what he calls "the 34 million U.S. poor." Some controversial proposals are recommended.

Kotz, Nick. LET THEM EAT PROMISES: THE POLITICS OF HUNGER IN AMERICA. Garden City, N.Y.: Doubleday, 1971. 261 p. HS.

This book describes the plight of hungry Americans, traces the development of programs designed to aid them, and analyzes the incredible political-economic battles which rage over the question.

Lebergott, Stanley, ed. MEN WITHOUT WORK: THE ECONOMICS OF UN-EMPLOYMENT. Modern Economic Issues. Englewood Cliffs, N.J.: Prentice-Hall, 1964. 183 p. HS.

Readings on unemployment, automation, growth, the unemployed, and on programs here and abroad designed to expand employment are included in this volume.

Lekachman, Robert. INFLATION: THE PERMANENT PROBLEM OF BOOM OR BUST. New York: Vintage Books, 1973. 121 p. HS.

The author explores the problem of inflation, its causes, and possible solutions.

_____. PUBLIC SERVICE EMPLOYMENT: JOBS FOR ALL. Public Affairs Pamphlets, no. 481. New York: Public Affairs Committee, 1972. 28 p. HS.

A look at the unemployment situation, including a discussion of jobs and skills, class and racial exclusions, teenagers and women, public service approach, historical precedent, controlling the jobs, and individual opportunity.

McCormack, Arthur. THE POPULATION PROBLEM. New York: Crowell, 1970. 246 p. HS.

The ratio between food supply and population increase is examined and some solutions to the problem are proposed. The author agrees that some form of population control will have to be practiced but hopes that the world can be saved from famine by the development of improved crops and better understanding of the technology necessary to put land to new and better uses.

McDonald, Stanleigh B. TEN WEEKS TO A BETTER JOB. Garden City, N.Y.: Doubleday, 1972. 239 p. HS.

This timely guide has a dual purpose: to assist in planning a

campaign for the job hunter and to dispel the discouragement felt
by most people who are looking for new employment.

McMurrin, Sterling M., ed. FUNCTIONAL EDUCATION FOR DISADVAN-
TAGED YOUTH. New York: Committee for Economic Development, 1971.
120 p. HS.

This volume is concerned with effectively tying education with
jobs to ensure employment that is both productive and satisfying.
The choice between "technical" and "academic" schooling should
not be a choice between poor and good education, but a choice
among the various patterns of life that education opens to the individual.

_____. RESOURCES FOR URBAN SCHOOLS: BETTER USE AND BALANCE.
New York: Committee for Economic Development, 1971. 146 p. HS.

Schools for the urban disadvantaged have been short-changed in a
variety of significant ways ranging from maldistribution of educational resources to poorly trained teachers because of the inadequacies of traditional teacher training institutions. Among the reme-
dies suggested by the authors are sweeping reforms of taxation
policies, new institutions for training teachers, an emphasis on
"outputs" rather than "inputs," and innovative approaches to school
design and land use.

Myrdal, Gunnar. THE CHALLENGE OF WORLD POVERTY: A WORLD ANTI-
POVERTY PROGRAM IN OUTLINE. New York: Pantheon Books, 1970.
518 p. HS.

The author summarizes his analysis of world poverty, with heavy
emphasis on anti-Communist India and Pakistan and develops suggested solutions on a world-wide scale. He examines problems of
population control, education, agriculture, trade, and capital investments.

O'Connor, John R., et al. EXPLORING THE URBAN WORLD. New York:
Globe, 1972. 432 p. Teaching guide. Elem.

This is a discussion of the cities of the world, their historical
development, current condition, and the outlook for the future.
There is a discussion concerning what is happening to cities today, the problems faced, the role of government in cities' existence,
and what changes the future may bring. Special attention is
given to the growth of cities across America.

Okun, Arthur M., ed. THE BATTLE AGAINST UNEMPLOYMENT. Rev. ed.
Problems in Modern Economy. New York: Norton, 1972. 248 p. HS.

This volume includes readings on such topics as unemployment, price stability, fiscal policy, and monetary policy.

Paradis, Adrian A. INFLATION IN ACTION. New York: Julian Messner, 1974. 190 p. Elem, JH.

Pointing up that inflation has occurred ever since Nero's time, this book is a readable and informative introduction to the problem which outlines reasons for inflation, its effects on individuals, and methods of control. Good definitions and extensive information on the problems which currently afflict labor, farmers, and municipal services add to the relevance of this survey.

Pitt, Valarie. LET'S FIND OUT ABOUT THE CITY. New York: Franklin Watts, 1968. 48 p. Elem.

Ways that a city can raise money are examined as are essential services which it must supply to its citizens.

Pringle, Laurence. ONE EARTH, MANY PEOPLE: THE CHALLENGE OF HUMAN POPULATION GROWTH. New York: Macmillan, 1971. 86 p. Elem.

The author presents the views of specialists in various fields about continued population growth. He discusses pollution, the "green revolution" in agriculture, the developing shortages of water and energy, and the reasons why an increasing population in the United States is a greater threat to the earth's resources than a similar growth in an underdeveloped nation.

PUBLIC SERVICE EMPLOYMENT: JOBS FOR ALL. Public Affairs Pamphlets, no. 481. New York: Public Affairs Committee, 1973. 28 p. HS.

The author of this pamphlet believes that private business cannot generate enough jobs to reduce the high rate of unemployment. He argues that many of the people in the United States who were jobless at the start of 1972 could be permanently employed in public service jobs and that it is the responsibility of the federal government to create these jobs. Unemployed men and women should be trained to work in areas of education, health, and social services.

Roby, Pamela, ed. THE POVERTY ESTABLISHMENT. Englewood Cliffs, N.J.: Prentice-Hall, 1974. HS.

This book describes and criticizes the maintenance of poverty and wealth in the United States. Historical perspective is provided as well as a survey of government subsidies to the rich and government programs for the poor. The exploitation of poverty programs by corporations and the attempts of the poor to work within the system are examined. The causes of poverty are discussed and steps suggested to reduce poverty and inequality.

Spengler, Joseph. POPULATION CHANGE, MODERNIZATION AND WEL-
FARE. Englewood Cliffs, N.J.: Prentice-Hall, 1974. 182 p. HS.

This is an introductory review of the major socioeconomic consequences of current world-wide demographic trends. The author
examines the growth, age, composition, and distribution of population throughout the world; the environmental aspects of demographic growth; the costs and benefits from continued population
growth; the pros and cons of stationary versus a growing population.

Stein, Herbert. UNEMPLOYMENT AND INFLATION. Bedford Hills, N.Y.:
Teaching Resources Films in Cooperation with the Joint Council on Economic
Education, 1972. 46 p. HS.

Topics discussed are the following: unemployment and inflation,
meaning of unemployment, inflation, what determines total spending, instruments for stabilizing total spending, and strategy of
stabilization policy.

STEPS FOR A BALANCED ECONOMY, INFLATION CAN BE STOPPED. New
York: Joint Council on Economic Education, 1969. 32 p. HS.

Monetary and fiscal policy and their relationships to the individual are introduced. There is a discussion of how actions taken
at the national level can achieve a balanced economy and how
the individual can influence these decisions.

Stewart, Maxwell S., and Duffy, Helene. WHAT INFLATION AND TIGHT
MONEY MEAN TO YOU. Public Affairs Pamphlets, no. 416. New York:
Public Affairs Committee, 1968. 20 p. HS.

The many and far-reaching facets of inflation and the programs
designed to combat inflation are discussed. It is hoped that by
helping the public to recognize the underlying causes of inflation,
it will be possible to develop wiser policies.

Tannenbaum, Beulah, and Stillman, Myra. FEEDING THE CITY. New York:
McGraw-Hill, 1971. 63 p. Illus. Elem.

This presents basic information about how food is transported from
rural areas to the city and about the preservation and grading of
food to ensure quality and to make shopping easier.

Terborgh, George. THE INFLATION DILEMMA. Washington, D.C.: Machinery and Allied Products Institute and Council for Technological Advancement, 1969. 70 p. HS.

This pamphlet considers the control of inflation. It reviews the record of wage and price control.

U.S. Bureau of the Census. SOCIAL AND ECONOMIC STATUS OF NEGROES IN THE UNITED STATES. Washington, D.C.: 1971. 156 p. Sold by the Government Printing Office. HS.

This report prepared jointly by the Bureau of the Census and the Bureau of Labor Statistics is one of a series about the social and economic conditions of Negroes in the United States, and brings together the statistics available for the period between 1960 and 1970. During the 1960s Negroes continued to make substantial economic and social gains and to consolidate advances made in the 1950s in health, education, employment, and income. Despite these gains, Negroes remain behind whites in most social and economic categories, but the differences in a number of areas continue to narrow.

U.S. Congress. Senate. Select Committee on Nutrition and Human Needs. "HUNGER 1973" AND PRESS REACTION. Washington, D.C.: Government Printing Office, 1973. 91 p. HS.

The effectiveness of federal food programs in helping the hungry and the poor in America and the press reaction to these programs are subjects of this report.

WHAT ARE ECONOMIC PROBLEMS? Iowa City: Bureau of Business and Economic Research, State University of Iowa, 1966. 19 p. HS.

The way in which a society organizes to produce desired goods and services is introduced and clearly analyzed.

World Bank. POPULATION PLANNING: A SECTOR WORKING PAPER. Washington, D.C.: 1972. 83 p. HS.

This paper describes the World Bank's effort to help member countries reduce population growth rates. The paper also outlines the economic effects of reducing population growth in developing countries and summarizes available information on the global demographic situation, world population trends and projections, and the accomplishments and potential of family planning programs.

MEDIA

AMERICA'S URBAN CRISIS. Chicago: Singer/SVE, 1974. 6 filmstrips, 15-16 mins. ea. Sound. Color. JH, HS.

On-site photography in six major U.S. cities, comparative charts, and narration provide a survey of pressing environmental problems. Students examine urban dilemmas where industrial and technological achievements and personal irresponsibility have created by-products which menace the quality of urban life. Titles: "The Roots of Our Urban Problems"; "The Air Pollution Menace"; "Water Pollution--a Complex Problem"; "Solid Waste--a New Pollutant"; "The Transportation Crisis"; "The Housing Crisis."

CAN THE EARTH PROVIDE? New York: McGraw-Hill, 1960. Film. 30 mins. Sound. B&W. HS.

This film portrays the race between population and productivity. The frightening question of whether the earth can provide enough to feed the rapidly growing population is discussed.

THE CHANGING CITY. Los Angeles: Churchill-Wexler Production Films, 1963. Film. 16 mins. Sound. Color. HS.

This film, an introduction to urban economics, describes the unplanned growth of the city and its surrounding suburbs. The major problems confronting central cities are also depicted.

THE CITIES: TO BUILD THE FUTURE. Santa Monica, Calif.: BFA Educational Media, 1968. Film. 60 mins. Sound. Color. HS.

This film produced for CBS News describes the urban renewal program of Philadelphia and discusses urban planning in Columbia, Maryland, and Irvine, California. A systematic approach to urban planning and renewal is developed.

CITIES AND HISTORY: CHANGING THE CITY. New York: McGraw-Hill, 1967. Film. 8 mins. Sound. Color. Teacher's guide. Elem.

Some of the reasons for change in the city are discussed. It is explained that change can mean both improvement and decay, and that city planning can affect the deterioration or growth of neighborhoods.

CITIES AT WORK. Chicago: Science Research Associates, 1970. 12 filmstrips. Sound. Color. Elem, JH.

Each of these filmstrips, concerned with some aspect of city life, contain some economic analysis. The titles are: "The City and Transportation"; "The City, Water, and Air"; "Dots on the Earth"; "Keeping Cities Up to Date"; "Marketplace of Goods and Services"; "Marketplace of Ideas"; "What Is a City"; "What Keeps People Together"; "Why a City Grows"; "Why a City Is Where It Is"; "Why Most Cities Plan"; "The City and Government."

CITY IN THE MODERN WORLD. Stamford, Conn.: Educational Dimension Corp., 1973. 2 filmstrips. Sound. HS.

This unit offers a comparative analysis of urban development patterns, industry, housing, architecture, traffic, and communications. The concept of the global village is introduced and investigated.

CRISIS IN URBAN DEVELOPMENT. Wilton, Conn.: Current Affairs Films, 1968. Filmstrip. 45 frames. B&W. HS.

A brief study of the nature, causes, extent, and effects of the urban crisis, and a look at some approaches and programs that are attempting to deal with it.

ECONOMICS OF THE CITY. Santa Monica, Calif.: BFA Educational Media, 1971. 6 filmstrips, 51-73 frames ea. Sound. Color. Elem.

This series examines how cities grow, how goods and services are provided, how people get goods and services they need, and how community problems are resolved by elected officials. Titles: "Life Cycle of the City"; "Economics of Change, Westwood Village"; "City Needs Goods"; "City Needs Services"; "Specialization and Mass Production"; "Cities are Run by People."

FEEDING THE WORLD'S PEOPLE. Wilton, Conn.: Current Affairs Films, 1966. Filmstrip. 42 frames. B&W. HS.

The unprecedented growth of the population in both the developed and underdeveloped countries is described. The prospect of achieving a balance between the growth of population and the growth of output through the use of modern technology is explored.

FOOD, WILL THERE BE ENOUGH? Holyoke, Mass.: Scott Education Division, 1973. 2 filmstrips. Sound. Teacher's guide. JH, HS.

The study of this critical problem attempts to create in the students an awareness of the nature of the global food problem, helps them to analyze the fundamental causes and effects of the problem, and introduces them to some of the technological attempts to cope with the problem.

GHETTOS OF AMERICA. Tarrytown, N.Y.: Schloat Productions, 1967. 4 filmstrips, 12 mins. ea. Sound. Color. Guide. JH.

Life in America's two largest ghettos is shown through the eyes of an inhabitant of each; Jerry in Harlem and Anthony in Watts. Each child is followed through his daily routine in overcrowded dwellings, filthy street playgrounds, and substandard schools. This program aims to develop an understanding of how ghettos are created and sustained.

INDIA: URBAN CONDITIONS. New York: McGraw-Hill, 1968. Film.
19 mins. Sound. Color. Teacher's guide. Elem, JH, HS.

The problems, frustrations, and general living conditions of a typical workman and his family in a large Indian city are pictured.
The film portrays the urgent need for industrial growth and the
fact that the population growth is so rapid that it tends to negate
the government's attempts to increase food production and stimulate
industry.

INDIA'S POPULATION. Santa Ana, Calif.: International Communication
Films, 1963. Filmloop. 4 mins. Color. Elem, JH, HS.

This film depicts the tremendous size of the Indian population
through a survey of crowded streets and groups performing everyday functions. A religious celebration which draws a huge crowd
is seen as well. The student can understand the effect of the
population on the economy and culture of India.

INFLATION. Chicago: Encyclopaedia Britannica Films, 1953. Film. 20
mins. Sound. Color. HS.

The causes of an inflationary spiral in the immediate post-World
War II period are described. The film suggests monetary and fiscal policies that were thought appropriate weapons to contain es-
calation of prices at that time.

INFLATION. New York: Committee for Economic Development. McGraw-
Hill, 1971. Film. 27 mins. Color. HS.

This film relates fundamental economic principles to the real
world of people and events. The film concerns Lunia, a mythical
land, where inflation overheats a gigantic production machine.
The lesson of Lunia is applied to the recent U.S. experience,
starting with the relatively stable period of the early 1960s, then
moving to the Vietnam commitment and the ensuing inflationary
upsurge, and finally, to a discussion of actions required to stabilize the economy and insure a more sophisticated response to economic events for the long term.

INFLATION AND THE STANDARD OF LIVING. Wilton, Conn.: Current
Affairs Films, 1960. Filmstrip. 36 frames. B&W. HS.

This filmstrip explains how inflation affects different groups in
society. Both demand-pull and cost-push inflation are described.

INFLATION AND YOU. Economics of Our Times. New York: McGraw-

Hill, 1962. Filmstrip. 36 frames. Color. HS.

This filmstrip correlates with the book ECONOMICS FOR OUR TIMES by Augustus H. Smith. It describes the causes of inflation and explains attempts by governments to control it at various times by wage and price controls and by monetary and fiscal policies. (See Smith, Augustus H. ECONOMICS FOR OUR TIMES. Chapter 10.)

INQUIRY INTO CONTEMPORARY AMERICAN PROBLEMS: POVERTY AND URBAN DECAY. New Rochelle, N.Y.: Pathescope Educational Films. Pictures. 2 sets of 6 photos in classroom quantities. Teacher's manual. JH, HS.

These sets of Associated Press photos are designed to involve students in meaningful discussions about the world they live in.

MUST THE WORLD GO HUNGRY? Wilton, Conn.: Current Affairs Films, 1974. Filmstrip. Sound. Color. Teacher's guide. JH, HS.

This filmstrip describes the present food shortage throughout the world. It provides a graphic description of food shortages, protein deficiencies, and the effects these have on human beings. The problem and several possible solutions are depicted authentically and with a high degree of objectivity.

ONE WAY TO BETTER CITIES. New York: Harold Mantell, 1969. Film. 29 mins. Sound. Color. Teacher's guide. HS.

The film discusses the economic influence of the property tax. It attributes to this tax: urban decay, suburban sprawl, and land speculation. The film advances suggestions as to how private industry might be motivated to renew, upgrade, and develop urban improvement programs.

OUR CHANGING CITIES: CAN THEY BE SAVED? Chicago: Encyclopaedia Britannica Films, 1974. Film. Sound. Color. HS.

This film contains cultural and historical background data concerning the labor market's reaction to the Industrial Revolution and increased mechanization of manual tasks, both rural and commercial. The film concentrates on the subsequent labor migration from rural to urban America. It compares life in the city to that in the suburbs and discusses the economic factors in present day urban societies.

PEOPLE IN MOTION: THE TRANSPORTATION DILEMMA. Holyoke, Mass.: Scott Education Division, 1973. 2 filmstrips. Sound. Teacher's guide. JH, HS.

This is an analysis of the problem of attempting to find efficient means of moving people to, from, and around large urban areas. This series could serve as a part of a larger study of the total energy crisis.

THE PEOPLE PROBLEM. Wilmette, Ill.: Films, 1972. Film. 17 mins. Sound. Color. HS.

This Canadian Broadcasting Corporation production both visually and verbally paints a pessimistic picture of the future for the earth's inhabitants. There are too many people and the population explosion continues unabated in the developing nations. The rich nations of the world have squandered the earth's resources and set a bad example for the developing nations. In this time of crisis the rich nations must provide the leadership to solve the people problem.

POVERTY. Pleasantville, N.Y.: Audio Visual Narrative Arts, 1972. 3 filmstrips. Sound. Color. Teacher's guide. HS.

These filmstrips portray various types of poor, including non-white ethnic groups, the aged, migratory workers, displaced blue collar workers, and marginal farmers. After identifying the poor, the filmstrips present reasons for poverty and attempts to eliminate poverty, from the time of the New Deal legislation to modern legislative efforts.

POVERTY, PROBLEM AND PROMISE. Wilton, Conn.: Current Affairs Films, 1964. Filmstrip. 42 frames. B&W. HS.

The causes, extent, and victims of poverty are identified. Some of the proposals to cope with the problem of poverty in the United States are discussed.

PROBLEMS IN OUR CITIES. New York: Miller Brody Productions. 6 filmstrips. Sound. Color. Teacher's guide. HS.

This is a complete study unit on urban problems, designed to stimulate discussion and motivate research and learning. Each filmstrip presents one aspect of the problem and suggests possible causes and solutions. The titles are: "Introduction"; "Housing"; "Pollution"; "Traffic"; "Social Problems"; "Urban Renewal"; and "City Planning."

PROBLEMS OF THE CITIES. Filmstrip on Current Affairs. New York: New York Times, 1968. Filmstrip. 75 frames. Sound. B&W. JH, HS.

Urban renewal, transportation, the flight to the suburbs, taxes, crime in the streets, and the problems associated with the departure of business from the cities are examined.

Economic Problems

UNEMPLOYMENT IN A FREE ECONOMY. Wilton, Conn.: Current Affairs Films, 1960. Filmstrip. 39 frames. B&W. HS.

A historical record of unemployment immediately after World War II is presented. Kinds of unemployment are described and some proposals for preventing it are discussed.

URBAN AMERICA AS WE SEE IT. Pleasantville, N.Y.: Guidance Associates. Filmstrip. 15 mins. Sound. HS.

The photos and script for this filmstrip were created by students. They convey an immediate sense of life on inner-city streets. Problems with housing, environmental services, crime and drugs, and police are described. The excitement of city life is projected.

URBAN EDUCATION STUDIES: BASIC ALBUMS. New York: John Day Co., 1965. HS.

Sets of photographs have been chosen to illustrate problems and attitudes towards living in big cities.

URBAN STUDIES. Chicago: Singer/SVE, 1973. 11 filmloops. Color. JH, HS.

This set of loops is designed to help students visualize the impor- tant elements found in a typical urban area. Onsite photography presents impressive surveys of the overall urban structure. Titles are: "Aerial View"; "Cross-section"; "Contrasts"; "Population"; "Occupations"; "Recreation"; "Culture"; "Government"; "Transpor- tation"; "Industry"; "Commerce."

VALUE OF YOUR DOLLAR. Wilton, Conn.: Current Affairs Films, 1968. Filmstrip. 43 frames. Color. HS.

The causes and consequences of inflationary pressures are described. The gold drain is discussed and suggestions for maintaining dollar stability are reviewed.

THE WAR AGAINST POVERTY. Old Greenwich, Conn.: Listening Library, 1966. Filmstrip. Sound, B&W. HS.

A look at the antipoverty programs of the 1960s is presented. The nature, extent, and distribution of poverty is discussed and the weapons used to attack the problems are reviewed.

WELFARE DILEMMA. Pleasantville, N.Y.: Guidance Associates. 2 film- strips, 10 mins. ea. Sound. HS.

Experts in this field examine the present system, pointing out its major inadequacies and suggesting new approaches.

WELFARE PROGRAM: PROBLEMS AND PROSPECTS. Old Greenwich, Conn.: Listening Library, 1972. Filmstrip. Sound. Color. Teacher's guide. HS.

> The ever-increasing burden on the taxpayer to support the ever-growing welfare program is discussed.

WHAT'S THE PRICE? Wilton, Conn.: Current Affairs Films, 1967. Filmstrip. JH.

> Some of the factors involved in changing the purchasing power of money, and thus causing either the inflation or depression of its value are examined.

WHERE WE LIVE: REGIONAL PLANNING AND THE HOUSING CRISIS. Holyoke, Mass.: Scott Education Division, 1973. 2 filmstrips. Sound. Color. Teacher's guide. JH, HS.

> Urban sprawl and growth without planning are universal problems but perhaps most acute in the United States. This series provides an analysis of the problem of urban growth and its interrelatedness to other concerns.

WORK IN THE CITIES. New York: New York Times, 1970. Filmstrip. 66 frames. Sound. Color. HS.

> In exploring the effects of rising unemployment upon cities, this filmstrip considers factors influencing job opportunities; the job search; subemployment; training programs; the hard-core unemployed; and the cities' economic burdens.

Chapter 6
ECONOMIC SYSTEMS

Barach, Arnold B. THE U.S.A. AND ITS ECONOMIC FUTURE. New York:
Macmillan, 1964. 148 p. HS.

> Charts and maps illustrate the nature, growth, and extent of all
> kinds of economic resources and factors in the United States.
> Some projections are made into the future. The book aims to
> stimulate interest in economics and economic institutions.

Berle, Adolf A. THE AMERICAN ECONOMIC REPUBLIC. New York:
Harcourt, Brace, & World, 1965. 274 p. HS.

> An analysis of the American economic system, explaining how it
> works, why it is successful, and how it can become even greater.

Bloom, Clark C. HOW THE AMERICAN ECONOMY IS ORGANIZED. Primer of Economics Series, no. 2. Iowa City: Bureau of Business and Economic
Research, State University of Iowa, 1961. 34 p. HS.

> An introduction to the functioning of a market economy, explain-
> ing the interrelationships among business, consumer, and govern-
> ment. An analysis of change in tastes, resource supplies, and
> technology is followed by a consideration of the role of profits.

Chamber of Commerce of the United States of America. THE POWER OF
CHOICE. Understanding Economics Series, no. 10. Washington, D.C.:
1966. 46 p. HS.

> This pamphlet presents the ideas and values which undergird our
> American way of life. It explains how the constitutional princi-
> ples of a voluntary economy to enlarge human power to choose
> and to act.

_____. WHY PRICES? Washington, D.C.: 1966. 31 p. HS.

> This is an explanation of the basic elements involved in setting
> prices and the impact of prices on the organization and function

of a market economy. It shows why prices of goods and services affect supply, as well as demand, and why demand and supply, in turn, affect prices; it points out that, in a competitive market, balance is achieved between supply and demand.

Council for the Advancement of Secondary Education. CAPITALISM AND OTHER ECONOMIC SYSTEMS. Washington, D.C.: 1962. 110 p. HS.

An economic analysis of the market economy and of Communist and Socialist economies.

Forman, Brenda. AMERICA'S PLACE IN THE WORLD ECONOMY. New York: Harcourt, Brace, & World, 1969. 127 p. HS.

The implications of America's position as a dominant power in the world economy are examined. The author focuses on the extent and nature of this country's wealth and the responsibilities and limitations inherent in its power.

Friedman, Milton. CAPITALISM AND FREEDOM. Chicago: University of Chicago Press, 1965. 202 p. HS.

The book opens with a discussion of the nature of freedom and of the role of government. The author discusses his view of the proper role of competitive capitalism in achieving economic free- dom and maintaining political freedom. Problems considered in- clude these: monetary and fiscal policy, international trade, ed- ucation, discrimination, monopoly, distribution of income, social welfare, and poverty.

Galbraith, John K. THE AFFLUENT SOCIETY. New York: New American Library, 1963. 286 p. HS.

This is one of the most talked-of economic books of our time. The analysis of poverty and abundance reflects the social and economic changes of the past decade. The book's central theme of public versus private wants leads to thought on the allocation of resources and to the heart of economics.

_____. AMERICAN CAPITALISM: THE CONCEPT OF COUNTERVAILING POWER. Boston: Houghton Mifflin, 1965. 208 p. HS.

The author looks at society in terms of the balance of power and is ready to use the power of government to build a better eco- nomic society, one in which the power of government is used to neutralize the economic powers of business and labor.

_____. THE NEW INDUSTRIAL STATE. 2d ed. Boston: Houghton Mifflin, 1971. 423 p. HS.

The author believes that the imperatives of technology and growth of giant corporations are bringing about a planned economy. He sees government increasingly allied to industry and sees the displacement of the entrepreneur. Management is viewed as the new directing force, its decision making assisted by the "technostructure" of the educated, experienced specialist. He poses questions regarding the impact of these changes on education and social and political behavior.

Gay, Kathlyn. MONEY ISN'T EVERYTHING: THE STORY OF ECONOMICS AT WORK. New York: Delacorte, 1967. 96 p. Elem.

The author describes our economic system as a vast network of interdependent producers and consumers. She discusses such topics as profit and loss, taxes, savings and investments, and points out how each individual plays an important part in the whole system.

Glassner, Sherwin, and Grossman, Edward N. HOW THE AMERICAN ECONOMIC SYSTEM FUNCTIONS. Westchester, Ill.: Benefic, 1968. 96 p. Elem, JH.

The various aspects of the American economic system are presented and compared to communism and socialism. How goods and services are produced and distributed in the American capitalistic system is described in conjunction with an explanation of the organization of one-man businesses, partnerships, and corporations. Roles of labor, unions, and government in the American economy are also discussed. (See HOW THE AMERICAN ECONOMIC SYSTEM FUNCTIONS, p. 66.)

Heilbroner, Robert L. MAKING OF ECONOMIC SOCIETY. 4th ed. Englewood Cliffs, N.J.: Prentice-Hall, 1972. 272 p. HS.

The author, tracing the development of the market society from antiquity to the present, gives a strong background in economic history. Chapters analyze the pros and cons of capitalism and relate the problems of today's America to the development of economic history. He gives a picture of historic change and an insight to economics as a key to understanding the past and present.

Hoover, Calvin B. THE ECONOMY, LIBERTY AND THE STATE. Garden City, N.Y.: Doubleday, 1961. 408 p. HS.

This is a comparative study of modern economic systems. The focus is on the degree to which the economies of the West and Communist Russia meet the basic desires for liberty and justice.

Industrial Relations Center. COMPETITIVE PRICES IN ACTION. Basic Economic Series. Chicago: University of Chicago, 1965. 30 p. HS.

Starting with the problem of unlimited wants and limited resources, the pamphlet explores the purpose of competitive prices, how competitive prices work, and the competitive price system. Restrictive practices of government interference, monopolistic business practices, and monopolistic labor practices are discussed.

_____. PRODUCING FOR BETTER LIVING. Chicago: University of Chicago, 1965. 38 p. JH, HS.

This pamphlet would be especially useful in junior high school. It contains a brief but excellent description of the market economy.

Lovenstein, Meno. CAPITALISM, COMMUNISM, SOCIALISM: COMPARATIVE ECONOMIC SYSTEMS. Studies in Economic Issues Series. Minneapolis: Curriculum Resources, 1962. 150 p. HS.

This booklet provides comparative views of the functions common to all economies and evaluates them in terms of socioeconomic goals. There are descriptions of U.S. capitalism, the USSR and other Communist economies, and mixed economies.

Maher, John E. LEARNING ABOUT PEOPLE WORKING FOR YOU. New York: Franklin Watts, 1969. 70 p. Elem.

The author defines and analyzes the many elements of our economic system. He shows how goods and services are produced, both privately and by government, and traces the modern trends in our economy and their effects upon society.

Oxenfeldt, Alfred R. ECONOMIC SYSTEMS IN ACTION: THE U.S., SOVIET UNION AND THE UNITED KINGDOM. New York: Holt, Rinehart & Winston, 1965. 288 p. HS.

With reference to the functions common to all economies, the author describes and evaluates three different types of economies: capitalism in the United States; Communist economic planning in the Soviet Union, China, and Eastern Europe; and rhe economy of Great Britain under the labor government.

Rosenblum, Marc. HOW A MARKET ECONOMY WORKS. Minneapolis: Lerner, 1970. 87 p. JH.

This book discusses the basic principles of a market economy--one in which most resources are owned by people or by corporations-- and its application in the United States.

U.S. Department of Commerce. THE MARKETING STORY. Washington,

D.C.: 1968. 50 p. Distributed by Government Printing Office. HS.

This booklet traces the role of marketing from producer through distributor to consumer. It tells how our marketing system works to bring goods from farm and factory to satisfy the everyday needs of the American home.

MEDIA

AMERICAN CAPITALISM: A FLEXIBLE AND DYNAMIC SYSTEM. Economics for Our Times Series. New York: McGraw-Hill, 1962. Filmstrip. 36 frames. Color. HS.

This filmstrip correlates with the book, ECONOMICS FOR OUR TIMES by Augustus H. Smith. Our economy is pictured as the most productive in the world. It is compared with early theories and practices of capitalism. Its history and evolution are described and the role of the federal government in today's economy is explained. (See Smith, Augustus H. ECONOMICS FOR OUR TIMES. Chapter 10.)

AUSTRIA, PAST AND PRESENT. Chicago: Coronet Instructional Films, 1966. Film. 11 mins. Sound. Color. Teacher's guide. JH.

The historical background, cultural heritage, and beautiful cities of this Alpine country are presented. It is explained how the economy is related to the mountains and hydroelectric power.

BOY OF SOUTHEAST ASIA. Los Angeles: Film Associates, 1967. Film. 16 mins. Sound. Color. JH.

The economy and customs of life in Southeast Asia are shown by following the activities of Geng and his friends.

COMMUNISM AND ECONOMICS. Chicago: Singer/SVE, 1963. Filmstrip. Sound. Color. Teacher's guide. JH.

The filmstrip compares a Communist-oriented economic system with an American style market-oriented system. It provides a basis for discussing two ways of organizing an economic system.

COMMUNIST CHINA. New York: McGraw-Hill, 1964. Film. 30 mins. B&W. HS.

The economics of Communist China, its organization and operation, is shown through newsreels. Factors that shaped decisions on the allocation of scarce resources are presented.

COMPARATIVE ECONOMIC SYSTEMS. World of Economics Series. New

65

York: McGraw-Hill, 1963. Filmstrip. 35 frames. Color. HS.

This filmstrip is correlated with THE WORLD OF ECONOMICS by Leonard [S.] Silk It describes how laissez-faire and mixed capitalism, Communist, Fascist, and Socialist systems decide the fundamental economic questions. (See Silk, Leonard S. THE WORLD OF ECONOMICS. Chapter 10.)

ECONOMIC GEOGRAPHY: COMPARING TWO NATIONS. Santa Monica, Calif.: BFA Educational Media. Film. 10 mins. Color. JH.

Why does one nation prosper, while another with apparently similar economic resources remains underdeveloped? This film answers this question by comparing the people and the economics of two nations. One nation is primarily dependent on just one major crop for its income, while the other has a diversified economy.

ECONOMICS. Santa Ana, Calif.: Doubleday Multimedia, 1972. 3 filmstrips, 55–60 frames ea. Sound. Color. Teacher's guide. JH, HS.

Three basic economic systems of today, namely, traditional, centralized, and market, are generally described. Our U.S. system is shown to be a combination of all three types. The differences between the Mexican system and ours are discussed.

EVERYONE HELPS IN THE COMMUNITY. Los Angeles: Churchill-Wexler Production Films, 1960. Film. 15 mins. Sound. Color. Prim, Elem.

The coming of the railroad transforms the life of a farm family. It is now possible for them to specialize in the production of strawberries and as a result, they become dependent on others for goods and services. The farm becomes more productive and the family becomes involved in market processes.

HELPERS WHO COME TO OUR HOUSE. Chicago: Coronet Instructional Films, 1955. Film. 12 mins. Sound. B&W. Prim.

Goods and services delivered to the home are shown. The connection can be made between income and the goods and services that a family can enjoy.

HOW THE AMERICAN ECONOMIC SYSTEM FUNCTIONS. Westchester, Ill.: Benefic, 1969. Filmstrip. Color. Elem.

This filmstrip was designed for use with the Glassner book of the same title. The organization of American businesses, labor's involvement, and regulations of the government are shown. (See Glassner, Sherwin, and Grossman, Edward W. HOW THE AMERICAN ECONOMIC SYSTEM FUNCTIONS, page 63.)

INDIA AND PAKISTAN. New York: New York Times, 1969. Filmstrip. 60 frames. Sound. B&W. HS.

The political, economic, and social life and customs of India through the years are shown.

JAPAN'S GEOGRAPHY: HUMAN AND ECONOMIC. New York: Sterling Educational Films, 1962. Film. 13 mins. Sound. Color. JH.

From the green Boso Peninsula to the congested railway confluence in the urban Tokyo, the country is pictured in a panorama that highlights its age-old topography and its changing economy.

MARKETS IN A FREE ECONOMY. World of Economics Series. New York: McGraw-Hill, 1963. Filmstrip. 35 frames. Color. HS.

This filmstrip is correlated with THE WORLD OF ECONOMICS by Leonard S. Silk. It defines the market system and describes how the system functions to allocate scarce resources to fulfill human desires. Instances when government intervention has modified market results are described. (See Silk, Leonard S. THE WORLD OF ECONOMICS. Chapter 10.)

MONEY TALKS: ALLOCATING OUR RESOURCES. New York: Carousel Films, 1962. Film. 30 mins. Sound. B&W. HS.

In the mixed economy of the United States, fundamental questions of what shall be produced and who shall enjoy the benefits of production are decided by the private decision making of individuals and institutions. In some instances the government does intervene to influence what shall be produced and who shall enjoy the benefit of production.

MONEY TALKS: CASE FOR COMPETITION. New York: Carousel Films, 1962. Film. 30 mins. Sound. B&W. HS.

The case of competitive markets versus monopolistic markets is presented. The difficulty of trying to achieve the benefits of both systems is discussed.

OUR ECONOMIC SYSTEM. New York: Filmstrip House, 1963. 6 filmstrips, 34-40 frames ea. Color. JH, HS.

Titles in this series are: "Freedom and Responsibility"; "Private Capital"; "Profit Motive"; "Competition"; "Labor"; "The Role of Government."

STATE ENTERPRISE IN EASTERN EUROPE. Santa Ana, Calif.: International Communications Films, 1966. Filmloop. 4 mins. Color. JH, HS.

Examples of large and small state-owned enterprises are shown. Urban industries and farms are seen which are state-owned, affording the government control over the economy. This film illustrates various stages of economic development among these countries.

SUPPLY AND DEMAND. New York: McGraw-Hill, 1950. Filmstrip. 34 frames. B&W. HS.

This filmstrip describes the determination of equilibrium prices under competitive conditions. The relationship between the extent of competition and price elasticity of demand is depicted and the elasticity of supply is described.

Chapter 7

ENVIRONMENT AND NATURAL RESOURCES

Bardach, John. HARVEST OF THE SEA. New York: Harper & Row, 1968. 301 p. HS.

In this popular study of developments in ocean science of sea life and its potential for food and industry, the author traces the development of the fishing industry from the family boat operation to the modern factory afloat. He discusses fisheries research, conservation, and utilization of marine resources.

Bixby, William. A WORLD YOU CAN LIVE IN. New York: McCay, 1971. 130 p. Elem.

In this book the author comments on America's ecological past, present, and future. He contends that this generation must stop pollution, promote conservation, and stress the importance of ecology in general.

Burke, William. KNOWLEDGE, SCIENCE AND AEROSPACE. San Francisco: Federal Reserve Bank, 1966. 29 p. HS.

This pamphlet discusses the costs and economic roles of higher education and of research and development. The role of defense and especially aerospace in the economies of California and other parts of the western United States is explained. Attention is also given to the problems of conversion to nondefense activity.

Davies, Delwyn. FRESH WATER: THE PRECIOUS RESOURCE. Garden City, N.Y.: Natural History Press, 1969. 155 p. HS.

The author explains the properties, distribution, and uses of water, including purification, irrigation, desalination, and reuse. He also examines some of the problems arising from increased demands of the world's water supply in the light of man's essential physiological needs and modern industrialized society's requirements.

ECOTACTICS: THE SIERRA CLUB HANDBOOK FOR ENVIRONMENT ACTIV-
ISTS. Edited by John G. Mitchell with Constance L. Stallings. New York:
Simon & Schuster, 1970. 288 p. HS.

Ecotactics is the science of arranging and maneuvering all available forces in action against enemies of our planet Earth. This
collection of essays tells how the individual can fight to save the
earth via the law, the media, rapping, teach-ins, and education.
Many of the essays were written by college student activists in
this field as well as by veterans such as Ralph Nader.

Fenton, D.X. HARVESTING THE SEA. New York: Lippincott, 1970. 63 p.
Elem.

The natural resources found in the sea, present methods of harvesting them, and prospects for the future utilization of the sea
are discussed. The author includes information on various methods used to catch fish, to produce fresh water from salty sea water,
and to collect minerals and oil.

Hitch, Allen S., and Sorenson, Marian. CONSERVATION AND YOU.
Princeton, N.J.: Van Nostrand Co., 1964. 126 p. Illus. Elem.

The need for preserving wildlife and wilderness areas and for
maintaining the delicate balance of nature upon which mankind's
survival depends is presented.

Landsberg, Hans H. NATURAL RESOURCES FOR U.S. GROWTH: A LOOK TO
THE YEAR 2000. Washington, D.C.: Johns Hopkins Press for Resources for
the Future, 1964. 260 p. HS.

Much of the folklore that passes for fact in the areas of natural
resource use is disposed of in this book. How we are using our
natural resources and what will be required for continued development of the U.S. economy is discussed. A look toward the year
2000, based on what has been done and what is still in the developmental stage, is presented.

Lauber, Patricia. DUST BOWL: THE STORY OF MAN ON THE GREAT
PLAINS. New York: Coward-McCann, 1958. 96 p. Illus. Maps. Elem.

A dramatic account of the Great Plains region and its development into a "dust bowl" is given. The region before the coming
of the settlers is described, the factors that caused the erosion are
traced, and action being taken to prevent further erosion is mentioned. New conservation methods are also noted.

McClellan, Grant S., ed. LAND USE IN THE U.S.: EXPLOITATION OR
CONSERVATION. Reference Shelf, vol. 43, no. 2. Bronx, N.Y.:
H.W. Wilson, 1971. 253 p. HS.

The first section touches on our emerging land use policies. Section 2, "A Land to Live In," briefly raises the issue of a new
urban-rural balance and the building or rebuilding of our cities.
Questions of conservation and proper use of our water, forest, and
mining resources are dealt with in section 3. Brief reference in
section 4 is made to our national parks, wilderness areas, and
other scenic lands.

Mattison, C.W., and Alvarez, Joseph. MAN AND HIS RESOURCES IN
TODAY'S WORLD. Mankato, Mich.: Creative Educational Society, 1967.
144 p. Illus. Elem.

When our continent was discovered by European settlers, it revealed a hoard of natural treasures greater than the gold sought.
An introduction in clear text and excellent photographs, to the
present problem of preserving different resources--air, water, forests, wildlife, and minerals is presented.

Pollock, George F. THE CONSERVATION STORY: A BACKGROUND FOR
UNDERSTANDING TODAY'S CRISIS. Columbus, Ohio: American Education
Publications, 1969. 47 p. HS.

Contemporary case studies focus on major conflicts in conservation:
the pollution of Lake Erie, the fight over DDT, the California
redwoods issues, and others. The history of conservation is traced
from Thoreau's day to the present.

Pringle, Laurence. THE ONLY EARTH WE HAVE. New York: Macmillan,
1969. 86 p. Elem.

This book stresses the importance of living with nature. It explains clearly how polluted air affects human beings, property,
climate, plants, and animals. It shows how water becomes polluted and unusable, points out the dangers of long-lasting bio-
cides to wildlife, and discusses the problem of the disposal of used
materials.

Stead, William H. NATURAL RESOURCE USE IN OUR ECONOMY. Rev.
ed. New York: Joint Council on Economic Education, 1960. 88 p. HS.

The basic problem dealt with in this booklet is this: How can we
manage our renewable and nonrenewable resources wisely enough
to maintain a high standard of living?

U.S. Department of Agriculture, Soil Conservation Service. MEASURE OF
OUR LAND. Washington, D.C.: Government Printing Office, 1971. 22 p.
HS.

This is a discussion of the uses of our land for roads, factories,

towns, and farms and which lands can be best used for all of
these purposes.

_____. OUR AMERICAN LAND, USE THE LAND, SAVE THE SOIL. Agri-
cultural Information Bulletin, no. 321. Washington, D.C.: Government
Printing Office, 1968. 29 p. HS.

Our growing population needs more of the products of the land.
If we are going to be able to meet these needs we must use wis-
dom, skill, and technology to keep the land productive.

_____. SOIL CONSERVATION AT HOME, TIPS FOR CITY AND SUBURBAN
DWELLERS. Agricultural Information Bulletin, no. 244. Washington, D.C.:
Government Printing Office, 1967. 29 p. HS.

This bulletin is about conservation for the small pieces of land
that surround urban and suburban homes. It provides some hints
about coping with some of the soil and water problems of these
places.

_____. WATER AND THE LAND, FACTS ABOUT OUR WATER PROBLEM.
Washington, D.C.: Government Printing Office, 1965. 15 p. HS.

The national aspect of the water problem is discussed as is the
need to conserve and manage the available water in each community to best serve the long-time needs of its people.

Zimmerman, Erich W. INTRODUCTION TO WORLD RESOURCES. New York:
Harper & Row, 1964. 220 p. HS.

The author believes resources are not only raw materials but also
include factors necessary to utilize them, such as labor, power,
and marketing.

MEDIA

BEER CAN BY THE HIGHWAY. Tarrytown, N.Y.: Schloat Productions.
Filmstrip. 12 mins. Sound. Color. Guide. Elem.

This filmstrip presents a thoughtful examination of the conflict
between America's extremely high standard of living and dread-
fully low standard of conservation. Students will gain a new
awareness of the psychology and economics of our throwaway culture and the conspicuous waste so ingrained in American life.

CONSERVATION: A JOB FOR YOUNG AMERICA. New York: McGraw-
Hill, 1968. Film. 19 mins. Sound. Color. Teacher's guide. JH.

This film points out that the uncontrolled by-products of technology and industry are affecting air, water, soil, and wildlife. The responsibility for control of these by-products and for conservation lies with society.

CONSERVATION FOR BEGINNERS. Chicago: Coronet Instructional Films, 1967. Film. 11 mins. Sound. Color. Prim.

Students observe through field trips and experimental work in class the effects of erosion, crop rotation, contour planting, preserving woods, and other essential conditions affecting the output of land and productivity.

CONSERVATION FOR TODAY'S AMERICA. Chicago: Singer/SVE. 1967. 7 filmstrips, average 44 frames ea. Sound. Color. Elem.

An analysis of the importance of conservation of natural resources including urban and land conservation is presented. There is also an explanation of the causes of these problems and what can be done about them.

CONSERVATION IN THE CITY. Chicago: Encyclopaedia Britannica Films, 1968. 3 filmstrips, average 54 frames ea. Color. Elem.

Conservation as it affects people, birds, animals, insects, plants, and trees is discussed. It is important to plan for open spaces when living spaces are developed as an aid to health, protection from weather, and to preserve the beauty of our cities.

CONSERVING OUR FORESTS TODAY. Chicago: Coronet Instructional Films, 1960. Film. 11 mins. Sound. Color. Teacher's guide. Elem, JH.

The advances in forest conservation such as the use of helicopters in fighting fires, new insecticides and chemicals for the control of disease, aerial seeding, and mechanical transplanting are pointed out. The value of forests for lumber, grazing, water, and recreation is shown.

CONSERVING OUR MINERAL RESOURCES TODAY. Chicago: Coronet Instructional Films, 1966. Film. 11 mins. Sound. Color. JH.

This film shows that costs of production have increased because of inefficient use of mineral metals. Some that were once available in the United States must be imported. Better utilization of resources and use of alternative sources of supply must be brought about to contain increasing costs.

CONTROVERSY OVER INDUSTRIAL POLLUTION: A CASE STUDY. Chicago: Encyclopaedia Britannica Films. Film. 17 mins. Color. Teacher's guide. JH, HS.

This film tells of the scientific, social, and economic issues involved in the case of the Anaconda Aluminum Company's plant in Columbia Falls, Montana.

THE EARTH'S RESOURCES. New York: McGraw-Hill, 1970. 6 filmstrips. Color. Elem.

Information about such topics as minerals and other resources from the oceans, the hydrologic cycle, minerals and metals from the ground, coal and fuels underground, weathering and erosion and gases in the atmosphere is presented. The titles in this series are: "Ocean Resources"; "Fresh Water Resources"; "Mineral and Rock Resources"; "Fuel Resources"; "Atmospheric Resources"; "Soil Resources."

ENERGY AND ECONOMIC GROWTH. New York: American Petroleum Institute. 6 wall charts. Booklet. Teacher's guide. HS.

This unit is a compendium of standard, authoritative statistics and relevant ideas concerning energy and economic growth. Chart titles: "Factors Contributing to Economic Growth"; "Economic Growth--How Measured"; "Energy Use and Economic Growth"; "Energy Use and the National Income"; "Changing Picture of Energy Use"; "Future Growth and Energy Needs."

ENERGY AND YOUR FUTURE ENVIRONMENT. Norwood, Mass.: Edward Perry. Kit. 2 filmstrips. 4 transparencies. Spirit duplicator master. Worksheets. 2 wall charts. Games. Teacher's guide. Elem.

This program centers attention on the wise use of energy resources and the improvement of our environments. Students become involved in the issues and in the discovery of possible solutions at home and in their communities.

ENERGY CRISIS: DEPLETING THE WORLD'S RESOURCES. Wilton, Conn.: Current Affairs Films, 1973. Filmstrip. 64 frames. Sound. Color. HS.

The shortage of natural resources in the United States and the possible effects on people's lives as well as on progress are investigated in this filmstrip.

ENVIRONMENT AND THE ECONOMY. Bedford Hills, N.Y.: Teaching Resources Films. Filmstrip. Sound. Color. Teacher's guide. JH.

This is a discussion of industry's role in pollution, the individual's ambivalence when pollution control measures bring higher prices, less convenience, and questionable quality.

FOOD, CLOTHING AND SHELTER IN THREE ENVIRONMENTS. Los Angeles:

Film Associates, 1969. Film. 16 mins. Sound. Color. Elem, JH, HS.

A comparison is presented of the basic living conditions of people in the dry deserts of West Pakistan, hot tropical islands of the Pacific, and the cold northern mountains of Japan, showing how people adjust their clothing, food, and homes to their environment.

FORESTS. Rochester, N.Y.: Ward's National Science Establishment. Filmstrip. 65 frames. Color. Teacher's guide. Elem, JH, HS.

The uses to man of forests and their products are discussed. The filmstrip illustrates how forests help to control erosion and some of the dangers confronting our forests.

THE GREAT SWAMP. Bloomington, Ind.: Audio-Visual Center, 1968. Film. Sound. Color. Elem, JH.

The experiences of a young city boy during a visit to the Great Swamp in New Jersey stress the importance of conservation, the balance of nature, and the values of a wilderness area.

THE HOUSES OF MAN: OUR CHANGING ENVIRONMENT. Chicago: Encyclopaedia Britannica Films, 1964. Film. 17 mins. Sound. Color. JH, HS.

The waste of natural resources in cities, woodlands, and farmlands and the pollution of our rivers and the air are discussed. Wasteful methods and intelligent conservation techniques are compared. The film shows how and why man must apply these techniques to save his world.

LAND USES AND VALUES. Tarrytown, N.Y.: Schloat Productions. 3 filmstrips, 13 mins. ea. Sound. Color. Guide. Elem.

This program aims to stimulate discussion toward responsible uses of land. Today's environmental and urban problems demand that land usage--whether for playgrounds or for skyscrapers--be carefully planned to avoid future complications. The titles are: "What Gives Value to Land?"; "How is Land Owned?"; "Land and the United States."

LEARNING ABOUT CONSERVATION. Chicago: Coronet Instructional Films, 1968. 6 filmstrips, average 48 frames ea. Sound. Color. Elem.

An explanation of the importance of our natural resources, their use and misuse, and what can be done to conserve and preserve them is given. Ways are shown to assist the work of conservation officials. Contents: "Some Problems We Face"; "Our Soil"; "Our Water and Air"; "Our Forests"; "Our Grasslands"; "Our Minerals and Energy Resources."

Environment and Natural Resources

MAN USES AND CHANGES THE LAND. Chicago: Coronet Instructional Films, 1967. Film. 11 mins. Sound. Color. Elem.

A discussion of land as a factor of production is presented. The film focuses on the persisting problem of making the best use of this resource, with the aid of modern technology, for mankind's increasing need for food, clothing, and shelter.

NEIGHBORHOOD SERIES. Chicago: Coronet Instructional Films, 1967. 6 filmstrips. Sound. Color. Prim.

This series describes the various kinds of neighborhoods and it depicts their interrelationships. The sixth filmstrip analyzes why neighborhoods change. Titles: "Neighborhoods of Many Kinds"; Neighborhoods in the Country"; "Neighborhoods in Small Towns"; "Neighborhoods in the City"; "Neighborhoods in the Suburbs"; "Neighborhoods Change."

OCEANS, THE LAST FRONTIER. Bedford Hills, N.Y.: Teaching Resources Films. Filmstrip. Sound. Color. HS.

An analysis of the political and economic significance of the oceans as a source of minerals, food, and living space is given.

OIL IN THE MODERN WORLD. East Providence, R.I.: Avid Corp. Filmstrip. 36 frames. Color. Elem, JH.

The production of oil is followed from the field to refinery to distributor; drilling and refining processes and the use of the final product are discussed.

OUR NATURAL RESOURCES. New York: Filmstrip House, 1973. Filmstrip. Sound. Color. Elem, JH.

Decreasing supplies of natural resources of Canada, the United States, and Mexico are discussed. These include petroleum, iron ore, copper, other scarce metals, forests, water, and agricultural products.

OUR POLLUTED WORLD: THE PRICE OF PROGRESS. Wilton, Conn.: Current Affairs Films. Filmstrip. 18 mins. Sound. Color. Discussion guide. JH, HS.

The problem of pollution in the United States, Italy, and India is considered. Some of the ways in which the earth has been polluted are shown. There is a discussion of the relation between pollution and economic growth.

OUR PRODUCTIVE RESOURCES. Pasadena, Calif.: Arthur Barr Productions, 1968. Film. 10 mins. Sound. Color. Teacher's guide. Prim.

The need of resources for the fulfillment of human desires is shown. Scarcity is defined and the young viewer is challenged to identify the productive resources used in the things that are found in the home and school.

SQUANDERED RESOURCES. Old Greenwich, Conn.: Listening Library, 1971. Filmstrip. Sound. B&W. Teacher's manual. JH, HS.

Current needs and natural resources are discussed and some projections are made for the future. Man's chances for survival on his home planet are examined.

Chapter 8
GENERAL

Alexander, Albert. ECONOMICS. Young Adult Library. New York:
Franklin Watts, 1963. 66 p. HS.

   How the American economy manages natural, human, and capital
   resources to produce the most worthwhile goods and services is
   discussed. The government's role in our economy is explained
   and the Russian and American systems compared.

Barron, J.F., and Hoff, Marilyn L. SOME CONCEPTS ESSENTIAL TO BASIC
UNDERSTANDING OF ECONOMICS. Cincinnati: South-Western Publishing
Co., 1964. 41 p. HS.

   This pamphlet introduces concepts that provide the essential framework for an elementary course in economics. An understanding of
   these concepts will facilitate the understanding and analysis of
   most practical economic problems.

Chamber of Commerce of the United States of America. WHY ECONOMICS?
Washington, D.C.: 1966. 31 p. HS.

   This pamphlet shows clearly what economics is all about. It explains why every nation, every human society, needs an economic
   system of some sort. There is a discussion of the basic problem
   of the scarcity of the factors of production and how the American
   society has tackled this problem with a free enterprise system in
   which supply and demand determine what is to be produced. It
   also explains how private enterprise operates, and shows the advantages of a private market economy over other economic systems.

Colm, Gerhard, and Geiger, Theodore. THE ECONOMY OF THE AMERICAN
PEOPLE. 3d ed. Washington, D.C.: National Planning Association, 1967.
218 p. HS.

   To show how the American economy has achieved its high productivity and living standards, the authors discuss its history, its performance at home and in the world economy, and American aspirations and outlook. Part 1 provides a useful discussion of the factors basic to our high level of production. Part 2 centers on discussion of current issues, the booklet should also be a useful guide to current economic problems, in addition to providing a valuable supplement to the study of American history.

Douglas, Paul H. IN OUR TIME. New York: Harcourt Brace Jovanovich, 1968. 228 p. HS.

This is a former senator's comments on economic inequities in society such as tax loopholes, political financing, consumer credit abuses, truth in lending, and poverty.

Gill, Richard T. ECONOMIC DEVELOPMENT: PAST AND PRESENT. Modern Economic Series. Englewood Cliffs, N.J.: Prentice-Hall, 1964. 120 p. HS.

This booklet is usable as an introduction to economics for the general reader. It is a short survey of the contributions of economics to an understanding of the process of growth and development. It includes an explanation of economic development factors and theories, a review of problems of underdeveloped nations, and a comparison of Indian and Chinese approaches to economic problems.

Heilbroner, Robert L. THE GREAT ASCENT: THE STRUGGLE FOR ECONOMIC DEVELOPMENT IN OUR TIME. New York: Harper & Row, 1963. 160 p. HS.

This volume expresses a controversial view of political conditions for economic development. Economic problems of today and the challenge of these problems to America are discussed.

_____. MAKING OF ECONOMIC SOCIETY. 4th ed. Englewood Cliffs, N.J.: Prentice-Hall, 1972. 272 p. HS.

The author presents the basic elements of economic thought, tracing economic evolution from the slave system and feudalism through the industrial revolution to the present. The main theme is the rise and development of the market system.

Horton, Byrne J., et al. DICTIONARY OF MODERN ECONOMICS. Washington, D.C.: Public Affairs Press, 1948. 365 p. HS.

An effort to assemble for the layman and student reasonably lucid definitions of "those terms which cover the economic facts of life." Included in a single alphabetic arrangement are the meanings of terms used extensively in business and economic affairs, brief descriptions of more important forces and institutions that profoundly affect economics, and short biographies of persons who have made significant contributions to economic thought.

Howard, Willard W., and Dale, Edwin L., Jr. CONTEMPORARY ECONOM-
ICS. Lexington, Mass.: Heath, 1971. 537 p. HS.

Students are introduced to basic economic problems facing all societies and to alternative economic systems. They are also introduced to the basic analytical tool of microeconomics, supply and
demand analysis, and the basic analytical tools of microeconomics,
--national income accounting and input-output economics. International economics and the economics of growth and development
are also discussed.

Industrial Relations Center. A LOOK AT OUR ECONOMY. Basic Economic
Series. Chicago: University of Chicago, 1965. 37 p. HS.

This pamphlet, especially useful for high school students, is an
introduction to economics. It relates the individual to basic
principles and problems. The basic wants of a useful job, a rising standard of living, and financial security are discussed. There
is also a consideration of the economic problems of depressions,
inflation, unequal opportunities, government debt, capital for investment, and group conflicts.

Inman, Raymond S., and Murphy, R.E., eds. THE ECONOMIC PROCESS:
INQUIRY AND CHALLENGE. Glenview, Ill.: Scott, Foresman, 1969.
224 p. HS.

Each of the twelve chapters begins with an introduction that sets
forth the problem and briefly introduces the author. A series of
questions designed to help the student comprehend the material
precedes each reading. Some of the issues discussed are these:
Is the consumer pawn or king? What should be the role of government in the economy? How can we rescue our cities?

Kaminsky, Ralph, ed. INTRODUCTION TO ECONOMIC ISSUES. Garden
City, N.Y.: Doubleday, 1970. 270 p. HS.

This is a collection of essays by the nation's top economists, illustrating broad principles of economics and examining the political context of economic decisions. Some of the articles included
are: economic systems, price-directed economic activity, government role, economic performance and growth, economic stabilization, employment, distribution of income, United States in the
world economy, and urban economics.

Leamer, Laurence E., and Thomson, Dorothy L. AMERICAN CAPITALISM:
AN INTRODUCTION. CASE Economic Literacy Series, no. 1. New
York: McGraw-Hill, 1968. 116 p. HS.

This is a realistic appraisal of the American economy and its free
enterprise system, presented so the student can relate economics to
his own life. Major economic goals are defined and applied.
Important analytical devices and statistical tools are explained.

McGRAW-HILL DICTIONARY OF MODERN ECONOMICS: HANDBOOK OF
TERMS AND ORGANIZATIONS. New York: McGraw-Hill, 1965. 697 p.
HS.

Over a thousand frequently used modern economic and related
terms are alphabetically arranged in part 1 of this dictionary.
Definitions were written for the reader with no previous knowledge
of the subject. Part 2 lists and describes private and public organizations concerned with economics and marketing.

Maher, John E., and Symmes, S. Stowell. IDEAS ABOUT CHOOSING.
New York: Franklin Watts, 1969. 48 p. Illus. Prim.

This is a simple explanation of the meaning of an economic
choice of time or money. It discusses the terms goods, services,
earned income, and producers and tells why people have to learn
to make wise economic choices of goods and services.

_____. IDEAS ABOUT OTHERS AND YOU. New York: Franklin Watts,
1969. 48 p. Illus. Prim.

Economist Maher explains briefly to the young reader the basic
concept of natural, machine, social, political, and man-machine
systems, and their frequent interlocking with one another for the
purpose of producing the things that we need and want.

_____. LEARNING ABOUT WHY WE MUST CHOOSE. New York: Franklin
Watts, 1970. 68 p. Illus. Elem.

A more advanced discussion than IDEAS ABOUT CHOOSING (see
above), this book goes into the need for choices in getting the
greatest returns from our resources. The author defines "economic
scarcity" and explains how consumers make "economic choices"
concerning the use and distribution of economically scarce items,
including natural, human, and capital resources.

_____. WHAT IS ECONOMICS? New York: John Wiley & Sons, 1969.
174 p. HS.

The author presents this book in response to the difficult question
of what economics is and what economics is not.

Mark, Shelley, and Slate, Daniel, eds. ECONOMICS IN ACTION: READ-
INGS IN CURRENT ECONOMIC ISSUES. 4th ed. Belmont, Calif.: Wadsworth, 1969. 564 p. HS.

A volume that could be used with standard high school texts, contains articles on private decisions versus public policies, economic growth, resource allocations, income distribution, and policy toward economic sectors, both national and international.

Mayer, Martin. UNDERSTANDING AND USING ECONOMICS. Washington, D.C.: National Consumer Finance Association, 1966. 41 p. HS.

This pamphlet is designed to bridge the gap between the study of social economics and personal economics. The topic range includes jobs, borrowing, saving, insurance, taxes, public debt, business cycles, and personal security. The overall orientation, toward family money management, makes it a most useful supplement for classes in consumer economics, home economics, and problems of democracy.

Miller, Herman P. RICH MAN, POOR MAN. New York: Thomas Y. Crowell, 1971. 305 p. HS.

The author has analyzed U.S. income statistics and has produced some interesting comparative studies of poverty, wealth, occupational trends, and earning power based on age, sex, race, education, and other factors. Though he mainly evaluates past and present conditions, he does venture some predictions for the decades ahead.

Miller, Roger. AMERICAN ECONOMIC LIFE: YESTERDAY AND TODAY. San Francisco: Canfield Press, 1974. 320 p. Illus. HS.

A very simple introduction to economics. A historical approach is used to introduce economics and economic problems. The book is illustrated with photographs.

Nemmers, Erwin E., and Janzen, Cornelius C. DICTIONARY OF ECONOMICS AND BUSINESS. Totowa, N.J.: Littlefield Adam and Co., 1966. 160 p. HS.

This book contains a careful identification or brief explanation by two well-qualified authors of nearly 4,000 terms. It will be a comprehensive aid to students and teachers who need to check the meanings of terms in the two broad subject areas.

North, Douglas C., and Miller, Roger. THE ECONOMICS OF PUBLIC ISSUES. New York: Harper & Row, 1973. 184 p. HS.

In thirty brief chapters the authors show how the basic tools of economics can be used to classify such social and political issues as abortion, the draft, ecology and conservation, crime prevention, and the population crisis.

OUR NATION'S WEALTH. Englewood Cliffs, N.J.: Scholastic Book Services, 1968. 192 p. JH.

This is a brief text that combines economic theory and interesting illustrations. It can be used with students who have a limited background in economics.

Paradis, Adrian A. THE ECONOMICS REFERENCE BOOK. Philadelphia: Chilton Book Co., 1970. 191 p. HS.

This book was written for the high school student and the layman who may be puzzled by the meanings of various economic terms encountered in their daily study or reading. Terms are defined and there are also sketches of leading economists and the part they played in monetary and sociological systems.

Shay, Arthur. WHAT HAPPENS WHEN YOU SPEND MONEY. Chicago: Reilly and Lee, 1970. Unp. Illus. Elem.

A child and her mother go to the supermarket to do the weekly shopping. This book relates their purchases in the shopping center in Detroit with the production of workers in New Jersey, Japan, and Tanzania as well as with the work of local farmers and dairy-men. It explains in simple terms the concepts of labor, salary, capital, profit, production, distribution, and taxes.

Spadero, Louis M. ECONOMICS: AN INTRODUCTORY VIEW. Milwaukee: Bruce, 1969. 209 p. HS.

The principles as well as the dynamic, developing, and controversial aspects of economics are stressed in an attempt to help students comprehend what the subject is basically all about.

Stanek, Muriel. HOW PEOPLE LIVE IN THE SUBURBS. Westchester, Ill.: Benefic, 1970. 48 p. Prim.

A simple explanation of a suburb is presented. Families that live in a suburb are described. It tells where the people work, what they do for fun, and how they commute to the city, and deals with suburban schools, policemen, and firemen.

Theobald, Robert, ed. SOCIAL POLICIES FOR AMERICA IN THE SEVENTIES. Garden City, N.Y.: Doubleday, 1968. 216 p. HS.

Nine divergent proposals are presented on how to insure the well-being of all citizens in a world that is being fundamentally altered by science and technology.

Thomas, Dana L. THE MONEY CROWD. New York: G.P. Putnam & Sons, 1972. 365 p. HS.

This is an account of the "money crowd," inheritors of huge
global fortunes amassed over many generations, together with self-
made multimillionaires who have accumulated their wealth since
World War II.

U.S. Department of Commerce. TRAVEL/U.S.A. Washington, D.C.: 1965.
40 p. Distributed by Government Printing Office. HS.

This booklet tells the story of tourism in the United States, its
impact on the balance of payments, and its benefits to the economy.

U.S. Department of Commerce, Bureau of the Census. POCKET DATA BOOK,
U.S.A. Washington, D.C.: 1969. 360 p. Distributed by Government
Printing Office. HS.

This handbook is published biennially. It is a compendium of
tables and charts on basic U.S. economic and related data.

Venn, Grant. MAN, EDUCATION AND MANPOWER. Washington, D.C.:
American Association of School Administrators, 1970. 281 p. HS.

The changing role of education in manpower development to meet
the needs of people in a changing technological society are described.

Wagner, Lewis E. WHAT ARE ECONOMIC PROBLEMS? Primer of Economic
Series, no. 1. Iowa City: Bureau of Business and Economic Research, State
University of Iowa, 1958. 19 p. HS.

This introduction to economics, for high school students, concerns
the nature of economics, of the economy as a whole, and of the
goals an economy may serve.

MEDIA

AMERICAN ECONOMY. New York: McGraw-Hill, 1969. Filmstrips.
3 sets, 4 filmstrips ea. Sound. Color. HS.

This series describes the mechanisms relied upon in the United
States to answer the basic economic questions of what shall be
produced, how scarce resources shall be used, and how products
shall be allocated. The last titles are for advanced students;
there is an assumption that some work has already been done in
economics. Theory is presented on a demanding level. Titles:
(1) "The Economy and You"; (2) "Process: Balance Wheel of the
Economy"; (3) "Productivity: the Key to Better Living"; (4)
"Capital: Foundations of the Economy"; (5) "Wages in a Market

Economy"; (6) "Profits: Fuel of the Economy"; (7) "Money and Banking"; (8) "Business Cycles"; (9) "The United States and International Trade"; (10) "Comparative Economic Systems"; (11) "How to Manage Your Income"; (12) "Personal Economic Security."

BASIC CONCEPTS IN ECONOMICS. Santa Monica, Calif.: BFA Educational Media, 1973. 6 filmstrips, 7-10 mins. ea. Sound. Teacher's guide. Elem.

Basic concepts are explained, using an inquiry approach and emphasizing decision making. Titles: "Factors of Production"; "Specialization"; "Economic Independence"; "Saving and Lending"; "Our Market Economy."

BASIC ECONOMICS. Duluth, Minn.: Instructor Publishers, 1967. Charts. Elem.

Twenty colorful display charts illustrate fundamental concepts important to understanding our economic system.

BASIC ECONOMICS. East Orange, N.J.: Tweedy Transparencies, 1969. 38 transparencies with 114 overlays divided into 6 major categories. Multicolor. HS.

These transparencies are in the areas of economic problems; market economy; the role of the household, firm, and government; the circular flow of economic activity; money, banking, and monetary policy; and economics around the world.

A COLLAR FOR PATRICK. New York: AVI Associates, 1970. Filmstrip. 50 frames. Sound. Color. Teacher's guide. Prim.

Daniel's need to buy a collar for his duck so that his duck would be clearly identified leads him to an explanation of a market society, production, and the need to earn income in order to be able to buy goods and services.

CROSSROADS. New York: Educational Media Services. Film. 14 mins. Sound. Color. Elem.

The film describes the circular flow of income and output and supply and demand in the labor markets and provides guidance for students making career choices.

DANIEL'S BIRTHDAY. New York: AVI Associates, 1970. Filmstrip. 50 frames. Sound. Color. Teacher's guide. Prim.

This filmstrip deals with opportunity cost and occupational specialization. It explains the distinction between goods and services. This information is related in connection with a young boy's birthday.

ECONOMIC GEOGRAPHY: THREE FAMILIES IN DIFFERENT ENVIRONMENTS.
Santa Monica, Calif.: BFA Educational Media, 1971. Film. 14 mins.
Sound. Color. JH.

The film deals with the ways three families in different environments (rain forest, western rural, and western urban) have met
basic needs. An organized comparison of homes, customs, resources, family roles, and economic systems is presented. The
viewer is able to make definite assumptions for himself as to the
effect of environment upon each family's way of life.

ECONOMIC ISSUES IN AMERICAN DEMOCRACY. Bedford Hills, N.Y.:
Teaching Resources Films in cooperation with the Joint Council on Economic
Education, 1972. 4 filmstrips. Sound. Color. Teacher's guide. HS.

The titles in this series are: "Unemployment and Inflation"; "The
Profit System"; "Government and Our Economic System"; "The
World Economy."

This series explores several important aspects of the economics of
modern society. The program develops understanding about the
interaction among various areas of economic activities and how
the results of these activities affect the lives of everyone. The
benefits and problems of world trade are analyzed in an easily
comprehensible manner. A discussion of profits, inflation, and
unemployment clarifies complicated concepts.

ECONOMIC PROBLEMS. East Orange, N.J.: Tweedy Transparencies, 1968.
7 transparencies with 19 overlays. Color. HS.

This set of transparencies explores the nature of economics; the
scarcity of resources in relation to human wants; the role of production in satisfying them; the kinds of resources needed; and the
basic types of economic systems.

ECONOMICS, Glenview, Ill.: Educational Projections Corp. Filmstrip.
Elem.

Four facets of modern economics are covered: the role of unions
in the economy; the purpose of taxes; the ways of saving money;
and the usefulness of a budget.

ECONOMICS. 2 pts. New York: AEVAC. Pt. 1, 6 transparencies and
23 overlays. Pt. 2, 6 transparencies and 29 overlays. Color. HS.

Part 1 graphically presents and unfolds the following economic
concepts: resources and wants; classical economic thought; circular flow; national income accounting; the business cycles; and
Marxism.

Part 2 illustrates and clarifies such factors as: the new econom-

General

ics; the creation of money; Federal Reserve monetary controls; supply and demand; deflation and inflation; and international trade.

ECONOMICS: THE SCIENCE OF CHOICE. World of Economics Series. New York: McGraw-Hill, 1963. Filmstrip. 34 frames. Color. HS.

Central economic problems of scarcity of resources relative to human desires are introduced. Different kinds of economic choices are reviewed and the role of economics in analyzing and solving economic problems is described. This filmstrip is coordinated with the Leonard S. Silk text, THE WORLD OF ECONOMICS. (See Silk, Leonard S. THE WORLD OF ECONOMICS. Chapter 10.)

ECONOMICS FOR PRIMARIES. Burbank, Calif.: Q-ED Productions, 1973. 4 filmstrips. Sound. Color. Teacher's guide. Poster. Prim.

The children pictured are involved in real situations with real people. The products and services produced or utilized in the filmstrips are all relevant to the student's world. Emphasis is placed on the advantages of working together, the importance of community workers, and the interdependence of individuals. Titles: "The Toy Store"; "The Doghouse"; "The Breakfast"; "The Garden."

ECONOMICS FOR THE CONCERNED CITIZEN. Lincoln: University of Nebraska, 1968. 12 films, 30 mins. ea. Sound. B&W. HS.

The twelve lessons in the series are designed to make the workings of our economic system understandable to all citizens. The emphasis is on the considerations facing a decision-maker in his private role as a consumer and in his public role as a citizen. The titles are: "What Economics is All About"; "The American Economy"; "Markets and Prices"; "The Realities of a Mixed Economy"; "How We Raise Our Living Standards"; "Fiscal Policy"; "The United States in the World Economy"; "International Monetary Problems"; "Other Economic Systems"; "Some Problems of a Growing Economy"; "Economic Stability"; "Money, Banking and Monetary Policy."

ECONOMICS IN OUR WORLD. Bedford Hills, N.Y.: Teaching Resources Films, 1971. 8 filmstrips, average 45 frames ea. Color. Teacher's guide. Flash cards. Wall chart. Elem.

This kit of materials was designed to develop the importance of economics in everyday living. Each filmstrip gives children certain basic economic concepts as well as the vocabulary to express economic ideas. Titles: "Specializing and Exchanging"; "We Are All Consumers"; "Working and Earning"; "Economic Systems"; "Money and Exchange"; "Labor Unions"; "International Trade"; "Government Goods and Services."

ECONOMICS--IT'S ELEMENTARY. Hollywood, Calif.: Charles Cahill & Assoc., 1964. Film. 11 mins. Sound. Color. Study guide. Elem, JH.

The activities of a vacationing family are used to introduce basic principles of economics. They plant, grow, and sell vegetables to aid in covering their vacation expenses. Expenses are estimated, profits figured, and profits exchanged for services and supplies.

FUNDAMENTALS OF ECONOMICS. Jamaica, N.Y.: Eye Gate House. 8 filmstrips. Sound. JH, HS.

Essential to the understanding of our democratic form of government is an understanding of our economic institutions. Some basic elements of the dynamics of these institutions are covered in this series of filmstrips. Titles: "What is Economics"; "Money"; "Banks and Banking"; "Business Organization"; "Labor and Labor Unions"; "Credit Buying"; "Population."

FUNDAMENTALS OF MODERN ECONOMICS. Washington, D.C.: Washington Tapes, 1969. Tape. HS.

Various facets of current economic theory and practice discussed on this tape include the following: the roles of the president and Congress in stabilizing the economy; inflation; budget deficits; the national debt; and taxation.

INDEX NUMBER AND ECONOMIC STATISTICS. New York: McGraw-Hill, 1962. Filmstrip. 37 frames. Color. HS.

The filmstrip demonstrates the essentiality of statistics; it also emphasizes how similar data can be differently interpreted. It shows how a price index can be constructed and the various uses to which such an index can be put.

OUR COMMUNITY SERVICES. Chicago: Encyclopaedia Britannica Films, 1969. Film. 14 mins. Sound. Color. Prim.

The film shows how the organized community provides many services for people which it would be difficult for them to provide for themselves and explains how payments for these services are secured.

OUR ECONOMY. New York: Westinghouse Learning Press, 1971. 6 filmstrips. Sound. Color. Elem.

Various phases of our economy explained through everyday situations that young children can easily understand and relate to. Titles: "Medium of Exchange, 'Left Wing Catches On'"; "Labor and Its Value, 'Up a Tree'"; "Supply and Demand, 'Jimmy's Hot

Idea'"; "Banks, Loans, and Interest, 'A Rewarding Experience'";
"Taxes, 'The Lost Vacation'"; "Free Enterprise, 'Bridal Party'."

OUR GROWING AMERICA. New York: Joint Council on Economic Education,
1963. Filmstrip. 152 frames. Color. HS.

This three-part filmstrip explains (1) growth of the American economy, and interrelationships among the various sectors; (2) inter-
flows of goods, services, and money among the major sectors, and
economic influences on investments, population, profits, and
government activity on the country's economic growth; (3) roles of
government and monetary and banking systems in promoting stability and growth; and (4) some of the economic problems related to
national economic growth in the 1960s.

PRIMARY ECONOMICS. New York: Holt Media, 1970. 4 filmstrips. Sound.
Prim.

Common problem-solving experiences of young children are used to
introduce basic concepts fundamental to the understanding of economics. Concepts of goods, services, money, consumers, producers, businesses, taxes, savings, borrowing, and interest are introduced.

TOWNS AND CITIES. Palo Alto, Calif.: Field Educational Publications.
11 filmstrips, 13-74 frames ea. Sound. Color. Teacher's guide. Study
prints. Elem.

This series stresses the interdependence of people. Various city
services are identified and explained. Titles: "Cities are People";
"City Problems are People Problems"; "Water Watchers"; "People
Solve City Problems"; "Fire"; "Keeping People Healthy"; "Quiet
Please"; "Going Places"; "What Shall We Do Now"; "People,
People Everywhere"; "Where the Action Is."

UNDERSTANDING OUR ECONOMY. Washington, D.C.: Washington Tapes,
1968. Cassette. 30 mins. Teacher's guide. HS.

Two differing views on the degree to which government should
intervene in the market place are put forth on this cassette. Dr.
Kermit Gordon explains America's modified free enterprise system
and government influence on the economy. Carl H. Madden
advocates less government regulation of process and wages, and a
curtailment of the power of labor. He analyzes proposals for a
guaranteed annual income.

U.S. ECONOMIC HISTORY. Bedford Hills, N.Y.: Teaching Resources
Films. 2 filmstrips. Sound. Color. HS.

The filmstrips look at American economic history in terms of the country's great growth and the search for a stable monetary system. The program shows the roles of natural resources, a productive labor force, increasing capital, technology, and research, all of which interact to produce economic growth. The effect of a large population, consumer demands, the shorter work week, technological advances, and the environmental crises are pondered.

THE U.S. ECONOMY. New York: New York Times, 1967. Filmstrip. Sound. B&W. Teacher's manual. HS.

This is a bird's-eye view of the American economy. It briefly touches upon many problems such as inflation, taxation, big business, poverty and unemployment, and the impact of the new technology.

U.S.A. TODAY: CITY--SUBURB--COUNTRY. Freeport, N.Y.: Educational Activities. 6 filmstrips. Sound. Color. Elem.

The disciplines of anthropology, economics, and political science are combined in this comprehensive study of the United States today. Students are taken into the homes, schools, families, and communities of people in different areas of our country. Titles: "A City Grows"; "City, Suburb, Country"; "Services"; "Occupations"; "Homes"; "Communications."

A VISUAL ANALYSIS OF THE AMERICAN ECONOMY. Boston, Mass.: Heath, 1968. 54 transparencies. Color. Teacher's guide. HS.

These transparencies endeavor to explain in depth the following basic economic concepts: production possibilities curve; circular flow of the economy; demand and supply; elasticity of demand; simplified theory of the firm; functional theory of income determination; money and prices; business cycles; balance of payments.

WE MAKE CHOICES. Pasadena, Calif.: Arthur Barr Productions, 1969. Film. 10 mins. Sound. Color. Teacher's guide. Elem.

An elementary economics film showing that our productive resources are limited so we must choose what we will produce, and that we choose by spending money to buy the things we want, or by making choices through our government.

WHO HELPS US? Santa Monica, Calif.: BFA Educational Media, 1969. 10 filmstrips. Sound. Color. Elem.

Excellent photographs tell what happens behind the scenes of different community services: fire department, police department, supermarket, bakery, laundry, service station, dentist, library, and post office.

Chapter 9

GOVERNMENT

Chamber of Commerce of the United States of America. GOVERNMENT AND
THE ECONOMY. Understanding Economics Series, no. 7. Washington, D.C.:
1966. 36 p. HS.

> This pamphlet is largely a description of the federal tax system of
> the United States. State and local financing are discussed briefly.
> Functions carried out by the government are vital to the operation
> of the economy. These activities are financed with revenues col-
> lected as taxes.

Committee for Economic Development. BUDGETING FOR NATIONAL OB-
JECTIVES: EXECUTIVE AND CONGRESSIONAL ROLES IN PROGRAM PLAN-
NING AND PERFORMANCE; A STATEMENT ON NATIONAL POLICY BY THE
RESEARCH AND POLICY COMMITTEE. New York: 1966. 65 p. HS.

> This statement proposes modernization of the federal budgetary pro-
> cess so that both legislative and executive centers of authority
> may contribute more effectively to the public interest through bet-
> ter planning and execution.

_____. A FISCAL PROGRAM FOR A BALANCED FEDERALISM; A STATE-
MENT ON NATIONAL POLICY. New York: 1967. 70 p. HS.

> This statement is concerned with ways for improving the financing
> of state and local governments and possible actions of the federal
> government. Some of the topics discussed are: the roles of state
> and local governments; prospects for growth of expenditures and
> revenue from existing systems; federal grants-in-aid; and state ac-
> tions which would strengthen local financial independence.

_____. RESHAPING GOVERNMENT IN METROPOLITAN AREAS. New
York: 1970. 28 p. HS.

> It is proposed to provide guidelines for redesigning the present
> structure and organization of government in metropolitan areas, in

---

the belief that new programs are likely to fail unless we have a more rational, more flexible system than now exists.

Congressional Quarterly Service. FEDERAL ECONOMIC POLICY. Washington, D.C.: 1969. 116 p. HS.

Important economic topics that are dealt with and analyzed are: major economic developments since World War II, current economic legislation, budget controversy, the president's economic report, and the budget.

Council of Economic Advisers. ECONOMIC REPORT OF THE PRESIDENT. Washington, D.C.: Government Printing Office, annual. HS.

This report is a valuable source of information on current economic conditions, problems, and policy. Each includes a review of the state of the economy during the prior year and an analysis of economic problems expected in the year ahead. The president's message at the beginning of each volume provides a summary of the documents. Charts, tables, and statistical information are included. A study of this report is prepared annually by the Joint Economic Committee of Congress (see below).

Federal Reserve Bank of Philadelphia. NATIONAL DEBT. Philadelphia: 1965. 10 p. HS.

This pamphlet analyzes the national debt and maintains that those who see government debt as all bad are wrong but clearly states that national indebtedness must be managed with care and prudence.

Heaps, Willard A. TAXATION, U.S.A. New York: Seabury Press, 1971. 200 p. JH, HS.

A survey of American taxation written for young people.

Heilbroner, Robert L., and Bernstein, Peter [L.]. A PRIMER ON GOVERN-MENT SPENDING. 2d ed. New York: Random House, 1971. 106 p. HS.

This easily read book discusses such topics as wealth and waste, spending and borrowing, inflation and foreign complications.

Heller, Walter. NEW DIMENSIONS IN POLITICAL ECONOMY. New York: W.W. Norton, 1967. 203 p. HS.

A former chairman of the Council of Economic Advisers describes the role economists played in getting the American economy to grow and presents a plan for returning some of the federal revenue to the states.

Industrial Relations Center. GOVERNMENT SPENDING IN THE U.S. Basic
Economic Series. Chicago: University of Chicago, 1965. 34 p. JH, HS.

A beginning description of the government's role in our economy.
Topics discussed are goals, patterns of action, place in the market,
and accounting for tax dollars.

_____. TAXES IN THE UNITED STATES. Chicago: University of Chicago,
1964. 29 p. HS.

This pamphlet presents a clear discussion of the general subject of
taxes. It points up what taxes predominate at the three levels of
government: federal, state, and local. It also deals with the
expenditures made by the three levels of government.

Joint Economic Committee of Congress. JOINT ECONOMIC REPORTS.
Washington, D.C.: Government Printing Office, annual. HS.

An annual study of the ECONOMIC REPORT OF THE PRESIDENT
(see above), prepared by the Joint Economic Committee of the
two houses of Congress.

Kershaw, Joseph A. GOVERNMENT AGAINST POVERTY. Studies in Social
Economics. Washington, D.C.: Brookings Institution, 1970. 174 p. HS.

This is an account of government efforts on behalf of the poor,
through the Office of Economic Opportunity and through the
broadening of social security, aid to education, public assistance
in housing, and other ways. The author describes the successes
and failures of the antipoverty campaign and contemplates its future.

Lewis, Ben. GOVERNMENT AND OUR ECONOMIC SYSTEM. Economic
Issues in American Democracy. Bedford Hills, N.Y.: Teaching Resource
Films and Joint Council on Economic Education, 1972. 76 p. HS.

The nature of the economic problems we face, various economic
systems, and the nature of the U.S. economy in the 1970s are
surveyed. There is also a discussion of economic systems in other
countries. A filmstrip is available to be used with this pamphlet.
(See GOVERNMENT AND OUR ECONOMIC SYSTEM, page 96.)

Miller, Glenn H. THE FEDERAL BUDGET AND ECONOMIC ACTIVITY.
Kansas City, Mo.: Federal Reserve Bank, 1969. 77 p. HS.

This booklet is meant to aid citizens interested in understanding
the relationships between federal fiscal action and economic performance. It explains something about the presentation of expen-
diture and revenue plans in the budget, about the process by

which the plans are transformed into actions, and about the impact of such actions on economic activity.

Miller, Roger. NEW ECONOMICS OF RICHARD NIXON: FREEZES, FLOATS AND FISCAL POLICY. New York: Harper's Magazine Press, 1972. 88 p. HS.

Most of the text is devoted to providing economic background against which the Nixon policies can be viewed. The appendixes contain the text of the president's speech on economic controls, text of the executive order on the subject of prices and wage controls, and the presidential proclamation regarding the 10 percent import tax.

Nikolaieff, George, A., ed. TAXATION AND THE ECONOMY. Reference Shelf, vol. 39, no. 6. Bronx, N.Y.: H.W. Wilson, 1968. 212 p. HS.

The purpose of this book is to view the role of taxation as an economic tool. The book also concerns itself with the fundamental economic assumptions that underlie our government's actions in the economic sphere.

TAXATION IN THE UNITED STATES. Economic Topics Series. New York: Joint Council on Economic Education, 1969. 18 p. HS.

Three articles, "Federal Revenue and Income Tax," "Tax Revenues for State and Local Governments," and "New Directions," cut through the complexities of the tax apparatus to give the student a manageable basic introduction to the subject of taxation.

MEDIA

BIG GOVERNMENT AND PRIVATE ENTERPRISE IN THE 70'S. Hackensack, N.J.: Valiant IMC, 1972. Filmstrip. Sound. Color. HS.

Wage price controls, growing involvement by the government in economic and social sectors, and the extensive powers of government regulatory agencies are changing the role private capital has traditionally played in America's development. This strip explores the impact of these changes on the lives of average Americans.

GOVERNMENT AND OUR ECONOMIC SYSTEM. Bedford Hills, N.Y.: Teaching Resource Films, 1972. Filmstrip. Sound. Color. HS.

TAXES: WHO NEEDS THEM? Hollywood, Calif.: Handel Film Corp., 1969. Film. 20 mins. Color. Teacher's guide. JH.

The services that citizens use every day and that are made possible by tax collection are described. The uses of taxes on the local, state, and federal levels are explained.

WHAT ARE TAXES ALL ABOUT? New York: Carousel Films, 1968. Film. 25 mins. Sound. JH, HS.

A camera follows a TV newsman from the time he receives his check to the moment he mails a completed tax return. He explains the U.S. tax system, kinds of taxes, why they exist, who pays them, and where the tax money goes.

YOUR TAX DOLLAR. New York: New York Times, 1971. Filmstrip. Sound. B&W. HS.

This is a broad study of taxation that considers the economic needs of the government on one hand and the staggering tax load of the people on the other hand. Tax reforms, loopholes, taxpayers' unrest, and how taxes are paid in other countries are covered. An explanation is given of the American system of taxation in terms of the needs facing American society today.

Chapter 10
HIGH SCHOOL TEXTS

Abbott, Lawrence. ECONOMICS AND THE MODERN WORLD. 2d ed.
New York: Harcourt Brace Jovanovich, 1967. 876 p. Student guide.
Instructor's manual. Test item file.

> An introductory text in which facts and theories are interwoven
> and the concepts, techniques, and laws of economics are related
> to the modern world. Stress is on economic theory, especially
> microtheory. It is cumulative in construction, each chapter being
> built on its predecessor. Terms and concepts are carefully defined.

Alexander, Albert. THE CHALLENGE OF ECONOMICS: A GUIDE FOR THE
PERPLEXED. New York: Pitman, 1970. 227 p.

> This is an attempt to illustrate the theory and practice of how one
> system--the market economy--attempts to provide goods and ser-
> vices that people need and desire. By way of contrast, an anal-
> ysis has been included of how others attempt to solve the chal-
> lenge of economics, determining what a society shall produce,
> how it will be produced, and for whom it shall be produced.

Ammer, Dean S., ed. READINGS AND CASES IN ECONOMICS. Boston:
Ginn, 1971. 330 p.

> This supplementary reader can be used in conjunction with any
> standard high school economics text. The emphasis is on modern
> economics and problem situations, taken from a wide diversity of
> viewpoints and sources; from the Chamber of Commerce to the
> AFL-CIO, from both conservative and liberal journals, from col-
> lege textbooks, popular magazines, and daily papers. Each of
> the more than sixty readings has a short introduction suggesting
> its significance, and its relationship to text book principles.

Attiyeh, Richard, et al. BASIC ECONOMICS: THEORY AND CASES.
Englewood Cliffs, N.J.: Prentice-Hall, 1973. 440 p.

The essential principles of economics are considered in this text. It integrates the study of basic economics with the application of theory to contemporary, real world issues. The book provides a direct approach combining three integral teaching strategies: programmed learning chapters; analytical review questions; and actual case studies. The student's continuous participation and involvement in the material are encouraged. Teacher's manual is available.

Bach, George L. ECONOMICS--AN INTRODUCTION TO ANALYSIS AND POLICY. 8th ed. Englewood Cliffs, N.J.: Prentice-Hall, 1974. 832 p.

More than most texts, this problem-oriented text emphasizes the importance of a clear understanding of economic goals. It stresses a systematic approach to the study of economic problems and the use of analytical tools.

Brown, James E., and Wolf, Harold A. ECONOMICS: PRINCIPLES AND PRACTICES. Columbus, Ohio: Charles Merrill Publishing Co., 1968. 528 p.

This volume aims to give students a fundamental understanding of economic issues and theories and teaches them to analyze current economic problems rationally and objectively. The meaning of economics is discussed. Microeconomics, macroeconomics, international matters, including foreign exchange and other economic systems are examined and current economic issues such as poverty, inflation, unemployment, pollution, and urban problems are discussed.

Calderwood, James D. ECONOMICS IN ACTION. New York: Macmillan, 1968. 531 p.

The book focuses on economic problems and seeks to increase the student's understanding of the world of economics and to help him become an active participant in it. The scope and content of economics is defined. Individual and national economic goals of the American people are identified.

Calhoun, Donald W. SOCIAL SCIENCE IN AN AGE OF CHANGE. New York: Harper & Row, 1971. 529 p.

This is an integrated social science text for the high school. One part is devoted to political and economic processes. Economic and political institutions and their complex interrelationships are discussed.

Chalmers, James A., and Leonard, Fred H. ECONOMIC PRINCIPLES: MACROECONOMIC THEORY AND POLICY. Riverside, N.J.: Collier-Macmillan, 1971. 460 p.

This comprehensive, up-to-date volume both reflects all recent progress in quantitative methodology and thoroughly summarizes the important principles in macroeconomics.

Daugherty, M[arion].R., and Madden, C[arl].H. THE ECONOMIC PROCESS. Glenview, Ill.: Scott, Foresman, 1969. 504 p.

The text consists of six units; it begins by discussing the basic principles of the science of economics and concludes by examining international problems and policymaking. A series of nine articles describing the theories of the world's foremost economists is included. Six of the articles describe the interrelationship between economics and other fields. There is a teacher's resource book.

Freund, John E., and Perles, Benjamin M. BUSINESS STATISTICS: A FIRST COURSE. Englewood Cliffs, N.J.: Prentice-Hall, 1974. 359 p.

This is an introductory statistics textbook. The authors emphasize "instruction in the understanding, use and appreciation . . . of statistical techniques." The topics dealt with include summarizing data, probabilities, normal distributions, sampling analysis of data, basic measurements, and time series analysis.

Hailstones, Thomas J. BASIC ECONOMICS. 4th ed. Garden City, N.Y.: Doubleday, 1972. 654 p.

A primer and guide to our economic system, covering every significant topic in the field: the role of money; business fluctuations and their causes; production, employment, income, and how they are measured; modern methods of economic analysis; and the impact of government policies.

Harriss, Clement Lowell. THE AMERICAN ECONOMY: PRINCIPLES, PRACTICES, AND POLICIES. 6th ed. Homewood, Ill.: Richard D. Irwin, 1968. 998 p.

Unlike other texts, there is great emphasis on business organization and institutions in this volume. Topics discussed are: macrotheory and problems, price theory and problems, distribution theory and problems, domestic and international institutions and problems.

_____. ECONOMICS: AN ANALYTICAL APPROACH. 3d ed. Boston: Ginn, 1969. 566 p.

This scholarly, objective text focuses on current economic life, the problems of today, and the prospects for tomorrow. Wage and price guideposts, urban renewal, costs of urban riots, budget cuts in the space program, training programs for the "hard core" unemployed, and transportation problems are among the many relevant topics considered and carefully analyzed. Over a dozen case studies, supplemented with abundant graphs, tables, and study help charts are included.

Heilbroner, Robert L. THE ECONOMIC PROBLEM. 3d ed. Englewood Cliffs, N.J.: Prentice-Hall, 1972. 747 p.

This relevant and readable introductory examination of economics focuses on a broad understanding of economic history and basic concepts of microeconomics and macroeconomics. The meaning of the history and analysis in present day contexts is discussed.

_____. UNDERSTANDING MACROECONOMICS. 4th ed. Englewood Cliffs, N.J.: Prentice-Hall, 1972. 274 p.

The author presents in detail the main themes of current macro-economic thought complete with charts and diagrams.

Heller, Robert. ECONOMIC SYSTEM. New York: Macmillan, 1972. 302 p.

This well-organized text places stress on analysis, both macro and micro.

Kennedy, John Wesley, and Olsen, Arthur R. ECONOMICS: PRINCIPLES AND APPLICATIONS. 8th ed. Cincinnati: South-Western Publishing Co., 1972. 611 p.

This basic discussion of our economic system should enable the student to understand the nature of our economic system and to compare it with other economic systems including socialism, com-munism, and fascism. Some of the subjects explained are: our economic and political institutions and practices, production, re-sources, income and income distribution, business organization, organized labor, monopolies, production of gross national product, income and its components, the functions and cost of government, and our international relations.

Lipsey, Richard C., and Steiner, Peter O. ECONOMICS. 3d ed. New York: Harper & Row, 1972. 806 p.

This text reflects the enormous changes that have taken place in economics in recent years. The relationship between economic theory and economic policy is discussed. Particular stress is placed on scientific methodology and the role of economists as scientists. Topics discussed are: price system, demand, supply, market price, distribution, international trade, market economy, circular flow of income, money, banking and prices, economic growth, economic development, and contemporary problems of macroeconomic policy.

Lynn, Robert A. BASIC ECONOMIC PRINCIPLES. 2d ed. New York: McGraw-Hill, 1970. 375 p.

This text presents a survey of economic analysis issues and institutions. It is intended to help the reader acquire some basic familiarity with tools that economists have devised to aid our understanding of this many-sided and ever-changing aspect of our world. The author has attempted to relate the material presented to the important issues before our nation at this time.

McConnell, Campbell R. ECONOMICS: PRINCIPLES, PROBLEMS AND POLICIES. 5th ed. New York: McGraw-Hill, 1972. 838 p.

Clarity, currency, and the introduction of new ideas are stressed. Principles and problems of economics are presented in a straightforward, logical fashion. New to this edition are chapters on urban economy and economy of war industry. Instructor's manual, study guide, book of readings, test file, overhead transparency set, and transparency masters are available.

Robinson, Marshall A., et al. INTRODUCTION TO ECONOMIC REASONING. Rev. ed. Garden City, N.Y.: Doubleday, 1967. 306 p.

This is an introduction to economics for laymen. Its purpose is to help the reader explore the meanings of economic events and acquire the skills for thinking economic issues through to some conclusion. Originally, this book was prepared for use by adult discussion groups. It is a way of thinking about economic issues rather than a full review of economics. Its purpose is to show how to examine an economic question. Essentials of fact and formal definition are presented and then the reader is led to a consideration of selected problems on which he may exercise his powers of analysis.

Rogers, Augustus J. CHOICE: AN INTRODUCTION TO ECONOMICS. 2d ed. Englewood Cliffs, N.J.: Prentice Hall, 1974. 271 p.

An introductory text primarily designed for a one semester course in economics. It emphasizes choosing among scarce alternatives as the main problem in economics. Essentials of micro and macroeconomics are explained. The second edition has additional material on topics such as comparative economic systems, competitive and noncompetitive markets, and the theory of macroeconomics.

Sampson, Roy J., et al. AMERICAN ECONOMY: ANALYSIS, ISSUES AND PRINCIPLES. Boston: Houghton Mifflin, 1972. 518 p.

This book uses an issue-oriented problem-solving approach to the economy of the 1970s. After systematically grounding the pupil in basic economic laws, the text applies the principles learned to the "bread and butter" problems of individual, family, community, and nation. Teacher's guide and key, work guide, progress test, and duplicating masters are available.

Samuelson, Paul A. ECONOMICS: AN INTRODUCTORY ANALYSIS. 9th ed. New York: McGraw-Hill, 1973. 917 p.

This basic text places special emphasis on making economics relevant to student interests. Topics treated are: microeconomics, macroeconomics, national income, income distribution, business and labor, international trade, and finance. The new edition focuses on issues facing the economy in the new decade, theoretical and policy sections have been substantially rewritten, and new chapters have been added in an overall attempt to help the student to understand and to cope with the issues of poverty, inequality, economics of race, and problems of the urban economy.

Silk, Leonard S., and Saunders, Phillip. THE WORLD OF ECONOMICS. New York: McGraw-Hill, 1969. 560 p.

Designed for a twelfth grade economics course, this text provides the fundamental concepts and analytical tools which students will need to understand the economic problems they are likely to confront as adults. Basic principles of economic theory are presented. Major units cover microeconomics, macroeconomics, comparative economic institutions, and international economics. Teacher's manual, study guide, workbook, book of readings, filmstrips, and transparencies are available.

Smith, Augustus H. ECONOMICS FOR OUR TIMES. 4th ed. New York: McGraw-Hill, 1966. 569 p. HS.

See "Controlling the Business Cycle" in chapter 2; "Inflation and You" in chapter 5; and "American Capitalism: A Flexible and Dynamic System" in chapter 6.

Trenton, Rudolph W. BASIC ECONOMICS. 3d ed. New York: Appleton-Century-Crofts, 1973. 400 p.

This is an introductory textbook in economics, written in nontechnical language for students who do not wish to pursue the subject beyond a basic minimum course. It gives a comprehensive view of the operations of the American economy.

Weitzman, David, and Gross, Richard E. THE HUMAN EXPERIENCE. Boston: Houghton Mifflin, 1974. 608 p. HS.

This is an interdisciplinary social studies text for high school. Fundamental concepts and skills of anthropology, sociology, political science, economics, and history are presented. Various sections discuss the origins of humankind; its evolution and nature; the development of economics; the origin and transition of cities; patterns of communications. Each chapter includes exercises designed to enable students to understand concepts, collect data, and develop analytical skills.

Chapter 11
HISTORY

Boardman, Fon W. ECONOMICS: IDEAS AND MEN. New York: Henry
Z. Walck, 1966. JH, HS.

This straightforward, readable survey is a useful introduction to
the field of economics. It traces the development of economic
ideas from ancient Greece to the present. Attention is given to
economic systems and to the men such as Adam Smith, John Maynard Keynes, Karl Marx, and others who have influenced economic
theory.

Cipolla, Carlo M. THE ECONOMIC HISTORY OF WORLD POPULATION.
Baltimore: Penguin Books, 1970. 135 p. HS.

A short readable account of man's development through three
types of economic activity--hunting, agricultural, and industrial--
and of his experiences with different standards of living, with
rising levels of population, and with cultural-social changes from
a global point of view.

Davis, Lance E. GROWTH OF INDUSTRIAL ENTERPRISE 1860-1914. Economic Forces in American History Series. Chicago: Scott, Foresman, 1964.
72 p. HS.

Factors of growth from the time of the Civil War are discussed.
Topics presented are: Civil War and reconstruction, industry and
agriculture, forces that brought change, growth in the national
market, efficient use of resources, increase in production resources,
effects of change, benefits of change, and costs of growth.

Dowd, Douglas F. MODERN ECONOMIC PROBLEMS IN HISTORICAL PER-
SPECTIVE. 2d ed. Boston: Heath and Co., 1965. 198 p. HS.

Each of the nine chapters traces the historical background of an
economic problem such as American capitalism, labor, agriculture,
underdeveloped areas, and the changing role of government. If

a student has a knowledge of U.S. history, this book could provide a useful means by which he can bring that knowledge to
bear on economics.

Elting, Mary. ALL ABOARD: RAILROAD TRAINS THAT BUILT AMERICA.
Rev. ed. New York: Four Winds, 1970. 127 p. Photos. Elem.

America's trains from the first experimental engine to today's enormous diesels and the jet-powered trains of the future are described.
The impact of rail transportation on our development and history
is discussed.

Freidel, Frank, ed. THE NEW DEAL AND THE AMERICAN PEOPLE. Englewood Cliffs, N.J.: Prentice-Hall, 1964. 151 p. HS.

A cross-section of popular opinion on the New Deal, the book
includes the writing of small men and critical analysts such as
Sherwood Anderson, William Kiplinger, migrant workers, midwestern pig farmers, and CCC campers.

Fusfeld, Daniel R. THE AGE OF THE ECONOMIST. Glenview, Ill.: Scott,
Foresman, 1966. 147 p. HS.

The author discusses various schools of modern economic thought in
historical context, and the philosophers who have contributed to
them.

Galbraith, John [K.]. THE GREAT CRASH: 1929. Boston: Houghton Mifflin,
1961. 199 p. HS.

The author makes the episode of the Great Depression in our history come alive for students who have had no first-hand knowledge of a general depression.

General Motors Corp. AMERICAN BATTLE FOR ABUNDANCE, THE
STORY OF MASS PRODUCTION. Detroit: 1955. 103 p. JH, HS.

The steps that lead to mass production are traced. Inventions of
past centuries have led to new methods of producing materials in
large quantities. The importance of accuracy and interchangeabil-
ity in manufacturing is stressed.

Hacker, Louis M. AMERICAN CAPITALISM: ITS PROMISE AND ACCOM-
PLISHMENT. Anvil Book, no. 20. Princeton, N.J.: Van Nostrand Co.
1957. 185 p. HS.

Part 1 is a short history of the American economy from colonial
times through the 1950s. Part 2 consists of thirty important documents having great economic significance, most of them being
reduced to short excerpts.

_____, ed. MAJOR DOCUMENTS IN AMERICAN HISTORY. 2 vols. Princeton, N.J.: Van Nostrand Co., 1961. 187 p. HS.

Volume 1, FROM AN AGRARIAN TO AN INDUSTRIAL ECON-OMY (1785-1900), and volume 2, PROBLEMS OF A WORLD POWER (1900-1961), trace the progress of U.S. economy. The documents in both volumes are prefaced with paragraphs concerning the historical settings of the readings.

Heilbroner, Robert L. WORLDLY PHILOSOPHERS, THE LIVES AND TIMES AND IDEAS OF THE GREAT ECONOMIC THINKERS. New York: Simon & Schuster, 1967. 320 p. HS.

This introduction to economic thought dramatizes the biographies of the great economists and their ideas which, translated into political action, helped shape the modern world.

Hiebert, Ray, and Hiebert, Roselyn. STOCK MARKET CRASH, 1929 PANIC ON WALL STREET ENDS THE JAZZ AGE. New York: Franklin Watts, 1970. 66 p. JH, HS.

The functioning of the New York Stock Exchange during the crash of 1929 is explained. Representative stocks are followed from record highs on September 3, 1929, to the record lows on November 13. The book explains how the stock market worked and exposes the men that manipulated it behind the scenes.

Hoag, Edwin. AMERICAN CITIES: THEIR HISTORICAL AND SOCIAL DE-VELOPMENT. Philadelphia: J.B. Lippincott Co., 1969. 160 p. Elem.

The history and growth of major American cities are traced and the role of geography, industry, and population in their economic and social futures are discussed.

Holland, Ruth. MILL CHILD. New York: Crowell-Collier, 1970. 138 p. JH, HS.

The invention of machines simple enough to be operated by children made it possible for mill and factory owners to employ children for wages less than those paid to adults. This moving account describes the bitter working conditions of these children and tells how the efforts of concerned settlement house workers, "muckrakers," and ministers helped to put an end to these cruel practices. The concluding chapter deals with the plight of the children of today's migrant workers and points out the need for legislation to protect them.

Leuchenburg, William E. FRANKLIN ROOSEVELT AND THE NEW DEAL, 1932-40. New York: Harper & Row, 1963. 393 p. HS.

The great changes brought about in the thirties to combat the effects of the Depression are discussed. These changes include: the growth of big government of labor and farm group empires, of new concern for social welfare, and of the increased political and social importance of ethnic groups.

_____. THE PERILS OF PROSPERITY, 1914-32. Chicago: University of Chicago Press, 1958. 313 p. HS.

This book traces the political, economic, social, and cultural phenomena that transformed America from an agrarian, primarily decentralized, moralistic, isolationist nation into an industrial, urban, morally liberalized nation, involved in foreign affairs in spite of itself.

McDougall, Duncan M. WORLD POWER AND NEW PROBLEMS, 1914-30. Economic Forces in American History. Glenview, Ill.: Scott, Foresman, 1964. 64 p. HS.

The developments in the United States from World War I to the time of the Depression are discussed, including: American industry, American agriculture, problems of labor, international finance, the market collapse, the collapse of the economy, and foreign trade.

Meltzer, Milton. BROTHER CAN YOU SPARE A DIME? THE GREAT DE-PRESSION, 1929-1933. New York: Alfred A. Knopf, 1969. 181 p. Elem.

Beginning with the stock market crash of 1929 and concluding with the election of Franklin D. Roosevelt, this book presents the human side of the Great Depression. It tells what happened to auto workers, farmers, white collar workers, professional people, miners, and sharecroppers--both black and white.

North, Douglas C. GROWTH AND WELFARE IN THE AMERICAN PAST: A NEW ECONOMIC HISTORY. Englewood Cliffs, N.J.: Prentice-Hall, 1966. 210 p. HS.

Economic theory and statistics are employed in the evaluation of data in the formation of historical generalizations with a reappraisal of some basic issues and interpretations of America's past.

Oliver, Donald W., and Newmann, Fred M. THE NEW DEAL: FREE ENTERPRISE AND PUBLIC PLANNING. Columbus, Ohio: American Education Publications, 1968. 64 p. HS.

The meaning of economic desperation was quickly learned in the early 1930s by investors who had lost all their capital, farmers with mortgages due, and former businessmen selling apples. Major cases in this book cover the creation of the New Deal, its

attempt to balance freedom and central controls in the name of
the public welfare, and the consequences of Depression issues.

Paradis, Adrian A. THE HUNGRY YEARS: THE STORY OF THE GREAT
AMERICAN DEPRESSION. Philadelphia: Chilton, 1967. 183 p. Elem.

> The first part of this book covers the years after World War I and
> discusses the events which helped create the Depression in the
> United States. Part 2 tells what happened to people who lost
> their jobs, went hungry, and became homeless during the Depres-
> sion years. The last part summarizes the social and economic re-
> forms that resulted from the Depression.

Pike, E. Royston. ADAM SMITH: FATHER OF THE SCIENCE OF ECONOM-
ICS. New York: Hawthorn Books, 1966. 128 p. JH.

> In this simple introduction to the free enterprise philosophy, the
> author shows how the founder of scientific economics formed his
> ideas in an age of freedom and rugged individualism.

Place, Marian T. THE COPPER KINGS OF MONTANA. Landmark Books.
New York: Random House, 1961. 184 p. Elem.

> Marcus Daly, William A. Clark, and Fredrick A. Heinze, the
> copper kings, worked the "richest little hill in the world" and grew
> rich. This book presents the background of social, political, and
> economic life in the far West during the nineteenth century.

Rublowsky, John. AFTER THE CRASH: AMERICA IN THE GREAT DEPRESSION.
New York: Crowell-Collier, 1970. 186 p. HS.

> In this account of the crash of 1929 and the Depression that fol-
> lowed, the author describes the collapse of the American economy,
> and the early efforts of President Roosevelt to start his New Deal.

Smolensky, Eugene. ADJUSTMENTS TO DEPRESSION AND WAR, 1930-1945.
Economic Forces in American History Series. Glenview, Ill.: Scott, Foresman,
1964. 72 p. HS.

> Economic conditions of the Hoover and Roosevelt administrations,
> from the Depression through the end of World War II, are dis-
> cussed.

Taft, Philip. ORGANIZED LABOR IN AMERICAN HISTORY. New York:
Harper & Row, 1964. 818 p. HS.

> A history of American labor from its infancy, covering the Knights
> of Labor, dual unionism, the I.W.W., and the AFL-CIO and the
> labor leaders.

U.S. Department of Labor. BRIEF HISTORY OF THE AMERICAN LABOR
MOVEMENT. Washington, D.C.: 1964. 10 p. Distributed by Government
Printing Office. HS.

This pamphlet traces the development of the labor movement from
its earliest organization to the modern labor movement. Major
figures and important labor legislation are discussed. The general
outlook of the labor movement is presented.

Victor, R.F. JOHN MAYNARD KEYNES: FATHER OF MODERN ECONOM-
ICS. Charlotteville, N.Y.: SamHar Press, 1972. 31 p. Elem.

A very brief introduction to Keynes and his theories.

Wass, Philmore, et al. THE SEARCH FOR ECONOMIC SECURITY: AMERI-
CA'S EVOLVING PATTERN OF FAMILY SECURITY FROM COLONIAL TIMES
TO THE PRESENT. New York: Institute of Life Insurance, Educational Divi-
sion, 1968. 64 p. HS.

This booklet traces the evolution of American economic security
system, examining the contribution made by each period in our
nation's history to our attitudes and institutions for dealing with
economic risk.

Werstein, Irving. A NATION FIGHTS BACK: THE DEPRESSION AND ITS
AFTERMATH. New York: Julian Messner, 1962. 191 p. Elem.

The events that led to the 1929 stock market crash and Depression
are presented. Roosevelt's efforts to restore the country's prosperity and the resulting rise of social awareness in the nation are
discussed.

MEDIA

AMERICAN CIVILIZATION AND MAN'S QUEST FOR WEALTH. Stamford,
Conn.: Educational Dimensions Corp., 1972. Filmstrip. Sound. Color.
Teacher's guide. JH, HS.

Examples are shown of writings, satirical cartoons, "yellow journal-
ism" inspired by businessmen, politicians, farmers, miners, bosses,
robber barons, and others involved in the frantic drive for wealth
during America's development.

AMERICA'S FIRST FACTORY. Chicago: Denoyer-Geppert, 1961. Filmstrip.
Color. Teacher's guide. JH.

The effects of the factory system upon American society is viewed,
beginning with the establishment of Samuel Slater's original textile
mill.

BEGINNINGS AND GROWTH OF INDUSTRIAL AMERICA. Chicago: Coronet Instructional Films, 1960. Film. 11 mins. Sound. B&W. Elem, JH.

This film concentrates on the period from the Revolutionary War to the Civil War, describing some of the evolutionary process that transformed the United States from an agricultural to an industrial nation. It deals in some detail with the economic, political, social, and technological factors that contributed to this change.

COLONIAL SHIP BUILDING AND SEA TRADE. Chicago: Coronet Instructional Films, 1958. Film. 11 mins. Sound. Color. Elem, JH.

The film traces the evolution of the shipping industry in New England during colonial times. Because of its location and because of the skill of its population, New England emerged as the shipping center of colonial America. Trade brought employment, increasing incomes, and rising levels of living, not only to the colonies in New England but throughout colonial America.

THE CORPORATION. Pleasantville, N.Y.: Guidance Associates, 1969. 2 filmstrips, 14 mins. ea. Sound. HS.

Through a review of the evolution of business organization from the eighteenth century to the present time, the filmstrips describe advantages and disadvantages of the corporate form of business organization.

THE DEPRESSION. New York: Grossman Publications. Kit, collected by Andrew Bronin. JH, HS.

This kit is made up of twelve exhibits and five broadsheets that bring back the black days of the Depression both in the cities and on the farms. Exhibits include: Depression script, a photo sequence of a Texas dust storm, an NRA poster, and the front page of the Emporia Gazette of May 11, 1934.

ECHOES: THE GROWTH OF THE NATION AND ITS ECONOMY. Cambridge, Mass.: Pathways of Sound, 1972. 9 cassettes. Teacher's guide. JH, HS.

This program was designed to enlighten students as to how the individual is affected by government, employment, investment, and consumption. The titles are: "The Colonists and the Economic Beginnings of Our Country"; "What Is the Stock Market"; "Growth and Industrialization of the Country"; "What Was Good about Life in the Twenties?"; "The Stock Market Collapse"; "The Roosevelt Administration and the Beginning of a New Economic Philosophy"; "Financing and Banking Controls"; "Investment"; "Corporate Growth."

ECONOMIC GROWTH FROM OUR HISTORY 1789-1860 AND 1860-1945. New York: Filmstrip House, 1962. 2 filmstrips, 40 frames ea. Color. JH, HS.

The first filmstrip shows the southern economy, industrial growth of New England, expanding frontier, growth of canals, toll roads, and railroads. The second one is concerned with the rise of corporations, laws to control monopolies, the growth of big business and the transition from agricultural to industrial economy.

ECONOMICS IN AMERICAN HISTORY. Bedford Hills, N.Y.: Teaching Resources Films in cooperation with Joint Council on Economic Education, 1973. 120 slides. Color. Teacher's guide. HS.

This set of slides is designed to help the secondary teacher incorporate economic facts, concepts, principles, and problems into the American history course. The set is divided into twenty-one topics.

ERA OF WATER COMMERCE. New York: McGraw-Hill, 1960. Film. 11 mins. Sound. Color. Elem.

This film covers the period from 1750 to 1850 with emphasis on the importance of water transportation in the development of commerce and economic growth in the United States.

EVOLUTION OF AMERICAN INDUSTRY, ENTERPRISE AND WELFARE, 1650-1960. Chicago: Singer/SVE, 1966. 4 filmstrips. Sound. Color. Teacher's guide. JH.

Photographs, dioramas, paintings, and documents are used to show hardy pioneers, ingenious inventors, and dedicated educators who contributed to the growth of the United States. It is also shown that innovations in transportation, communication, industry, agriculture, commerce, and public welfare gave rise to the high standard of living in the United States.

THE GREAT DEPRESSION. New York: Grossman Publications, 1968. Kit, collected by Charles Humphries. 10 exhibits. 5 broadsheets. JH, HS.

This kit pictures the Depression as it was experienced in the United States and Canada. People's feelings of fear, discouragement, futility, and anger as they attempted to survive these black days of the 1930s are vividly recreated. Exhibits include: WALL STREET JOURNAL for October 30, 1929; liberal election poster, 1930; a collection can label for the hunger marches, 1935; and voices of the Depression on a record.

IMPACT OF THE GAY NINETIES: FOOTNOTES TO THE TIMES. Bronx, N.Y.: H.W. Wilson, 1969. 6 tapes, 18-22 mins. Teacher's guide. JH.

These tapes portray the transition in the United States from an agricultural to an industrial society. They depict the living styles of people from the affluent to the poor. The panic of 1893 is used as a vehicle to develop insights into business cycles, unemployment, and causes of instability.

INDUSTRIAL REVOLUTION IN ENGLAND. Chicago: Encyclopaedia Britannica Films, 1960. Film. 25 mins. Sound. B&W. JH.

The evolution of manufacturing in England from the cottage system is described. Among essential questions discussed are why the development first took place in England, and how the transformation of industry in England affected levels of living there.

MEANING OF THE INDUSTRIAL REVOLUTION. Chicago: Coronet Instructional Films, 1950. Film. 12 mins. Sound. B&W. JH.

England was the first nation in the modern world to move from the domestic to the factory system of production. This film is the story of that evolution. Benefits from explorations and colonization stimulated trade, rising incomes, increased demand, scientific investigations, and technological change.

THE NEW DEAL. New York: Grossman Publications. Jackdaw kit, collected by James Compton. 10 exhibits. 6 broadsheets. JH, HS.

This kit examines Franklin Roosevelt's "New Deal for the American People," a program of recovery, rehabilitation, and reform. The excitement and ferment of the 1930s are shown. Exhibits include: a recording of President Roosevelt's first inaugural address; an excerpt from a speech by Senator Huey Long; a fireside chat; and a leaflet announcing a United Automobile Workers protest meeting.

THE SOUTHERN NEW ENGLAND REGION: NEW INDUSTRIES. New York: McGraw-Hill, 1963. Film. 13 mins. Sound. Color. Elem, JH.

The economic recovery of the New England states following World War I is discussed. The interrelationships among transportation, water, power, skilled labor, and research centers in the new economic development are shown.

THE '29 BOOM AND THE '30'S DEPRESSION. New York: McGraw-Hill, 1960. Film. 15 mins. Sound. B&W. JH, HS.

Through news clips, the film presents a historical view of the causes and attempted cures of the Great Depression. In addition to providing insights into this specific experience, the film develops a rationale for contra-cyclical policies.

U.S. ECONOMIC HISTORY. Bedford Hills, N.Y.: Teaching Resources
Films. 2 filmstrips. Sound. Teacher's guide. HS.

 The contributions to America's economic growth patterns of technology, research, abundant natural resources, a qualitative labor
 force, and increased capital resources are described.

U.S. IN THE 20TH CENTURY 1932-1940. Chicago: Coronet Instructional
Films, 1957. Film. 21 mins. Sound. B&W. HS.

 The film pictures the state of the economy at the depth of the
 Depression. It describes the policies the Roosevelt administration
 used to grapple with the nation's economic difficulties.

Chapter 12

INTERNATIONAL

American Federation of Labor and Congress of Industrial Organizations.
WAGES AND FOREIGN COMPETITION. Washington, D.C.: 1967. 6 p.
HS.

> The role of wages, wage rates, labor costs, prices, and efficiency
> of production in determining whether or not American workmen are
> harmed by lower tariffs is discussed. The general position taken
> is that the relationship between wages and foreign competition is
> a complex one.

BALANCE OF PAYMENTS CRISIS. Public Affairs Pamphlets, no. 387A. New
York: Public Affairs Committee, 1968. 20 p. HS.

> This pamphlet discusses the implications of the deficit in our in-
> ternational balance of payments. Proposed solutions to the defi-
> cit problem are individually presented along with the pros and
> cons of each.

Barach, Arnold B. THE NEW EUROPE AND ITS ECONOMIC FUTURE. New
York: Macmillan, 1964. 114 p. HS.

> This volume is based on the Twentieth Century Fund's study of
> EUROPE'S NEEDS AND RESOURCES. The magnitude, distribution,
> and growth of all kinds of economic resources and factors in to-
> day's Europe, including some projections into the future are dis-
> cussed. There are many maps and charts to illustrate this discus-
> sion.

Berkowitz, Monroe. INDIA: STRUGGLE AGAINST TIME. Area Studies in
Economic Progress. Minneapolis: Curriculum Resources, 1963. 72 p. HS.

> The author deals with questions of India's ability to make the
> transition from an agricultural to an industrialized economy, to
> eliminate hunger, poverty, and disease, to build factories, defend
> her borders, and satisfy her people's need for goods and services.

117

International
===

Brown, Lester. WORLD WITHOUT BORDERS. New York: Vintage Books, 1972. 395 p. HS.

> The author discusses the diverse and complicated developments of the past decades to document the growing interdependence of nations in a world in which problems are increasingly of global dimension (food shortages, world environment crisis, and so forth) which only global responses can meet the challenges posed by these problems.

Calderwood, James D. INTERNATIONAL ECONOMIC PROBLEMS. Economic Series, no. 52. Minneapolis: Curriculum Resources, 1961. 71 p. HS.

> This short survey of the U.S. international economic problems was written for high school students. It includes a discussion of the magnitude, nature, and importance of our international trade, of trade barriers, of aid to underdeveloped nations, of our balance of payments, and relations with the Soviet Union.

_____. A TEACHER'S GUIDE TO WORLD TRADE. Economic Life Series, no. 1. Washington, D.C.: National Council for Social Studies in cooperation with the Joint Council on Economic Education, 1960. 128 p. HS.

> The purpose and objectives of studying this topic are discussed. The problem is analyzed with comments on the subjects of changing world economy, why trade takes place, barriers to world trade, economic development, and the monetary framework of world trade. Projects and activities, books, magazines, visual materials, and evaluation procedures are suggested.

_____. WESTERN EUROPE AND THE COMMON MARKET. Area Studies in Economics Progress. Minneapolis: Curriculum Resources, 1963. 72 p. HS.

> The activities of Western Europe in the Common Market and the effect of these actions on the prosperity and security of the United States are discussed. Economic history, current economic issues, and Western Europe and the world are examined.

_____. WORLD ECONOMY. Economic Issues in American Democracy. Bedford Hills, N.Y.: Teaching Resources Films, 1972. 79 p. HS.

> This pamphlet contains an overall look at the nature of world trade and its importance to the United States and other countries. The impact of international trade and finance on the American economy and the economic well-being of all the people in the world is discussed and some of the principles underlying it are examined. There is also a consideration of trade barriers and trade policies and the problem of international monetary relations. There is a filmstrip available to accompany this pamphlet.

Cerami, Charles A. ALLIANCE BORN OF DANGER: AMERICA, THE COM-
MON MARKET AND THE ATLANTIC PARTNERSHIP. New York: Harcourt
Brace Jovanovich, 1972. 181 p. HS.

A clear, concise analysis of the European economic community
for the general reader. The author's belief that a political as
well as an academic partnership is imminent is explained.

Chamber of Commerce of the United States of America. INTERNATIONAL
ECONOMICS. Washington, D.C.: 1966. 33 p. HS.

This pamphlet points out the basic reason for international trade.
It explains how our economy is related to the economics of other
countries, the benefits of world trade, balance of payments, and
problems that stem from international monetary and trade policies.

Chang, Perry P. CHINA, DEVELOPMENT BY FORCE. Area Studies in Economic Progress. Minneapolis: Curriculum Resources, 1964. 80 p. HS.

Communism's strengths and weaknesses from the standpoint of economic development are pointed out. The use of force, skills of
propaganda and persuasion, and a disregard for human suffering
are strengths and may bring some quick results. The weakness is
that there are no checks to prevent the leaders from making serious mistakes.

Committee for Economic Development. ASSISTING DEVELOPMENT IN LOW-
INCOME COUNTRIES. New York: 1969. 88 p. HS.

This statement offers a rationale for public support of the U.S.
economic assistance program and recommends a far-ranging set of
priorities for the U.S. government policy. It proposes better ways
by which the United States and other advanced nations can speed
the growth of low-income countries through the application of
public and private external resources--financial, managerial, and
technological.

_____. DEVELOPMENT ASSISTANCE TO SOUTHEAST ASIA. New York:
1970. 96 p. HS.

This statement deals with the special responsibility of the United
States, Japan, and Australia to contribute external resources--
financial, managerial, and technological--to the economic and
social development of southeast Asia.

_____. THE DOLLAR AND THE WORLD MONETARY SYSTEM: A STATE-
MENT OF NATIONAL POLICY BY THE RESEARCH AND POLICY COMMITTEE.
New York: 1966. 76 p. HS.

This statement is made to increase the understanding of the balance of payments problem and the effect it has on the internation-

al monetary system. It also indicates priorities and emphasizes
the relationship between sound domestic and international economic policies.

_____. ECONOMIC DEVELOPMENT OF CENTRAL AMERICA. New York:
1964. 128 p. HS.

There are Spanish and English texts on facing pages. This statement surveys the impact of the Central American Common Market
and outlines new steps to be taken to speed economic growth in
this area. A history of this common market and a summary of
agrarian reform laws are included.

_____. STRENGTHENING THE WORLD'S MONETARY SYSTEM: A STATE-
MENT ON NATIONAL POLICY BY THE RESEARCH AND POLICY COMMIT-
TEE. New York: 1973. 87 p. HS.

This statement discusses the monetary crisis and the events that
led to it. It suggests reforms to resolve the crisis and describes
essential changes that should be made in the monetary system.

Dalton, George, ed. ECONOMIC DEVELOPMENT AND SOCIAL CHANGE:
THE MODERNIZATION OF VILLAGE COMMUNITIES. Garden City, N.Y.:
Doubleday, 1970. 664 p. HS.

This is a collection of essays on the tribal and peasant communities of Africa, Asia, and Latin America, discussing their primitive economic structure, the impact of European colonization, and
the process of economic development and cultural modernization
now underway in these regions.

Ellis, Harry B. THE COMMON MARKET. Cleveland: World, 1965. 204 p.
Illus. Elem.

The attempts to unify Europe are surveyed. The men and the
contributions that they made to the establishment of the economic
community within which people and money move freely are described.

Federal Reserve Bank of Minneapolis. WHY FOREIGN TRADE? Minneapolis:
1970. 42 p. HS.

This is an analysis of the impact a new trade bill could have on
world economy with special emphasis on the effects that would be
felt by the people in the district.

Federal Reserve Bank of San Francisco. THE CHINA TRADE. San Francisco:
1972. 39 p. HS.

This supplement to the MONTHLY REVIEW, a regular publication of the Federal Reserve Bank of San Francisco, discusses old China trade (to World War II), Western trade, American trade, English trade, opium wars, and treaty ports growth.

First National Bank of Chicago. GOLD AND THE BALANCE OF PAYMENTS. Chicago: 1968. 24 p. HS.

A summary of trends in the U.S. balance of payments with emphasis on factors affecting the gold market. Information is presented in chart form and tables.

Foreign Policy Association. UNDERSTANDING THE INTERNATIONAL MONETARY SYSTEM. Headline Series, no. 182. New York: 1967. 63 p. HS.

This is an effort to explain the problem of international monetary reserves.

Gallant, Kathryn. MOUNTAINS IN THE SEA, THE CHALLENGE OF CROWDED JAPAN. New York: Coward-McCann, 1957. 95 p. Illus. Maps. Elem.

This is a survey of the geographical features of the island, its agriculture, industries, problem of overpopulation, and what the Japanese are doing to provide food for its many people.

Hirsch, Fred. MONEY INTERNATIONAL. Garden City, N.Y.: Doubleday, 1969. 420 p. HS.

This is an analysis of the international monetary crisis and its underlying causes, with specific regard to various economical, fiscal, industrial, and banking factors.

Industrial Relations Center. AMERICA AND THE WORLD ECONOMY. Chicago: University of Chicago, 1965. 34 p. HS.

This is an introduction to the principles of international trade. Regional specialization and comparative advantage are explained and illustrated with charts. The pros and cons of tariff protection are also discussed.

Isenberg, Irwin, ed. THE DEVELOPING NATIONS: POVERTY AND PROGRESS. Reference Shelf, vol. 41, no. 1. Bronx, N.Y.: H.W. Wilson, 1969. 205 p. HS.

Divided into four sections--the development decade; what underdevelopment means; too many people, too little food; and development and the future--this volume gathers together articles on the problems of nation-building and the prospects for the economic development of emerging nations.

_____. THE OUTLOOK FOR WESTERN EUROPE. Reference Shelf, vol. 42, no. 2. Bronx, N.Y.: H.W. Wilson, 1970. 213 p. HS.

This compilation deals mainly with Western Europe's economic conditions and the political questions it faces such as the possibility of federation. Western Europe's foreign relations with both East and West are also discussed in several articles.

Kenen, Peter B. GIANT AMONG NATIONS: PROBLEMS IN UNITED STATES FOREIGN ECONOMIC POLICY. Chicago: Rand McNally, 1963. 223 p. HS.

This book includes both historical background and economic analysis of U.S. foreign aid, foreign trade, foreign investment policies and programs. The author suggests the economic diplomacy and proposals whereby government and business through joint efforts can best utilize our economic resources.

Kenen, Peter B., and Lubitz, Raymond, eds. INTERNATIONAL ECONOMICS. 3d ed. Modern Foundations of Economics Series. Englewood Cliffs, N.J.: Prentice-Hall, 1971. 127 p. HS.

This is a volume of readings on industry, price theory, money and credit, labor, public finance, economic development, international economics, and national income analysis.

League of Women Voters of the United States. FOREIGN AID AT THE CROSS-ROADS. Washington, D.C.: 1966. 78 p. HS.

The political implications both at home and abroad and the influence of current political problems on foreign aid are discussed. Programs and organizations such as the Alliance for Progress, U.N. Development Program, and the World Bank are explained. The problems of deciding the type of aid and the selection of the countries to receive it are taken up.

Madden, Carl [H.]. LATIN AMERICA: REFORM OR REVOLUTION. Area Studies in Economic Progress. Minneapolis: Curriculum Resources, 1963. 72 p. HS.

Can a Latin America be created where free institutions are to be given a chance to work out long-term solutions to the problems of poverty, illiteracy and hopelessness? What is the best course to take? How are Latin Americans different from us? What kind of land is there? What has kept Latin America from developing faster? What are the obstacles that hold these nations back? How are they trying to help themselves? What are we doing to help them? What about their future? The author tries to answer all the above questions.

Myrdal, Gunnar. BEYOND THE WELFARE STATE: ECONOMIC PLANNING

AND ITS INTERNATIONAL IMPLICATIONS. New Haven, Conn.: Yale University Press, 1960. 281 p. HS.

The distinguished Swedish economist and politician analyzes the "welfare state" as it existed in three areas: the Soviet nations, the underdeveloped nations, and the developed Western nations. He points out the increase of economic planning everywhere and discusses the international implications of the activities in these three areas.

Paradis, Adrian A. INTERNATIONAL TRADE IN ACTION. New York: Julian Messner, 1973. 190 p. Elem.

This survey of international trade provides up-to-date material on oil and the energy crisis, the complicated U.S. balance of payments, the pros and cons of protectionism, Japan's emergence as an international giant, devaluation of the dollar, and trade with the Soviet Union, China, and the world's underdeveloped nations. The importance of world trade in terms of its effect on unemployment is explained.

_____. TRADE: THE WORLD'S LIFEBLOOD. New York: Julian Messner, 1969. 96 p. Elem.

This is a discussion of the history and importance of international trade from prehistoric to modern times, telling how it has brought about wars, great discoveries, and better understanding between nations.

Randall, Laura. ECONOMIC GROWTH, EVOLUTION OR REVOLUTION. Studies in Economics. Boston: Heath & Co., 1964. 144 p. HS.

This collection of essays treats the problems of economic development facing underdeveloped nations. The analysis of the problem of capital formation in societies with economic institutions different from ours is an excellent aid in understanding the problems of investment in a private enterprise economy.

RETHINKING ECONOMIC DEVELOPMENT. Headline Series, no. 208. New York: Foreign Policy Association, 1973. 63 p. HS.

This pamphlet concludes that new approaches to economic development and foreign aid are imperative in order to narrow the gap between the poor and rich nations in the decade of the seventies. Even before the U.S. cut its foreign aid, economic growth rates in the developing countries were uneven and vast regions containing the majority of the world's poor made little progress.

Salkever, Louis R., and Flynn, Helen M. SUB-SAHARAN AFRICA: STRUGGLE AGAINST THE PAST. Area Studies in Economic Progress. Minneapolis:

Curriculum Resources, 1963. 72 p. HS.

An account of the new patterns of trade, technology, education, and government that are promoting new ways of thinking and acting in Africa. The clash of the new world in which economic growth is sought and the old world which represents tribal stagnation is described.

Savage, Katherine. THE STORY OF THE COMMON MARKET. New York: Henry Z. Walck, 1969. 192 p. JH.

A history of economic conditions in Western Europe is presented, then the author discusses the circumstances that led to the formation of the Common Market and describes the development of the plan up to 1969.

Schwartz, Harry. SOVIET UNION: COMMUNIST ECONOMIC POWER. Area Studies in Economic Progress. Minneapolis: Curriculum Resources, 1963. 72 p. HS.

This booklet examines the Soviet economy. It attempts to explain how the economic power developed, to look at the economic accomplishments and setbacks, to discover the problems facing the Soviet economy and how their leaders are meeting these problems.

Snider, Delbert A. INTERNATIONAL MONETARY RELATIONS. New York: Random House, 1966. 141 p. HS.

Designed for the layman, the text suggests reforms of the present system and explains essentials of international monetary relations including the balance of payments, problems, and future.

Steinberg, David J. THE U.S.A. IN THE WORLD ECONOMY. CASE Economic Literary Series. New York: McGraw-Hill, 1966. 138 p. HS.

The position of the United States in world trade and economic relations is discussed in this pamphlet. Aspects of our international economic position, such as the flow of private capital, the role of U.S. military and economic aid, the balance of payments, and the dollar in world money and banking are treated in depth.

Theobald, Robert. THE RICH AND THE POOR: A STUDY OF THE ECONOMICS OF RISING EXPECTATIONS. New York: New American Library of World Literature, 1960. 180 p. HS.

A study of the economics of rising expectations showing how the great advances made by industrial nations tend to disturb balance in the world economy. The role that "rich" nations can play in economic aid and cooperation to help the "poor" nations acquire wealth without a breakdown in tradition and moral strength is analyzed.

U.S. Department of Commerce. U.S. BALANCE OF PAYMENTS. Rev. ed. Washington, D.C.: 1971. 44 p. Sold by the Government Printing Office. HS.

> The international economic position of the United States is examined based on its international, military, and economic commitments.

Ward, Barbara. RICH NATIONS AND THE POOR NATIONS. New York: Norton & Co., 1962. 195 p. HS.

> This is a very readable account by a well-known British economist of the problem of economic development. It describes both rich and poor nations, and the blueprint followed by Communists to absorb more countries through the impact of economics.

Wilcox, Clair, et al. ECONOMIES OF THE WORLD TODAY: THEIR ORGANIZATION, DEVELOPMENT AND PERFORMANCE. 2d ed. New York: Harcourt Brace Jovanovich, 1966. 171 p. HS.

> This volume describes the economic systems of China and India, in addition to those of the Soviet Union, Great Britain, and the United States. The actual performance of each is stressed. Types of economies in general are discussed.

MEDIA

AFRICA IN FERMENT. Filmstrip on Current Affairs. New York: New York Times, 1968. Filmstrip. 69 frames. Sound. B&W. HS.

> Sub-Saharan Africa, where tribalism is being confronted with nationalism, is discussed. The problems that the new nations face in attempting to enter the modern world are explained.

AMERICA'S NEW RIVAL: THE COMMON MARKET. Bedford Hills, N.Y.: Teaching Resources Films, 1974. 2 filmstrips. Sound. Color. Elem, JH.

> These filmstrips emphasize the growing strength of the Common Market. A historical review shows its growth, and good charts point up comparisons between it and this country.

ARCTIC FISHERMAN IN WORLD TRADE. Hollywood, Calif.: Bailey Films, 1964. Film. 12 mins. Sound. Color. Elem.

> Fishing in Arctic waters is shown. The importance of fishing to the Norwegians is explained. Norwegians export dried cod to many parts of the world. These exports enable them to pay for the imports they wish to receive from other countries.

BREAKING THE TRADE BARRIER. 2 pts. New York: McGraw-Hall, 1962. Film, 30 mins. ea. Sound. B&W. HS.

This is a CBS report. The film uses discussion between Presidents Eisenhower and Kennedy and between President Kennedy and business leaders to develop a rationale of closer economic ties between the United States and Europe. The costs as well as the benefits of freer trade are presented.

BUSY HARBOR. Chicago: Coronet Instructional Films, 1960. Film. 11 mins. Sound. Color. Elem.

A boy and girl visit a tugboat captain and learn about the flow of goods between Seattle, Washington, and places in the United States as well as between Seattle and other nations of the world.

CHILE. Our Latin American Neighbors Series. New York: McGraw-Hill, 1961. Film. 15 mins. Sound. Color. Teacher's guide. Elem.

The major geographic regions of Chile, the busy ports of Antofagasta and Valparaiso, and the vital role of overseas trade in the nation's economy are described.

COMMON MARKET. Bedford Hills, N.Y.: Teaching Resources Films, 1973. 2 filmstrips. Color. HS.

The history and growth of the European Economic Community from 1946 to 1973 is traced. The struggles of the early years, the aid to workers and industry, the free circulation of workers, the establishment of free trade with African nations, British trade agreements, and French opposition to British membership in the European Economic Community are discussed.

COOPERATION IS OUR BUSINESS. Chicago: International Film Bureau. Film. 22 mins. Color. HS.

Problems of both rich and poor countries today are explored and the need for international cooperation in solving these problems is stressed. The film shows how cooperative efforts at research and discussion among the twenty-three member countries of the Organization for Economic Cooperation & Development are leading to solutions for some of the problems.

THE DOLLAR IN TODAY'S WORLD. Wilton, Conn.: Current Affairs Films, 1972. Filmstrip. Sound. HS.

The American dollar, long the "king of international currencies," is under attack. Can the dollar stage a comeback or must new ways be found to finance international trade? The importance of the stability of the dollar is tied to continued domestic prosperity and the United States' ranking as the world's number one economic power.

ECONOMIC AND SOCIAL COUNCIL. New York: National Film Board of Canada, 1963. Film. 16 mins. Sound. B&W. JH, HS.

This film discusses how the Economic and Social Council of the United Nations strives to promote international cooperation in fighting economic and social misery.

ECONOMIC DEVELOPMENT IN AN AFRICAN NATION. Santa Monica, Calif.: BFA Educational Media. Film. 8 mins. Color. Elem, JH.

A discussion of new industrial and economic growth that is taking place in African nations today is presented. The growth is dependent upon effective use of resources, a skilled labor force, and new scientific or technological advances. As more workers are employed due to specialization, division of labor, and mass production, more jobs are available, more wages are earned, and more people are able to buy more goods.

ECONOMICS AROUND THE WORLD. East Orange, N.J.: Tweedy Transparencies, 1968. 6 transparencies. 9 overlays. Color. HS.

This group of transparencies analyzes common causes of world poverty; the role of imports and exports in a nation's economy; international payments; and the Soviet and British economic systems.

EGYPT AND THE ARAB WORLD. Wilton, Conn.: Current Affairs Films, 1969. Filmstrip. 44 frames. Color. HS.

International economic problems of Egypt and other Arab countries are described. The unified fear of Israel and the growing Soviet influence in this area are explained.

EUROPE AND THE COMMON MARKET. Santa Ana, Calif.: International Communication Films, 1962. 6 filmstrips. Sound. Color. Teacher's guide. Elem, JH, HS.

A set of maps and a four-page fact table and two background booklets accompany this set of filmstrips on Belgium, France, Germany, Italy, the Netherlands, and Europe and the importance of the Common Market.

EUROPEAN ECONOMIC COMMUNITY. Chicago: Coronet Instructional Films, 1965. Film. 14 mins. Sound. Color. HS.

The three economic goals of the European Economic Community are the elimination of tariffs, free exchange of labor and capital, and creation of a common market. The achievement of these

goals should result in more efficient allocations of scarce resources
and a higher level of living for all.

EUROPE'S COMMON MARKET: PROBLEMS AND PROSPECTS. Wilton, Conn.:
Current Affairs Films, 1972. Filmstrip. 66 frames. Sound. Color. HS.

The root causes of disagreement between member nations of the
Common Market are examined and the prospects for a concerted
policy that could help turn the Common Market into one of the
world's superpowers are assessed.

INTERNATIONAL TRADE. New York: McGraw-Hill, 1950. Filmstrip. 36
frames. B&W. HS.

The filmstrip explains how international trade transactions are recorded in a balance of payments account and advocates specialization of production as a means of improving the living conditions
of all people.

INTERNATIONAL TRADE: WORLD'S LIFELINE. Wilton, Conn.: Current
Affairs Films, 1969. Filmstrip. 43 frames. Color. HS.

The filmstrip describes the income and the employment effects of
international trade. It relates the story of the emergence of
freer trade in the contemporary world.

JAPAN: ASIA'S ECONOMIC SUPERPOWER. Wilton, Conn.: Current Affairs Films, 1973. Filmstrip. Sound. Color. Teacher's guide. HS.

Japan's meteoric economic development is examined. Extensive
investments in foreign industry and increased spending on defense
has led to increased independence.

MR. EUROPE AND THE COMMON MARKET. New York: Carousel Films,
1962. Film. 60 mins. Sound. B&W. HS.

Monnet, the French economist who is known as the architect
of United Europe, describes how the Common Market will, by re-
moving barriers to trade, make possible an international flow of
men and goods that will add to productivity and lead to a higher
level of living in Western Europe.

MONEY TALKS: EXPORTS, IMPORTS, DOLLARS AND GOLD. New York:
Carousel Films, 1962. Film. 30 mins. Sound. B&W. HS.

The mutual advantages of trade within and between nations is
pointed out. Difficulties imposed by government regulations on
international trade are cited. Relationships among international
trade, balance of payments, and gold flows are explained.

MOUNTING MILLIONS. Bloomington, Ind.: Audio-Visual Center, Indiana University, 1969. Film. 60 mins. B&W. HS.

This film focuses on the need for economic and agricultural development and social change in India. Population growth makes these processes extremely difficult. Special emphasis is on food production shortages and alternative solutions to this severe problem.

NOT ENOUGH. New York: Modern Learning Aids, 1969. Film. 30 mins. Color. HS.

The need for wealthy nations to provide both financial and technical assistance to underdeveloped nations is shown. India and Thailand are examples. The film demonstrates how this results in construction projects such as dams and canals which supply life-sustaining water for people and their crops.

ROUND TRIP: U.S.A. IN WORLD TRADE. Chicago: Encyclopaedia Britannica Films, 1952. Film. 20 mins. Sound. B&W. HS.

The causes and benefits of foreign trade are described. The benefits in improved allocation of scarce materials and higher standards of living that could result from unhampered international trade are explained.

SOVIET CHALLENGE: INDUSTRIAL REVOLUTION IN RUSSIA. Chicago: Encyclopaedia Britannica Films, 1963. Film. 26 mins. Sound. B&W. HS.

The success of economic planning in the USSR is emphasized in this film. Official films tell the story of the drive to transform Russia from an agrarian to an industrial society.

TRADE BETWEEN NATIONS. Santa Monica, Calif.: BFA Educational Media, 1967. Film. 21 mins. Color. HS.

The theme that "bridges of trade bring nations and people closer together" is interwoven throughout this motion picture as students develop an understanding of the influence that world trade has on the economic development of the nations of the world. It highlights the economic interdependence among the Asiatic nations and the United States.

UNDERSTANDING INTERNATIONAL TRADE. Economics of Our Times Series. New York: McGraw-Hill, 1962. Filmstrip. 34 frames. Color. HS.

This filmstrip describes the advantages of international trade, the problems of financing this trade, and the sources of balance of payments problems.

WORLD TRADE FOR BETTER LIVING. Chicago: Encyclopaedia Britannica Films, 1951. Film. 20 mins. Sound. B&W. HS.

The beneficial results to nations of foreign trade are shown. An argument is developed for free international trade.

Chapter 13
LABOR

American Federation of Labor and Congress of Industrial Organizations. LABOR LOOKS AT AUTOMATION. Publication no. 21. Washington, D.C.: 1966. 36 p. HS.

> This pamphlet treats the topics of price and pace of technological progress, and the impact of automation on employment, job, and income security.

_____. WHY STRIKES? FACTS VS. FICTION. Washington, D.C.: 1965. 8 p. HS.

> The difficulty in judging the rights and wrongs of a management and labor dispute is discussed in this pamphlet. Basic issues common to all strikes are examined and arguments are presented for the "right to strike."

Barbash, Jack. THE LABOR MOVEMENT IN THE U.S. Public Affairs Pamphlets, no. 262. Washington, D.C.: Public Affairs Press, 1968. 27 p. HS.

> This pamphlet describes union goals, problems, and contributions to American society. There is a brief introduction to the role of union-management collective bargaining in our market economy.

Berger, Gilda. JOBS THAT HELP THE CONSUMER AND HOMEMAKER. New York: Lothrop, Lee & Shepard, 1974. 95 p. Elem.

> Jobs described deal with selling manufactured products or commercial services: insurance agents, interior designers, home products demonstrators, product designers, and dieticians employed by food producers.

Boucher, Bertrand P. HOW MAN PROVIDES. Finding-out Books. New York: Home Library Press, 1963. 56 p. Illus. Elem.

> This book tells where and how people all over the world make

their living including: farming, fishing, mining, lumbering, manufacturing, and trading. It emphasizes the need for world trade.

Bullock, Paul. EQUAL OPPORTUNITY IN EMPLOYMENT. Los Angeles: Institute of Industrial Relations, University of California, 1966. 114 p. HS.

A discussion of the problem of discrimination in the area of employment and the effect it has on the total economy with suggestions for overcoming the problem.

Cahn, Rhoda, and Cahn, William. NO TIME FOR SCHOOL, NO TIME FOR
PLAY: THE STORY OF CHILD LABOR IN AMERICA. New York: Julian
Messner, 1972. 64 p. Illus. Elem.

This book describes the lives of working children in the United
States before the passage of child labor laws.

CHILDCRAFT: WHAT PEOPLE DO. Childcraft: How and Why Library, vol.
7. Chicago: Field Enterprises, 1972. 366 p. Elem.

Children are taught about the world of work so that they can plan
for their role in it. There are sections on people who work in
special clothes, people who work with special tools, and people
who work together. Occupations from disc jockeys to stenotypists
are described.

Chilton, Shirley, et al. EVERYONE HAS IMPORTANT JOBS TO DO.
Chicago: Children's Press, 1970. 48 p. Illus. Prim.

This book shows the importance of everyday jobs. It shows the
child how he can compare these jobs and customs with those of
peoples of other cultures and in different periods of history.

Colby, Carroll B. NIGHT PEOPLE: WORKERS FROM DUSK TO DAWN.
Rev. ed. New York: Coward, McCann & Geoghegan, 1971. 48 p. Illus.
Elem.

The author describes some of the many important jobs that must
be carried out each night. Black and white photographs show
firemen and nurses, computer programmers and air traffic control-
lers, disc jockeys, and taxi drivers.

Davis, Daniel S. MR. BLACK LABOR: THE STORY OF A. PHILIP RANDOLPH.
New York: Dutton, 1973. 174 p. JH.

Philip Randolph played a leading role in the struggle for Negro
rights from the 1920s through the 1960s. He also became an important figure in the American labor movement.

Doherty, Robert E. THE EMPLOYER-EMPLOYEE RELATIONSHIP. Grass Roots

Labor

Guides on Democracy and Practical Politics, no. 25. Washington, Conn. Center for Information on America, 1966. 14 p. HS.

Interests common to management and labor and the areas of agreement and disagreement are identified. Changes in the nature of the management-labor relationships are discussed.

Fanning, Leonard M. FATHERS OF INDUSTRIES. New York: Lippincott, 1962. 256 p. Illus. Elem.

The lives of men important in the development of large industries are described. Some of the people included are: James Watt, Richard Arkwright, Samuel Slater, David Wilkinson, Eli Whitney, Nicholas-Louis Robert, John Loudon McAdam, John Stevens, and Robert Fulton.

Foss, Frank, Jr. JOBS IN MARINE SCIENCE: COMMERCIAL FISHING, MARINE CONSTRUCTION AND SALVAGE. New York: Lothrop, Lee & Shepard, 1974. 95 p. Elem.

This deals with technical and nontechnical marine careers--jobs in commercial fishing, salvage and marine construction, as well as the work of the marine geologist, physicist, chemist, and engineer. Students are advised of pertinent high school subjects. The book includes information on federal aid programs and opportunities in industry and government.

Galenson, Walter. A PRIMER ON EMPLOYMENT AND WAGES. 2d ed. New York: Random House, 1970. 140 p. HS.

This is a brief introduction to the manpower market, wages and employment, and problems of unemployment and poverty. The author is concerned with the problem of obtaining full employment without causing inflation.

Heaps, Willard A. WANDERING WORKERS: THE STORY OF AMERICAN MIGRANT FARM WORKERS AND THEIR PROBLEMS. New York: Crown Publishers, 1968. 192 p. HS.

This book consists of taped interviews of workers obtained by the author in migrant camps in New Jersey, Maryland, Virginia, Indiana, Illinois, Texas, and California. The migrants describe who they are, where they are from, where they travel, their work, their lives, and the problems of housing, health, community acceptance, and their children's welfare and education.

Holland, Ruth. FORGOTTEN MINORITY: AMERICA'S TENANT FARMERS AND MIGRANT WORKERS. New York: Crowell-Collier, 1970. 153 p. HS.

This book describes the backbreaking labor, poverty, and loneliness of the homesteader and the changes in farm ownership that came with the introduction of farm machinery. It deals with the dust storms and economic depression that forced the independent farmer to become a tenant and discusses the exploitation of migrant workers and the tenant farmer, their efforts to organize, and some needed reforms to improve their way of life.

Hutchinson, John. THE IMPERFECT UNION: A HISTORY OF CORRUPTION IN AMERICAN TRADE UNIONS. New York: Dutton, 1970. 477 p. HS.

The author surveys the history of unions and labor management relations from 1890 to the early 1960s. He focuses a magnifying glass on corruption in the building, longshoreman's, garment, service, and road transportation unions and offers commentary on the reasons for it.

Kaufmann, Carl. MAN INCORPORATE: THE INDIVIDUAL AND HIS WORK IN AN ORGANIZED SOCIETY. Rev. ed. Garden City, N.Y.: Doubleday, 1969. 268 p. HS.

The author documents historically the premise that work is essential to man and concludes that it is still true today that man needs work not simply for economic reasons but for his social and ethical development.

Kostyu, Frank A. SHADOWS IN THE VALLEY. Garden City, N.Y.: Doubleday, 1970. 192 p. HS.

The story of Ed Krueger and his migrant ministry to Mexican American laborers in the Rio Grande Valley, a heroic struggle to help these long-oppressed people gain justice and a decent standard of living.

Lavine, Sigmund A. FAMOUS INDUSTRIALISTS. Famous Biographies for Young People. New York: Dodd, Mead, 1961. 157 p. Elem.

The lives of men who built large industries are described. Included are: Cyrus Hall McCormick, Philip D. Armour, George Eastman, Andrew Carnegie, George Westinghouse, Henry Ford, Harvey Firestone, and Thomas J. Watson.

Lens, Sidney. WORKING MEN: THE STORY OF LABOR. New York: G.P. Putnam and Sons, 1960. 191 p. Illus. Elem.

This detailed history of American labor presents the growth of unions, their past successes, challenges of the future, and brief biographies of the leaders of the labor movement.

Lent, Henry B. MEN AT WORK IN NEW ENGLAND. New York: G.P. Putnam and Sons, 1967. 127 p. Illus. Elem.

A survey of the commerce and industry of New England, this volume covers the clock industry, fishing, shipbuilding, the making of maple syrup, tourist trade, textile industry, potato farming, and rope making.

_____ . MEN AT WORK IN THE GREAT LAKES STATES. New York: G.P. Putnam and Sons, 1971. 126 p. Illus. Elem.

This book deals briefly with the history of this area. It describes the work performed by men and women in the steel mills, paper mills, chemical plants, glass and furniture factories, cheese plants, farms, and research laboratories.

_____ . MEN AT WORK ON THE WEST COAST. New York: G.P. Putnam and Sons, 1968. 127 p. Illus. Elem.

Illustrated with photographs, this book surveys the many industries of California, Oregon, and Washington. Discussed are steel and aluminum mills, fisheries, fruit and vegetable farms, oil wells, aircraft, rocket and atomic reactor plants, Disneyland, and other industries.

Marx, Herbert L., ed. AMERICAN LABOR TODAY. Reference Shelf, vol. 37, no. 5. Bronx, N.Y.: H.W. Wilson, 1965. 208 p. HS.

This is a compilation of articles concerning American labor's position in the 1960s prosperous economic situation, the rise of membership, independence within unions, collective bargaining, and the development of labor law.

Miernyk, William H. TRADE UNIONS IN THE AGE OF AFFLUENCE. New York: Random House, 1962. 180 p. HS.

The author presents a nontechnical survey of trade unions discussing union political action, unemployment, and rising prices.

Paradis, Adrian A. LABOR IN ACTION: THE STORY OF THE AMERICAN LABOR MOVEMENT. New York: Julian Messner, 1963. 191 p. Illus. Elem.

The history of labor is told through accounts of the personalities who led the working men in the fight for the right to organize for improved working conditions.

Richardson, Reed C. AMERICAN LABOR UNIONS. 2d ed. ILR Bulletin, no. 30. Ithaca, N.Y.: School of Industrial and Labor Relations, Cornell University, 1970. 20 p. HS.

This is a summary of the history, goals, and influence on the total economy of labor-management relations throughout the nineteenth

Labor

century until the present era. Emphasis is put on current collective bargaining responses and the legal framework for collective bargaining that has been established at the federal level.

THE RIGHT TO STRIKE AND THE GENERAL WELFARE. New York: National Council of Churches in Christ in the U.S.A., 1967. 28 p. HS.

This discussion is based on concern for justice and freedom for workers. It includes a consideration of the right to strike, the responsible use of power, the general welfare, and the role of government.

Rossomando, Frederic, and Szymaszik, Marilyn. EARNING MONEY. Living and Working Together. New York: Franklin Watts, 1967. 48 p. Illus. Prim.

This simple guide to basic economics shows how people earn the money they need to pay for food to eat, clothes to wear, and a place to live. The authors tell how a man who works for the telephone company installing phones earns money to buy things he needs. Overtime pay and payroll deductions such as taxes and social security are explained.

Rowe, Jeanne A. CITY WORKERS. New York: Franklin Watts, 1969. 47 p. Illus. Prim.

Each of the major services in a big city is presented in a one-page description and a full-page photograph. Some of the different types of workers whose service jobs are described are: fireman, policeman, postman, sanitation worker, city planner, laundry attendant, file clerk, and waitress.

Rubicam, Harry. MEN AT WORK IN HAWAII. New York: G.P. Putnam and Sons, 1967. 127 p. Illus. Elem.

This book takes a look at the working people of Hawaii and the many jobs they do. Tourism; the production of sugar, pineapple, macadamia nuts, and coffee; cement manufacturing; orchid growing; and dairying are among the subjects discussed.

Schwartz, Alvin. THE NIGHT WORKERS. New York: Dutton, 1966. 64 p. Illus. Elem.

Photographs with text illustrate the many kinds of work people are doing at night when most of the city is asleep. Some of the jobs discussed are: policeman, tug boat pilot, baker, printer, and hospital worker.

Shippen, Katherine B. THIS UNION CAUSE: THE GROWTH OF ORGANIZED LABOR IN AMERICA. New York: Harper & Row, 1958. 180 p. Illus. Elem.

The story of leaders of labor and their struggle to bring the American working man good wages, fair working conditions, and respect is told in this book.

Sims, Carolyn. LABOR UNIONS IN THE UNITED STATES. New York: Franklin Watts, 1971. 85 p. JH.

Useful for poor readers, this book traces the history of labor unions in the United States and discusses their organization, goals, and methods of operation.

Smith, Frances C. MEN AT WORK IN ALASKA. New York: G.P. Putnam and Sons, 1967. 127 p. Illus. Elem.

This book presents a survey of the diverse industries which flourish in Alaska: forestry, trapping, airplane construction, farming, and mining. It also offers a glimpse of the military, government, and clerical work pursued in the more urbanized locales of this state.

Wakin, Edward. JOBS IN COMMUNICATIONS. New York: Lothrop, Lee & Shepard, 1974. 96 p. Elem, JH.

This is an introduction to career opportunities in mass media; newspapers, magazines, radio, television, movies, public relations, and advertising.

Weiner, Sandra. SMALL HANDS, BIG HANDS: SEVEN PROFILES OF CHICANO MIGRANT WORKERS AND THEIR FAMILIES. New York: Pantheon, 1970. 55 p. JH.

Seven profiles are drawn from taped interviews with Chicano workers in California. They reveal the unbreakable spirit of migrant workers who say, "Even though our lives are filled with so much work we love to have fun and have some happiness in our hearts."

Werstein, Irving. THE GREAT STRUGGLE: LABOR IN AMERICA. New York: Scribner, 1965. 190 p. HS.

This dramatic story of labor's growth from colonial times to the merger of AFL and CIO presents important people and events in the struggle to win the right to organize.

Winn, Marie. THE MAN WHO MADE FINE TOPS: A STORY ABOUT WHY PEOPLE DO DIFFERENT KINDS OF WORK. New York: Simon & Schuster, 1970. Unp. Illus. Prim.

The division of labor is explained in an easy-to-understand story. A father who makes unusually fine tops for his son agrees to make tops for the others in exchange for some services which they perform exceptionally well.

MEDIA

ADVENTURES IN THE WORLD OF WORK. New York: Random House Educational Media. 6 filmstrips. Sound. Color. Elem.

These filmstrips take students into the designer's workroom, the factory, and the marketplace to spotlight the many different kinds of work performed by people everyday. Each filmstrip emphasizes a different category of work. In one case, the engineering and inventive; in another, skilled and unskilled labor; in a third, planning and marketing. Each follows a commodity from the end point where the student comes in contact with it, back through ten or twelve stages to its origin. The emphasis throughout is on people and their jobs, rather than the steps involved in the manufacture of the product. Titles: "Who Puts the Print on the Page?"; "Who Puts the Ice in the Cream?"; "Who Puts the Blue in the Jeans?"; "Who Puts the Room in the House?"; "Who Puts the Grooves in the Record?"

BIG CITY WORKERS. Child's Life in the Big City. Irvington-on-Hudson, N.Y.: Hudson Photographic Industries, 1968. Filmstrip. 38 frames. Sound. Color. Teacher's guide. Prim.

The economic life of the city is explained to children by showing the many city workers that children come in contact with and the services that they perform. The street vendor, bus driver, policeman, teacher, custodian, and mailman are cited.

CAREER KITS FOR KIDS. Chicago: Encyclopaedia Brittanica Films, 1974. Sound filmstrips. Replicas of workers' hats. Posters. Duplicating masters. Sing-along songs. Teacher's guide. Prim.

These materials were designed to broaden children's knowledge of the world of work. Children learn about job choices, what different careers and training for them involve, and the language peculiar to various occupations.

COMMUNITY HELPERS. Rosslyn Heights, N.Y.: Urban Media Materials, 1973. Filmstrip. 30 frames. Color. Teacher's guide. Prim.

This filmstrip develops the concept that there are many kinds of workers in a community, some providing services, others producing goods, many requiring special training for their jobs. Some of the occupations pictured are: policeman, electrician, fireman, man repairing traffic light, dentist, mailman, teacher, entertainer, newscaster, auto mechanic, and laboratory technician.

COMMUNITY SERVICES. Hollywood, Calif.: AIMS Instructional Media Services, 1967. Film. 11 mins. Color. Prim.

The film shows how members of a community earn an income by providing services. Some of the workers are employed by the community and others work in private businesses.

ECONOMICS: WORKERS WHO BUILD HOUSES. Santa Monica, Calif.: BFA Educational Media. Film. Color. Prim.

This film uses the activity of building a house to illustrate division of labor, specialization, conversion of materials into products, payment of wages, pride of workmanship, cooperation, supervision, quality control, and use of the product by the buyer.

FAMILIES AND JOBS: RISA EARNS HER DIME. New York: McGraw-Hill, 1967. Film. 9 mins. Color. Prim.

A small girl is paid for doing a job. She uses the money to buy something she wants.

FATHERS--WHAT THEY DO. New York: AIMS Institutional Media Service. Film. 10 mins. Color. Prim.

Basic economics presented by viewing three fathers: a gas station attendant, a carpenter, and a hardware store owner.

FATHERS WORK. Los Angeles: Churchill-Wexler Production Films, 1968. 6 filmstrips, average 39 frames. Color. Prim.

Each filmstrip begins and ends with father at home with his family. It follows him through his day's work in the community and shows the responsibilities, skills, and personal relationships on the job. Titles: "My Dad is a Carpenter"; "My Dad Works in a Factory"; "My Dad is a Moving Man"; "My Dad Works in a Service Station"; "My Dad Works in a Shoe Store"; "My Dad Works in a Supermarket."

GROWTH OF AMERICAN LABOR. Wilton, Conn.: Current Affairs Films, 1964. Filmstrip. B&W. JH.

This filmstrip touches upon important events, personalities, legislation, and organizations involved in the rise and growth of labor unions in America.

GROWTH OF THE LABOR MOVEMENT. Pleasantville, N.Y.: Guidance Associates, 1970. 2 filmstrips, 17-20 mins. ea. Sound. Color. Teacher's guide. HS.

The development of craft and industrial unions, organizing methods, labor legislation, strikes, and collective bargaining are examined. Analyses are provided by labor, business, and government officials.

THE HOMES WE LIVE IN. Chicago: Singer/SVE, 1972. 6 filmstrips. Sound. Color. Elem.

This series uses a multidisciplinary approach to give students a clearer understanding of the homes they live in. Science, technology, and economics are all involved in the presentation. Special emphasis is placed on the various people whose occupations are involved in home-related industries. Titles: "Building a Community"; "Choosing and Buying a House"; "Moving into a House"; "Building an Apartment House"; "Choosing and Renting an Apartment"; "Moving into an Apartment."

JOBS FOR THE 1970'S. Washington, D.C.: U.S. Department of Labor, Bureau of Labor Statistics, 1971. 40 slides. Teacher's guide. HS.

This series of slides describes present and future job opportunities in the United States. Information is provided on the kinds of jobs available and the industries in which they are found as well as the qualifications for such jobs.

KNOWING OUR COMMUNITY HELPERS. South Holland, Ill.: H. Wilson Corp., 1969. 12 tapes, 18 to 20 mins. ea. Teacher's guide. Prim.

Specialization and the division of labor are explained for primary students in this series of tapes. The productive activities of neighbors in the community are used to illustrate interdependence and division of labor that are characteristic of our market economy.

LABOR: JOBS AND AUTOMATION. New York: New York Times, 1965. Filmstrip. B&W. JH.

Labor-industry problems of the sixties are reviewed. The effect of strikes upon public welfare and the impact of automation upon unionism and employment are touched upon. The need for a better educated and highly skilled labor force for the future is stressed.

LABOR AND UNIONS. New York: Modern Learning Aids, 1969. 6 filmstrips. Color. Elem.

This series traces the history of the labor movement from its beginnings through today's problems of employment. Titles in the series are: "Home Industry"; "Growth of Big Business"; "Early Labor Relations"; "The Birth of Unions"; "Farming Organizations"; "Machines Replace People."

LABOR IN WEST AFRICA. Los Angeles: International Communication Films, 1968. Filmloop. 4 mins. Color. Elem, JH, HS.

Men, women, and children are seen at various types of skilled and unskilled labor such as constructing bridges and houses, surveying roads, and packing nuts.

MAKING THE THINGS WE NEED--DIVISION OF LABOR. Chicago: Encyclopaedia Britannica Films, 1969. Film. 11 mins. Sound. Color. Prim.

The film discusses how consumption levels are raised by specialization and division of labor.

MOTHERS WORK. Lakeland, Fla.: Imperial Film Co., 1968. 6 filmstrips. Color. Elem.

Using the same format as FATHERS WORK (see above), this set shows six working mothers at home with their families and then follows each of them through her day at work. Titles: "My Mother is a Waitress"; "My Mother is a Dental Assistant"; "My Mother Works in a Bank"; "My Mother Works in an Office"; "My Mother Works in a Drugstore"; "My Mother Works at Home."

MOTHERS WORK TOO. Los Angeles: Churchill-Wexler Publication Films, 1968. 6 filmstrips, 39 frames ea. Color. Elem.

Each filmstrip follows a mother through her working day performing needed services in the community. She is shown meeting the needs of her family as well as fulfilling the responsibilities of her job. Interspersed among the captions on the frames are questions that lead the viewer to think about how the work is done.

MY DAD, THE FACTORY WORKER. What Does Your Dad Do? Detroit: Jam Handy, 1970. Filmstrip. Sound. Color. Prim.

In explaining the kind of work his father does, a boy touches upon different kinds of factories, complicated machines, the requirements needed by the workers, assembly lines, and labor unions.

ORGANIZED LABOR IN TODAY'S AMERICA. Wilton, Conn.: Current Affairs Films, 1970. Filmstrip. 44 frames. Color. JH.

The filmstrip studies the effect of labor unions on the U.S. economy from the 1930s to 1970. The unions' use of strikes and the future role of trade unionism are considered.

PEOPLE AT WORK. Set 1. Lakeland, Fla.: Imperial Film Co., 1974. 4 filmstrips. Sound. Color. Elem.

This set surveys four groups of related jobs to help young children become aware of the great variety of work performed in each career field. Titles: "At Work in Community Services"; "At Work in Your Neighborhood"; "At Work in Food and Clothing"; "At Work in Construction."

PEOPLE AT WORK. Set 2. Lakeland, Fla.: Imperial Film Co., 1974. 4 filmstrips. Sound. Color. Elem.

> This set examines four additional occupational areas. Its purpose is to make young children aware of the nature and scope of many jobs within broad career areas. At the same time it enables them to form a clear picture of how all the jobs within each field are related. Titles: "At Work in Transportation"; "At Work in Offices and Factories"; "At Work in Sports and Entertainment"; "At Work in Communications."

PEOPLE WHO HELP YOU. Holyoke, Mass.: Scott Education Division, 1969. 8 filmstrips. Sound. Color. Elem.

> From this series the student learns about the skills and services of workers in a community. He also discovers how goods and services are produced, exchanged, distributed, and consumed. Titles: "Who Are the People Who Help You"; "Your Fire Department"; "Your Police Department"; "Your Post Office"; "Your City Caretakers"; "Your School"; "Your Stores"; "Your Assembly-line Helpers."

THE ROLE OF OUR LABOR FORCE: THE PULSE OF THE NATION. New York: Joint Council on Economic Education, 1962. Filmstrip. 162 frames. Color. Booklets. HS.

> This three-part filmstrip deals with the following: the nature, growth, and interests of our labor force; background, development, functions, and impact of organized labor; and the problems of economic growth, stability, security, freedom, and justice in relation to our labor force.

SHELTER: ALMOST ANYONE CAN BUILD A HOUSE. New York: Learning Corp. of America, 1971. Film. 15 mins. Sound. Color. JH.

> Children building a tree house are compared with a developer constructing a modern suburban house in this film. As the film shifts from one to the other, the interrelatedness of job functions and the necessity of integrating the house into the suburban community become evident. Emphasis is placed on suburban shelter.

SO MANY JOBS TO THINK ABOUT. 2 sets. Lakeland, Fla.: Imperial Film Co., 1974. 8 filmstrips. Sound. Color. Elem, JH.

> In the first set, each filmstrip is a documentary profile of a specific job, seen through the daily experience of an individual jobholder. The occupations represent major and familiar job groups. Included are veterinarian, plant nursery salesperson, auto mechanic, and construction foreman. The second set in this series looks at four more representative occupations. Each filmstrip is an indepth profile of a job found in all communities, presented in a

format that helps young people become more fully aware of career opportunities and the day-to-day character of actual jobs. Included are park ranger, news reporter, teacher, and furniture designer.

STRIKE IN TOWN. New York: McGraw-Hill, 1955. Film. 30 mins. Sound. B&W. HS.

The background of a strike in a furniture factory is described. The two crucial items in the negotiations for a new contract are seniority and wages.

USE OF LABOR IN COLOMBIA. Santa Ana, Calif.: International Communication Films, 1965. Filmloop. 4 mins. Color. Elem, JH, HS.

This filmloop shows labor ranging from modern machine operators to hand labor, and includes mining, cotton, and fruit picking. The kinds of labor as well as the gradual progress toward an efficient use of labor in Colombia are pointed out.

THE USE OF LABOR IN EASTERN EUROPE. Santa Ana, Calif.: International Communications Films, 1966. Filmloop. 4 mins. Color. Study guide. Elem, JH, HS.

Thirty-one examples of labor in five countries of Eastern Europe offer a view of its economic condition. Individual hard labor is shown along with some modern methods.

USE OF LABOR IN MIDDLE AMERICA. Santa Ana, Calif.: International Communications Films, 1965. Filmloop. 4 mins. Color. Study guide. Elem, JH, HS.

A sampling of the way labor is used and the type of tools which extend each person's efficiency are shown.

VIEWPOINTS ON AMERICAN LABOR. New York: Random House. Filmstrip. Record. Resource books. Problem cards. Simulation game. HS.

A complete multimedia teaching unit, this kit focuses on the issues of labor and management and the conflicts between the two. The focal concepts of the kit are: (1) the issue of violence and why it is used as a weapon in the disputes; (2) the redefinition of the rights of opposing groups in the strikes; (3) the continuity and relationship between past and present labor disputes.

WAGES AND HOURS. World of Economics Series. New York: McGraw-Hill, 1963. Filmstrip. 37 frames. Color. HS.

Emphasizing that only increased productivity permits real wages to go up, this filmstrip studies real and money wages, factors having an effect on wages, and the reduction of the work week. This filmstrip is correlated with THE WORLD OF ECONOMICS by Leonard Silk. (See Silk, Leonard S. THE WORLD OF ECO-NOMICS. Chapter 10.)

WHO WORKS FOR YOU? New York: Random House. 6 filmstrips. Sound. Color. Elem.

The emphasis in this series is on the numerous types of services that American workers provide: in government, the airlines, for a television news program, health care, leisure time activities, and keeping America clean. Titles: "Who Puts the Plane in the Air?"; "Who Puts the News on Television?"; "Who Puts the Care in Health Care?"; "Who Puts the Fun in Free Time?"; "Who Keeps America Clean?"; "Who Works for You?"

WHY FATHERS WORK. Chicago: Encyclopaedia Britannica Films, 1969. Film. 14 mins. Sound. Color. Teacher's guide. Prim.

The film explains that in order for father to buy the goods and services his family desires, he must have an income. Father earns his income as a producer of goods and services.

THE WORK ETHIC: A VICTIM OF PROGRESS? Wilton, Conn.: Current Affairs Films, 1974. Filmstrip. 64 frames. Sound. Color. Teacher's guide. HS.

The theory that boredom, absenteeism, and shoddy production are on the rise challenges the concept that work ennobles. A new attitude toward work reflecting changing values is reviewed. Relief from dull, repetitive tasks is discussed, as well as the relationship between job selectivity and the economy.

WORKING IN U.S. COMMUNITIES. Chicago: Singer/SVE, 1970. 4 filmstrips. Sound. Color. Teacher's guide. Prim.

This series of filmstrips emphasizes economics at the elementary level for social studies classes. Different locations illustrate leading forms of economic activity. The series stresses people and their needs while showing how businessmen satisfy these needs, how history and geography of an area affect needs, how history and geography of an area affect business, and who profits by business activities. Titles: "Old Sturbridge and Mystic Seaport, Historic Communities"; "Douglas, Wyoming, Ranch Community"; "Rockland Maine, Coastal Community"; "Flagstaff, Arizona, Service Community"; "New Orleans, Marketing Community"; "San Francisco, Financial Community"; "Detroit, Manufacturing Community"; "Chicago, Transportation Community."

Chapter 14

MONEY, BANKING, AND FINANCE

American Bankers Association, Banking Education Committee. THE STORY OF
AMERICAN BANKING. New York: 1963. 76 p. HS.

> The book deals primarily with the historical development of bank-
> ing but it also tries to have the student acquire a better under-
> standing of the structure and operations of present-day banking
> and the monetary system. Explanations are given of such matters
> as the function of banks, the mechanics of bank lending, the re-
> lationship between bank credit and the money supply, bank re-
> serves, how banks are regulated, and the Federal Reserve System.

_____. USING YOUR MONEY WISELY--PLANNING, SAVING, SPEND-
ING, BORROWING. New York: 1967. 35 p. HS.

> This simple presentation was prepared as a reading source for stu-
> dents in adult education courses. It describes effective ways of
> budgeting, saving, spending, and borrowing, and explains banks
> and their services.

_____. YOU, MONEY AND PROSPERITY. New York: 1964. 31 p. HS.

> Easy to read and comprehend, this booklet examines the relationships
> between the individual, money, and prosperity. It gives clear-
> cut directions to the achievement of sustained economic growth
> without inflation, reasonable full employment, continuing pros-
> perity, and money we can depend on.

Arnold, Oren. MARVELS OF THE U.S. MINT. New York: Abelard-
Schuman, 1972. 128 p. Prim.

> This book traces the history and function of money in the United
> States from the creation of the United States Mint in 1792 to the
> present.

Axon, Gordon V. LET'S GO TO A STOCK EXCHANGE. New York:

G.P. Putnam and Sons, 1973. Unp. Prim.

An introduction to the stock exchange which covers securities,
bonds, dividends, bull and bear markets, and the role of the
stockbroker. Readers are guided through the stockbroker's office,
an order is placed to the trading floor, and the broker completes
the transaction at the trading post.

Babian, Haig. SAVINGS AND INVESTMENT, ESSENTIALS OF ECONOMIC
PROGRESS. Philadelphia: Invest in America Council, 1967. 33 p. HS.

Basic ideas about savings and investment and the savings and investment process in the context of the values of our society are
discussed.

Barr, Jene. WHAT CAN MONEY DO? Chicago: Whitman, 1967. Unp.
Prim.

A simple explanation of how people earn money; how money is
used; how men exchanged goods before there was much money;
what a budget is; the value of saving money; and the meaning of
interest.

Bernstein, Peter L. A PRIMER ON MONEY, BANKING AND GOLD. 2d ed.
New York: Random House, 1965. 180 p. HS.

This book, written for the general public, is concerned with
money, its creation, control, and theory. There is also a section
on gold here and abroad.

Black, Robert P. FEDERAL RESERVE TODAY. Richmond, Va.: Federal Reserve Bank, 1964. 24 p. HS.

The story of the Federal Reserve System today, its structure and
objectives, and its action.

Brindze, Ruth. INVESTING MONEY: FACTS ABOUT STOCKS AND BONDS.
New York: Harcourt, Brace, & World, 1972. 128 p. JH.

The stockholders of tomorrow can profit today from this clear and
readable guide that leads them through the complexities of the
language and procedure of financial operations, covering all
phases of the investment process.

Buehr, Walter. TREASURE--THE STORY OF MONEY AND ITS SAFEGUARD-
ING. New York: G.P. Putnam and Sons, 1955. 64 p. Illus. Elem.

A history of currency from the primitive days of a simple barter to
the present complex monetary structure. The currency systems used
in various countries and their origins are very clearly explained.

Burns, Scott. SQUEEZE IT TILL THE EAGLE GRINS: HOW TO SPEND, SAVE AND ENJOY YOUR MONEY. Garden City, N.Y.: Doubleday, 1972. 236 p. HS.

> This book examines and explains today's dollar and what it can buy. It also offers advice on mortgage payments, insurance, stocks, and mutual funds.

Campbell, Elizabeth. NAILS TO NICKELS: THE STORY OF AMERICAN COINS OLD AND NEW. Boston: Little, Brown and Co., 1960. 58 p. Elem.

> The story of coins, including the Roosevelt dime, the Jefferson nickel, the Lincoln penny, as well as older coins such as the Spanish silver dollar and the continental dollar, is told.

Chamber of Commerce of the United States of America. MONEY AND FINANCE. Understanding Economics Series, no. 4. Washington, D.C.: 1970. 26 p. HS.

> Prepared for an adult education course, this brief pamphlet contains much information. There is a description of the nature of money, the process of deposit creation, gold, and forces affecting the purchasing power of money. It summarizes the work of the Federal Reserve System.

Cheyney, William J. USING OUR CREDIT INTELLIGENTLY. Washington, D.C.: National Foundation for Consumer Credit, 1964. 54 p. HS.

> Written for young people, this pamphlet analyzes consumer credit, explaining the advantages and disadvantages of the numerous types of credit available. Family budgeting and the establishing and maintaining of a good credit standing are discussed as an advantage to the individual and as a contribution to the overall economy.

Cobb, Vicki. MAKING SENSE OF MONEY. New York: Parents' Magazine Press, 1971. 64 p. Prim.

> The author describes for young children the function of money in an economic system.

Cooke, David C. HOW MONEY IS MADE. New York: Dodd, Mead & Co., 1972. 64 p. Elem.

> The author describes step-by-step the paper used, the printings, the counting, and even the destruction of U.S. money. Also described is the making of coins. There are some valuable tips on how to identify counterfeit money.

Money, Banking, and Finance

Duesenberry, James S. MONEY AND CREDIT: IMPACT AND CONTROL. Foundation of Modern Economics Series. Englewood Cliffs, N.J.: Prentice-Hall, 1967. 119 p. HS.

A discussion of money including its nature, banking, capital markets, supply and demand, and monetary policy.

Federal Reserve Bank of Chicago. MODERN MONEY MECHANICS: A WORKBOOK ON DEPOSITS, CURRENCY AND BANK RESERVES. Rev. ed. Chicago: 1971. 31 p. HS.

The purpose of the booklet is to describe the mechanical process of money creation in a "fractional reserve" banking system. It illustrates the changes in bank balance sheets that occur when commercial bank deposits change as a result of monetary action by the Federal Reserve System. There is also a brief general description of the characteristics of money and how the U.S. money system works.

_____. TWO FACES OF DEBT. Chicago: 1972. 19 p. HS.

This booklet examines debt in the American economy, its composition and distribution between major groups of debtors and creditors. It shows the vital role debt plays in channeling savings into productive investment. While debt plays an essential role in our economic processes, it is important that it be managed intelligently.

Federal Reserve Bank of Minneapolis. YOUR MONEY AND THE FEDERAL RESERVE SYSTEM. Rev. ed. Minneapolis: 1973. 32 p. HS.

A discussion of money and banking and an explanation of the Federal Reserve System. Some of the topics treated are: modern forms of money, price of borrowed money, how banks influence the money supply, and services provided by the Federal Reserve Bank.

Federal Reserve Bank of New York. KEEPING YOUR MONEY HEALTHY. New York: 1966. 16 p. JH.

This is an easily understood pamphlet that provides a great deal of information on money and credit in the economy, the factors leading to inflation and recession, and the role and functions of the Federal Reserve System.

_____. MONEY AND ECONOMIC BALANCE. New York: 1967. 27 p. JH, HS.

This pamphlet illustrates how the balance of money in the economy is maintained by the Federal Reserve system, how the value of money changes, and the means by which the consumer price index is computed.

148

Federal Reserve Bank of Philadelphia. MONETARY POLICY--DECISION-
MAKING TOOLS AND OBJECTIVES. Philadelphia: 1961. 52 p. HS.

This is a series of articles which deal with some of the problems
encountered in implementing monetary policy.

Federal Reserve Bank of Richmond. READINGS ON MONEY. Richmond, Va.:
1965. 58 p. HS.

Some of the many phases of money described are: the nature of
money and changes in the supply, the nature of bank reserves,
the organization and work of the Federal Reserve, and types of
lending institutions.

Floherty, John J. MONEY-GO-ROUND. Philadelphia: Lippincott, 1964.
192 p. Illus. Elem.

The story of the various methods of exchange from earliest days
to present includes an explanation of credit, banking systems, and
international finance.

Friedlander, Joanne K., and Neal, Jean. STOCKMARKET ABC. Chicago:
Follett, 1969. 96 p. HS.

The authors discuss the operations on the floor of the New York
Stock Exchange, common and preferred stocks, mutual funds,
over-the-counter sales, the role of the stockholder, investments
other than stock, market terminology, and the translation of the
financial pages of the newspapers.

Gross, Ruth B. MONEY, MONEY, MONEY. New York: Four Winds,
1971. Unp. Prim.

A simple summary of the development of the use of money as a
medium of exchange. The book begins with trading and barter
and concludes with the use of credit cards.

Hine, Al. MONEY ROUND THE WORLD. New York: Harcourt Brace
Jovanovich, 1963. Unp. Illus. Prim.

In simple graphic text and striking illustrations, this book traces
the development of money from the barter system to the use of
metal coins and paper money, emphasizing U.S. currency but
describing the money of other countries also.

Industrial Relations Center. CAPITAL: KEY TO PROGRESS. Chicago: University of Chicago, 1964. 27 p. HS.

Modern methods of production are possible because of the investment of money in capital equipment, inventories, buildings, and the improved working conditions for human beings. Different sources of saving and related financial institutions are introduced.

_____. UNDERSTANDING MONEY AND BANKING. Chicago: University of Chicago, 1965. 31 p. JH.

A brief explanation of the use of money and its control.

Kane, Elmer R. HOW MONEY AND CREDIT HELP US. Westchester, Ill.: Benefic, 1966. Illus. Elem.

The history and use of money in the United States and the rest of the world is summarized. The development of systems of banking, the function of modern banks, and the functions money and credit play in making modern business possible are discussed.

Low, Janet. UNDERSTANDING THE STOCK MARKET: A GUIDE FOR YOUNG INVESTORS. Boston: Little, Brown and Co., 1968. 210 p. HS.

Basic information is given on stocks and bonds and factors to consider when choosing a stock.

Lowenstein, Dyno. MONEY. New York: Franklin Watts, 1963. 68 p. JH.

This book provides a description of American coins and paper money and how they are made, and an explanation of the meaning and value of money and how society uses and controls it.

Maher, John E. IDEAS ABOUT MEASURING AND ACCOUNTING. New York: Franklin Watts, 1974. 47 p. Illus. Elem.

An introduction to elementary concepts of keeping accounts. The reader establishes an income statement by adding earnings from odd jobs and birthday gifts and then enumerating the amount spent. A balance sheet is constructed with the same information. The need for both forms is developed through planning a trip and through examining a simplified U.S. government income statement and General Electric balance sheet.

_____. IDEAS ABOUT MONEY. New York: Franklin Watts, 1970. 47 p. Illus. Prim.

The author teaches the young learner about money. He describes how money serves us, the kind of money we use, where money comes from, and what the money of the future will be like. Aimed at the credit card society--cash is disparaged as a medium of exchange. Checks and credit cards are termed more useful for all purposes other than minor purchases.

_____. IDEAS ABOUT TAXES. New York: Franklin Watts, 1972. 31 p. Illus. Elem.

Information about taxes for the youngest reader is presented. Why we have taxes, how they are collected, and how they are used is explained. Income, social security, and excise taxes are defined. Problems involving taxation such as tax inequities and the problems faced by cities in raising enough money to provide needed public services are dealt with briefly.

Meek, Paul. OPEN MARKET OPERATIONS. New York: Federal Reserve Bank, 1969. 47 p. HS.

An explanation of the Federal Reserve open market operations in U.S. government securities is given.

Miller, Joseph. MONEY THEN AND NOW. 4th rev. ed. Alhambra, Calif.: Miller Books, 1971. 48 p. Elem, JH.

This text describes in simple terms the development of money and its place in an economic system.

New York Stock Exchange. JOURNEY THROUGH A STOCK EXCHANGE. New York: 1970. 23 p. HS.

This is a cartoon-type presentation of a boy's introduction to the stock exchange. It explains how a stock exchange operates, how the public buys and sells securities, and follows market information.

_____. YOU AND THE INVESTMENT WORLD. Rev. ed. New York: 1972. 44 p. HS.

This booklet describes how stocks and bonds are bought and sold; the structure, history, and function of the New York Stock Exchange; and how investment promotes economic growth.

Nitsche, Roland. MONEY. New York: McGraw-Hill, 1971. 128 p. Illus. Elem.

This is a fairly complete, illustrated history of money and banking in the Western world from the forerunners of money (weapons and tools) in prehistoric times, to the complicated systems of finance today.

Paradis, Adrian A. HOW MONEY WORKS: THE FEDERAL RESERVE SYSTEM. New York: Hawthorn, 1972. 90 p. Elem.

A discussion of money and banking and the part played by the Federal Reserve System in our economy.

Ratchford, B.U., and Black, R[obert].P. THE FEDERAL RESERVE AT WORK.
5th ed. Richmond, Va.: Federal Reserve Bank, 1971. 35 p. HS.

The objectives, structure, and operations of the Federal Reserve System are described. Tools of monetary policy and the effects of
different actions on economic activity are explained. The advantages and limitations of monetary policy are dealt with.

Rosenfeld, Sam. THE STORY OF COINS. Irvington-on-Hudson, N.Y.:
Harvey House, 1968. 126 p. Illus. Elem.

This broad survey of the historical development of coinage throughout the world covers past and present minting methods. There is
a photo story of commemorative coins of the United States.

Shay, Arthur. WHAT HAPPENS WHEN YOU PUT MONEY IN THE BANK.
Chicago: Reilly & Lees, 1967. Unp. Illus. Elem.

A brother and sister deposit in a commercial bank their earnings
from babysitting and lawnmowing. They learn why the bank can
afford to pay them interest and how their small funds help to
finance personal and business investments. Terms such as teller,
vault, deposit slip, and savings account are introduced.

Sobol, Rose, and Sobol, Donald. STOCKS AND BONDS. Young Adults
Library. New York: Franklin Watts, n.d. 61 p. Illus. Elem.

Different kinds of stocks, bonds, stock exchanges, and brokers
are discussed. The authors define stock terms and explain items
of stock quotations on the financial page of the newspaper.

Stanek, Muriel. HOW PEOPLE EARN AND USE MONEY. Westchester,
Ill.: Benefic, 1968. 48 p. Illus. Prim.

This simple introduction to economics tells how people earn money
to pay for goods and services they need every day. It explains
the terms: producer, consumer, credit, interest, and budget.
There is a brief discussion of the importance of spending one's
money wisely.

Sterling, Dorothy. WALL STREET, THE STORY OF THE STOCK EXCHANGE.
Garden City, N.Y.: Doubleday, 1955. 128 p. Illus. Elem.

The growth of the New York Stock Exchange and the American
Stock Exchange is traced. How securities are traded in these
exchanges and in over-the-counter market is explained.

THE STORY OF CHECKS. New York: Federal Reserve Bank, 1966. 20 p.
Illus. Elem.

This is a comic book. It tells about checks, how checks function in our economy, and the history of checks in Europe and in the United States. The pamphlet describes the Federal Reserve System as a clearinghouse by using true stories.

Tarshis, Barry. BARTER, BILLS AND BANKS. New York: Julian Messner, 1970. 80 p. Illus. JH.

The development of the use of money as a simple and convenient medium of exchange is traced. The function of money, inflation, supply and demand, the Federal Reserve System, credit cards, and checking accounts are explained.

Tussing, A. Dale. MONEY IN THE UNITED STATES: WHERE IT COMES FROM; HOW IT IS REGULATED; HOW IT AFFECTS OUR ECONOMY. Washington, Conn.: Center for Information on America, 1967. 14 p. HS.

The nature of money, the role of the Federal Reserve, and controversial issues are discussed in this brief pamphlet.

Tyler, Poyntz, ed. SECURITIES, EXCHANGES AND THE S.E.C. Reference Shelf, vol. 37, no. 3. Bronx, N.Y.: H.W. Wilson, 1965. 201 p. HS.

The purpose of this book is to introduce the reader to the methods used in trading securities and commodities, exchanges where such trading is conducted, and the federal government's machinery for regulating both trading and the exchange.

U.S. Board of Governors of the Federal Reserve System. THE FEDERAL RESERVE SYSTEM PURPOSE AND FUNCTIONS. 5th ed. Washington, D.C.: 1963. 297 p. HS.

This book aims to promote better understanding of the Federal Reserve System's trusteeship for the nation's credit and monetary machinery. Information on the organization of the Federal Reserve System for policy making, on the open market policy process, and on the balance of payments is given. There is an attempt to clarify the system's role and functioning in light of changes that have occurred in the national and world economics and in the light of further advances in monetary knowledge.

VINNY AND BILLY, THE BOYS WITH A PIGGY BANK. New York: American Bankers Association, 1963. Unp. Illus. Prim.

A primary book about children working for money, saving for something they wanted to buy, and finding out that saving in a bank had advantages over saving in a piggy bank.

Waage, Thomas O. MONEY: MASTER OR SERVANT. New York: Federal Reserve Bank, 1967. 44 p. HS.

Money, Banking, and Finance

An explanation of our monetary policy and the importance of money and banking in our society is given. Special emphasis is put on the part played by the Federal Reserve System in our economy.

Wade, William W. FROM BARTER TO BANKING--THE STORY OF MONEY. New York: Crowell-Collier, 1967. 136 p. Illus. Elem, JH.

Illustrated with photographs, this study in economics traces the history of money from its earliest forms to the present with emphasis on U.S. currency.

Welfing, Weldon. MONEY IN OUR ECONOMY. New York: McGraw-Hill, 1968. 106 p. HS.

This book consists of eight chapters containing essential understandings of the role of money, operations of the banking system, price-level change, and objectives and methods of monetary control.

Whittlesey, Charles, et al. MONEY AND BANKING: ANALYSIS AND POLICY. 2d ed. New York: Macmillan, 1968. 543 p. HS.

A widely respected text proceeds from a survey of financial structure to a careful examination of commercial banking, the Federal Reserve System, and other instruments of monetary management.

Winn, Marie. THE FISHERMAN WHO NEEDED A KNIFE: A STORY ABOUT WHY PEOPLE USE MONEY. New York: Simon & Schuster, 1970. Unp. Illus. Elem.

In the days before people used money they traded to get the things they wanted. This story concerns the many trades a fisherman must make before he gets the knife he wants. It is a simple introduction to money as a means of exchange.

MEDIA

BANK AND OFFICE WORKERS. Glenview, Ill.: Educational Projections Corp., 1973. 2 filmstrips. Color. Elem.

The work that is done in banks and offices is shown. Titles: "We Run a Bank"; "Office Workers."

BANKING AND MONETARY CONTROL. New York: McGraw-Hill, 1950. Filmstrip. 37 frames. B&W. HS.

The tools of monetary policy available to the Federal Reserve authorities, reserve requirements, rediscount rate, and open market operations are described.

THE BANK LOAN. Hollywood, Calif.: Bailey Films, 1968. Filmstrip.
Sound. Color. HS.

A simple introduction to the bank as a lending agency through the
case of a young girl applying for a loan in order to buy a used
car. Terms, procedures, and requirements involved in the transaction are described.

BANKS AND THE POOR. Bloomington, Ind.: National Educational Television, 1970. Film. 58 mins. Sound. B&W. HS.

The film discusses the question of whether banking institutions are
organized to meet the needs of the poor in respect to housing and
credit. A spirited dialogue between a member of the House of
Representatives and a banker focuses attention on the question of
how successful banks have been in solving community problems.

BEGINNING RESPONSIBILITY: USING MONEY WISELY. Chicago: Coronet
Instructional Films, 1967. Film. 11 mins. Sound. Color. Prim.

How money is earned and how it may be spent is shown in this
film. People are apt to have wants beyond what their income
can provide. It is therefore necessary to make wise choices to
make the best use of income.

BUILDING INDUSTRY. Glenview, Ill.: Educational Projections Corp. 2
filmstrips. Color. Elem.

This introduction to the building industry shows the operations of
a lumber mill and factories that produce bricks, beams, and
blocks. Titles: "We Visit a Lumber Mill"; "Bricks, Blocks and
Beams."

CURIOUS HISTORY OF MONEY. New York: Barclay's Bank, 1971. Film.
20 mins. HS.

Using primarily British examples, this film traces the uses of money
and the development of banks from earliest times to the present.
The film is a clear and precise exposition of the crucial role that
money and banks play in the development of a modern complex
economy.

DEVELOPMENT OF TRADE. Glenview, Ill.: Educational Projections Corp.
2 filmstrips. Color. Prim.

The story of the development of money as a medium of exchange
provides a basic explanation of trade; the story of a boy helping
his father run a grocery store gives a meaningful example of how
a business operates. Titles: "We Learn About Trade"; "We Run a
Store."

DOLLARS AND SENSE. Mahwah, N.J.: Educational Reading Service. 6 filmstrips. Sound. Color. Elem.

This unit is designed to help children gain a better understanding of concepts relating to money and to simple economic principles and procedures on a personal, municipal, and governmental level. Titles: "How Money Goes Round and Round"; "Different Kinds of Money"; "How Money is Made"; "How We Borrow Money"; "How Budgets Work"; "How Taxes Work."

ECONOMICS: THE CREDIT CARD. Santa Monica, Calif.: BFA Educational Media, 1971. Film. 9 mins. Color. Elem.

The use of credit cards is explained to children. The increasing use of such cards makes it important for children to understand that they must be used responsibly.

FEDERAL RESERVE SYSTEM: ORIGIN, PURPOSE AND FUNCTION. Chicago: Encyclopaedia Britannica Films, 1950. Film. 27 mins. Sound. B&W. HS.

The film describes the tools of monetary policy available to the Federal Reserve authorities and the development of the Federal Reserve System.

FRED MEETS A BANK. Chicago: Coronet Instructional Films, 1963. Film. 13 mins. Color. Elem.

Fred and his son go through phases of general banking services. They open a savings account, make a loan, discuss trust arrangements, and inspect a vault.

HOW MONEY AND CREDIT HELP US. Westchester, Ill.: Benefic, 1969. Filmstrip. Color. Elem.

This filmstrip is concerned with the part that money and credit play in our economy. It is designed to be used with the book of the same title by Elmer Kane. (See Kane, Elmer R. HOW MONEY AND CREDIT HELP US, page 150.)

HOW MONEY WORKS. Boulder, Colo.: Learning Tree Filmstrips, 1974. 4 filmstrips. Sound. Color. Teacher's guide. Elem.

Simple skits illustrate the meaning of such concepts as competition, money, credit, bargains, and a variety of topics related to economics and consumer education.

INVESTOR AND THE MARKET PLACE. New York: American Stock Exchange, 1969. Film. 21 mins. Color. HS.

The film describes how buying and selling take place on the American Stock Exchange and some of the consequences of this procedure for the American economy. It explains the role of the specialist, how prices are determined, and self-regulatory procedures.

IT'S ALL MINE. Los Angeles: John Sutherland Productions, 1969. Film. 10 mins. Sound. Color. JH.

Two boys learn about commercial banks when they decide to save their money. Through a visit and a discussion at a commercial bank, they learn how banks mobilize savings and lend these to business firms for investment spending.

LEARNING ABOUT MONEY. Elgin, Ill.: David Cook Publishing Co, 1964. 16 pictures. Color. Manual. Prim.

Economic facts are taught to children through their interest in money. Pictures: coins and bills; buying food, clothes, homes; children earning money; providing goods; providing services; banks; working at home; money travels; life necessities.

MANAGE YOUR MONEY. New York: American Bankers Association, 1966. Film. 14 mins. Sound. Color. HS.

The story of a typical banking day is told by the machines in a bank after closing time. The film seeks to develop an interest in personal money management but also explains opportunity costs, uses of savings, the relationship of savings to investment spending, and the determinants of interest.

THE MEANING OF MONEY. New York: Filmstrip House, 1967. Filmstrip. Color. JH.

The transition from barter to currency is explained. The history of money from the Lydian coin, 650 B.C. to twentieth-century silver coins is traced.

MONEY. Glenview, Ill.: Educational Projections Corp., 1968. 2 filmstrips. Sound. Color. Prim.

The story of the development of money and an explanation of the way money should be handled. Titles: "How Money is Used"; "How to Handle Money."

MONEY: DENARIUS TO DECIMAL. New York: Grossman Publications, 1971. Jackdaw kit, collected by Robin Grieve. 12 exhibits. 4 broadsheets. JH, HS.

The design, minting, and forging of coins from the days of ancient Greece and Rome to Britain's new decimal issue are traced. Exhibits include a map showing the dollar, picture sheets of gold, silver, and paper money.

157

Money, Banking, and Finance

MONEY AND BANKING. Los Angeles: John Sutherland Productions, 1968. Film. 28 mins. Sound. Color. Teacher's guide. HS.

The film defines money and describes how commercial banks operate in a market economy. The power of the Federal Reserve System to regulate the expansion and contraction of the monetary system is depicted.

MONEY AND BANKING. World of Economics Series. New York: McGraw-Hill, 1963. Filmstrip. 36 frames. Color. HS.

The nature of money and credit is described. The filmstrip explains the quality theory of money and discusses briefly Federal Reserve monetary policies.

MONEY AND ITS USES. Chicago: Encyclopaedia Britannica Films, 1962. Film. 11 mins. Color. Elem.

Dramatic situations illustrate the uses and value of money and explain the difference between barter and the use of a medium of exchange. A dollar bill is traced through a series of business transactions.

MONEY IN THE BANK AND OUT. Los Angeles: Churchill-Wexler Productions Films, 1965. Film. 15 mins. Sound. Color. Study guide. Elem, JH.

The film explains such procedures and terminology as deposits, checks, interest, loans, and money flow, and indicates how a bank helps the community by keeping money in circulation.

MONEY TALKS: SEARCH FOR STABILITY. New York: Carousel Films, 1962. Film. 30 mins. Sound. B&W. HS.

Money is defined. How a banking system can create money and credit and the tools for monetary policy are described. How the tools can be used to achieve the goal of economic stability is discussed.

ORIGINS OF MONEY. Stanford, Calif.: Multi Media Productions, 1974. Filmstrip. 51 frames. Sound. Color. Teacher's guide. Elem, JH.

Explains the barter system and the difficulties encountered which gradually led to the use of coins made from precious metals. The influence of coins on power and acceleration of trade is related. The change from wealth through land ownership to wealth through coinage affected the pre-Christian societies, just as basic economic concepts established with the minting of coins affect us today.

OUR MONEY SYSTEM. Pleasantville, N.Y.: Guidance Associates, 1967. Filmstrip. 21 mins. Sound. HS.

The filmstrip surveys American financial institutions, their interrelationships, and practical effects on daily life. It describes the banking system and depicts the powers of the Federal Reserve System to utilize monetary policy to counter inflation and recession.

THE ROLE OF CAPITAL INVESTMENT. New York: Joint Council on Economic Education, 1966. Filmstrip. 113 frames. Color. Booklet. HS.

This three-part filmstrip explains the importance of deferred consumption and the problems in capital accumulation, how balance is achieved between saving and investment, and how a nation accumulates publicly-owned capital.

THE ROLE OF THE COMMERCIAL BANKING SYSTEM. New York: Joint Council on Economic Education, 1960. Filmstrip. 112 frames. Color. Booklet. HS.

In three parts, this filmstrip deals with the evolution of money and banking, the uses of bank services, and the function of banking in the economy.

THE ROLE OF THE FEDERAL RESERVE SYSTEM--THE CREDIT MARKET. New York: Joint Council on Economic Education, 1960. Filmstrip. 111 frames. Color. Booklet. HS.

This three-part filmstrip explains the demand for credit; the supply of credit; and the problem of economic balance between supply and demand.

THE STORY OF A CHECK. Los Angeles: Film Associates, 1965. Film. 13 mins. Sound. Color. Study guide. Elem.

This film gives a detailed explanation of the checking system. It discusses the way in which banks cooperate with each other in exchanging checks, the processing of checks by trained workers, and points out the advantages of a checking account.

THE STORY OF OUR MONEY SYSTEM. Chicago: Coronet Instructional Films, 1958. Film. 11 mins. Sound. B&W. Elem.

The evolution of exchange from barter to the use of paper money is traced in the film. Many examples of how money functions are given.

WHAT MAKES US TICK? New York: New York Stock Exchange, 1952. Film. 12 mins. Sound. Color. HS.

Through a visit to the New York Stock Exchange, the film explains how securities are purchased and sold. The film describes how a growing company raises needed capital funds.

WHY WE USE MONEY: THE FISHERMAN WHO NEEDED A KNIFE. Santa Monica, Calif.: Steven Bosustow Productions, 1974. Film. 7 mins. Sound. Color. Elem.

This animated film explains the bartering process and the monetary system. It shows that in a village which had no monetary exchange system, a fisherman who wanted a new knife had to go through a series of time consuming trades in order to get the knife. The characteristics and uses of the system and money as a unit of exchange are discussed.

YOUR TOWN. New York: American Bankers Association, 1966. Film. 15 mins. Sound. Color. JH, HS.

The film describes the various banking services available and discusses how these services affect the economy of the community.

Chapter 15
COURSES OF STUDY AND TEXTS—ELEMENTARY

BAM. SOCIAL STUDIES SUPPLEMENT: WHY DO NATIONS ENGAGE IN WORLD TRADE? Oklahoma City: Public School System, 1971. 31 p. Available from ERIC.

This nongraded resource unit was prepared to give the teacher examples of social studies activities that emphasize economic concepts. It presupposes some knowledge of economics. The major themes are the following: producing, distributing, and consuming food, clothing and shelter, and service. Canada, United States, Mexico, Honduras, and Brazil are specifically considered on the question of world trade. It is assumed that people are interdependent and must help each other in obtaining and providing goods and services. The major question is followed by four subproblems: (1) what evidence of world trade do we find in our homes? (2) what are the productive resources necessary to provide goods for world trade? (3) how does market determine what products are imported and exported? (4) how do governmental policies influence trade among nations?

CHILD'S WORLD OF CHOICES. Iowa City: Bureau of Business and Economic Research, University of Iowa, 1968. 186 p.

This publication serves as a supplement to social studies guides in kindergarten through third grade; as such it provides a means of incorporating economic understandings into the social studies curriculum. The aim is to develop in a sequential and systematic fashion the student's ability to identify and analyze significant economic forces operating in the world around him. It is organized by grade level with five basic economic generalizations. While the statement of each generalization remains unchanged throughout the text, its treatment becomes more complex and sophisticated with each successive grade. An overview and a teaching guide follow each generalization at each grade level.

COMMUNITIES AROUND THE WORLD: OUR COMMUNITY; ECONOMIC

ASPECTS, TEACHER'S RESOURCE UNIT. Minneapolis: Minnesota University Minneapolis Project, Social Studies Curriculum Center, 1969. 203 p. Available from ERIC.

Teaching strategies for the study of the economic aspects of the student's own community are emphasized in this resource unit. It aims to teach children the following: (1) concepts including consumer, producer, capital goods, durable goods, productive resources and man's use of the physical environment, barter, money and banking, pricing and the cost of production, profits and economic goods, demand competition, economic model, individual proprietorship, partnership, corporation, cooperative, private enterprise system, taxes, division of labor and specialization; (2) generalizations evolving out of this conceptual approach to community study; and (3) inquiry skills.

COMMUNITIES AROUND THE WORLD: SOVIET COMMUNITIES, URBAN AND RURAL, TEACHER'S RESOURCE UNIT. Minneapolis: Minnesota University Minneapolis Project, Social Studies Curriculum Center, 1969. 182 p. Available from ERIC.

This social studies resource guide for grade four outlines one of four units on the theme of communities around the world, with emphasis on a comparative analysis of economic systems. Specific objectives for this unit on the Soviet Union are described in these areas: (1) economic geography and sociological concepts; (2) understanding and generalizations; (3) skills; (4) attitudes. Fifty-nine learning activities are outlined in a format designed to help teachers see the relationships among objectives, content, teaching strategies, and materials of instruction. A list of media is also included.

COMMUNITIES AROUND THE WORLD: THEIR ECONOMIC SYSTEMS, TEACHER'S GUIDE, GRADE 4. Minneapolis: Minnesota University Minneapolis Project, Social Studies Curriculum Center, 1969. 55 p. Available from ERIC.

This general guide to a grade four social studies course outlines goals, content, and teaching methods on the theme communities around the world, with an economic emphasis. Different communities are used as vehicles to teach about contrasting economic systems and the relationship between the economic system and the rest of culture. Four major units of study are: (1) our own community and economic emphasis; (2) a Soviet community--urban and rural; (3) the Trobriand Islanders; (4) a village in India.

COMMUNITIES AROUND THE WORLD: THE TROBRIAND ISLANDERS, A TEACHER'S RESOURCE UNIT. Minneapolis: Minnesota University Minneapolis Project, Social Studies Curriculum Center, 1969. 199 p. Available from ERIC.

The Trobriand society was chosen for study in this resource unit for upper elementary grades because its economic system illustrates the importance of reciprocal relationships which continue to be very important in many societies of the world. The system has some aspects of both a command and a market economy. Although the unit is focused upon the economic system, the Trobriand culture is presented as a total culture and the interdependence is made clear.

CONCEPTS AND INQUIRY: THE EDUCATIONAL RESEARCH COUNCIL SOCIAL SCIENCE PROGRAM. Edited by Mary Catherine McCarthy. Boston: Allyn and Bacon, 1971.

A planned, sequential, cumulative program designed to meet the need for a unified social science curriculum based on conceptual learning and the application of inquiry. The materials are paperback. The program has been field-tested as the Greater Cleveland Social Science Program. Basic integrated learning involving history, geography, economics, political science, sociology, anthropology, philosophy, and psychology are dealt with on each level.

The following materials are included: forty posters, ten color short strips, spirit duplicator master, teacher's guide.

OUR COUNTRY: EXPLORERS AND DISCOVERIES. Six sound filmstrips, three booklets, two teacher's guides. Grade 1.

OUR COMMUNITIES; AMERICAN COMMUNITIES. Six sound filmstrips, six booklets, teacher's guide. Grade 2.

METROPOLITAN COMMUNITIES. Two sound filmstrips, booklets, teacher's guide. Grade 3.

AGRICULTURE, MEN AND THE LAND; INDUSTRY, MEN AND MACHINE; INDIAN SUBCONTINENT. Filmstrips, vocabulary exercises, teacher's guide. Grade 4.

HUMAN ADVENTURE; LANDS OF THE MIDDLE EAST. Filmstrips, vocabulary exercises, teacher's guide. Grade 5.

HUMAN ADVENTURE; LANDS OF LATIN AMERICA. Filmstrips, vocabulary exercises, teacher's guide. Grade 6.

CHALLENGES OF OUR TIME; LANDS OF AFRICA. Filmstrips, vocabulary exercises, teacher's guide. Grade 7.

CONCEPTS IN SOCIAL SCIENCE. River Forest, Ill.: Laidlaw Brothers, 1972.

Conceptual, inductive, and interdisciplinary approaches to the social studies are used in this series. The texts for grades four through six contain material from economics, anthropology, and geography. There is an alternative text at the fourth grade level, USING THE SOCIAL STUDIES. This text could also be used in fifth and sixth grade.

CONSUMER EDUCATION: CURRICULUM GUIDE FOR OHIO GRADE K-12. Columbus: Instructional Materials Laboratory, Ohio State University, 1970. 145 p. Available from ERIC.

Units for regular high school and elementary school students are included with consumer education units for educable mentally retarded and socioeconomically disadvantaged students. Selected bibliographies accompany each unit. The guide is meant to help the teacher with ideas, not to be a structured sequence to follow. It is designed to examine the consumer's alternatives, both when he is earning money and when he is spending it, with emphasis on responsibilities, motivating forces, and the resultant effect of consumer decisions on the total economy. Each unit has been developed around economic systems, income procurement, consumer behavior determinants, and community resources.

CONTEMPORARY SOCIAL SCIENCE CURRICULUM. Morristown, N.J.: Silver Burdett Co., 1972.

This series is designed to be used in grades K-7. It is an interdisciplinary curriculum drawing on materials for history, geography, economics, political science, and other social disciplines. The inquiry method is used along with case studies and materials from original sources.

EARLY CHILDHOOD CONSUMER EDUCATION. Mt. Vernon, N.Y.: Consumer's Union of the U.S., 1973. 73 p.

This book is intended for parents and teachers who act as the chief educators and behavior models for three- to five-year-old children. A case study format is used to illustrate the different types of settings in which preschool children learn about the world around them. These cases include parent participation nursery schools, home-visit programs, community field trips, as well as parent organizations that deal directly with broadcasters in an effort to monitor the television programs and commercials reaching children. Included is a list of child experiences with consumer materials based on the developmental task concept.

ECONOMIC EDUCATION: A GUIDE TO NEW YORK SCHOOLS, GRADES K-11. Oneonta: Center for Economic Education, State University College of New York, 1970. Unp.

The main emphasis is on using the economics discipline to teach specific inquiry skills. Instructional strategies are geared to help students acquire basic thinking skills. Objectives are stated in behavioral terms.

ECONOMIC EDUCATION: A SUPPLEMENT TO THE SOCIAL STUDIES, K-2D

GRADE. Minneapolis: Minneapolis Public Schools, 1967. 177 p. Developed by the Minneapolis DEEP project.

By grouping the primary level guides into one volume, the supplements can help teachers plan for a greater continuity of concept development across grade levels. Included are suggested teaching-learning activities and a list of resources. Concepts developed within themes of home, school, and neighborhood.

ECONOMIC EDUCATION: A SUPPLEMENT TO THE SOCIAL STUDIES, 3RD AND 4TH GRADE. Minneapolis: Minneapolis Public Schools, 1967. 147 p. Developed by the Minneapolis DEEP project.

Economic concepts such as producer, consumer, and factors of production are identified; through suggested teaching-learning activities, strategies for instruction are provided.

ECONOMIC EDUCATION FOR ARKANSAS ELEMENTARY SCHOOLS, TEACHING GUIDE, GRADES 1–6. Little Rock: Arkansas Department of Education, Council on Economic Education, 1969. 317 p. Available from ERIC.

The primary objective of this guide is to set forth goals of learning that will contribute to student achievement of economic literacy. It is a skeletal structure which teachers can incorporate into a continuous social studies curriculum. Its main purpose is to develop the problem-solving ability of children as it relates to personal and social problems. To accomplish this, it is necessary to: (1) develop the child's ability to think analytically; and (2) help the child relate to his everyday knowledge of the basic structure of the subject so that a frame of reference can be established. A core of developmental concepts has been selected that can be extended through environmental, chronological, and logical sequences in line with grade progression.

ECONOMIC EDUCATION FOR WASHINGTON SCHOOLS, KINDERGARTEN THROUGH GRADE SIX. Olympia, Wash.: State Department of Public Instruction, 1966. 194 p.

This program was developed by the Seattle DEEP project under the supervision of the Northwest Council on Economic Education. There is a common format for the guidelines in which concepts are developed in terms of interpretations and suggested activities. Supplementary activities and a bibliography are listed at the end of each section. Each new concept has an explanatory note for the teacher. Concepts are restated into language appropriate for students at each grade level.

ECONOMIC EDUCATION SUPPLEMENTS, GRADES 3, 4, 5, and 6. Austin, Tex.: Independent School District, 1960. Supplements vary from 27 to 61 pages.

Each grade supplement is to be used in a unified program which includes social studies, health, and safety education. The supplements include basic content in economics, understandings to be taught, and activities and references to use.

ECONOMICS AND OUR COMMUNITY: A RESOURCE UNIT FOR GRADES 4, 5, and 6. Edited by George [G.] Dawson. New York: Joint Council for Economic Education, 1973. 25 p.

This unit pulls together the work done by teachers to promote economic literacy through studies of their communities. Basic interests that have been identified by teachers as being appropriate to the developmental learning levels of the students will be used as themes in future publications. Lists of initiatory, developmental, and cumulating activities, suggestions for evaluating the unit, glossary, and lists of materials are included.

ECONOMICS IN THE ELEMENTARY SCHOOL: WHY, WHAT, WHERE? A HANDBOOK FOR TEACHERS. Minneapolis: Minneapolis Public Schools, 1967. 21 p.

This primer of economics for elementary schools is a product of the Minneapolis DEEP project. It contains a rationale for economic education and suggestions for economic emphasis at each grade level.

ECONOMICS IN THE SOCIAL STUDIES, GUIDELINES FOR TEACHING THE ECONOMIC UNDERSTANDINGS IN THE N.Y. STATE SOCIAL STUDIES SYLLABUS. Albany: Center for Economic Education, State University of New York at Albany, 1968. Unp.

Key concepts are introduced at each grade level. Some concepts reappear at successive grade levels. The importance of each concept for economic understanding is discussed, followed by teaching objectives.

ECONOMIC SUPPLEMENT TO THE SOCIAL STUDIES: A TENTATIVE GUIDE FOR TEACHERS, GRADES 1–4. Indianapolis: Indiana Public Schools, 1962. 24 p.

This is a carefully worked out plan to supplement the regular social studies curriculum with appropriate economic concepts. The guide was developed by teachers who received in-service training in economics. It is an attempt to bring into focus economic concepts that are inherently part of the social studies program.

ELEMENTARY LEVEL CONSUMER EDUCATION. Consumer Education Materials Project. Mt. Vernon, N.Y.: Consumer's Union of the United States, 1972. 78 p.

This booklet, one of six in a series, includes descriptions of elementary level programs grouped under two headings: interdisciplinary approaches and teaching techniques. The selected case studies, representing the range of methods now being used in elementary schools to study the consumer's role in society, suggest a wide scope of possibilities for curriculum building, from individual lessons to year-long goals, from separated areas of inquiry to programs totally integrated into existing curricula.

EVERYDAY ECONOMICS. New York: Noble and Noble, 1967.

This six-unit economics program is designed for grades 1–6. All units deal with the same basic economic concepts. The basic economic concepts and understandings important to the social studies curriculum are presented at the appropriate grade level. At each successive grade, new, more sophisticated concepts are introduced. The units included are: the family; the community; early settlers; the nation; North America; and the world. Each unit contains sets of overhead transparencies with overlays, spirit duplicating masters, and a teacher's guide.

EXPLORING THE SOCIAL SCIENCES. Cincinnati: American Book Co., 1971.

This nongraded series aims to develop knowledge and skills in history, geography, sociology, economics, anthropology, political science, psychology, and other social science disciplines. The program's process approach confronts pupils with new situations to which they are required to offer solutions based on logical thinking processes rather than mere reliance on memory. Books are available in both cloth and soft bindings. Teachers' editions and tests are available at each level.

FIELD SOCIAL STUDIES PROGRAM FOR GRADES K–6. Palo Alto, Calif.: Field Educational Publications, 1970.

This program is based on the inquiry-conceptual approach to learning. Emphasis is on having students acquire social science concepts through a process of gathering information, asking questions, and analyzing, synthesizing, and evaluating data. The materials are multidisciplinary, treating the various social sciences throughout the program. Media kits are available for most levels containing filmstrips, records, photoprints, and so forth.

FIFTH GRADE SOCIAL STUDIES. Manitowoc, Wis.: Curriculum Development Center, Manitowoc Public Schools, 1967. 105 p.

This is a plan to use a basic economic model to introduce the concepts of scarcity, production, consumption, market, and interdependence, and subsequently to relate these and other economic concepts to studies of regions of the United States with emphasis given to regional specialization and capitalism.

Courses of Study, Texts—Elementary

GINN SOCIAL SCIENCE SERIES. Boston: Gill and Co., 1972.

This series is composed of eight textbooks and a set of kindergarten study prints which are accompanied by a teacher guide. Concepts are extracted from the subject disciplines of sociology, anthropology, geography, economics, political science, and history. This series represents a standard approach to social studies. It is divided into four areas: individuals and families, K-2; communities, grades 3 and 4; nations, grades 5 and 6; and personal and historic decisions, grades 7 and 8.

INQUIRING ABOUT TECHNOLOGY: STUDIES IN ECONOMICS AND ANTHROPOLOGY. New York: Holt, Rinehart & Winston, 1972.

This sixth grade text helps students understand basic contemporary problems in modern and nonmodern countries; the economic interdependence of rich and poor nations; food, populations, and the standard of living in India; poverty in America; and technological and environmental pollution. Complex issues become clear through carefully chosen examples, simple graphs, powerful illustrations, and a supplemental simulation game.

INVESTIGATING MAN'S WORLD. Glenview, Ill.: Scott, Foresman, 1970.

The content of the multidisciplinary series is drawn from the social science disciplines of anthropology, economics, geography, history, political science, and sociology. Basic concepts for each discipline are dealt with at each grade level.

IT'S ELEMENTARY--IT'S ECONOMICS. Quincy, Mass.: Quincy Public Schools, 1967. 117 p. Developed by the Quincy DEEP project.

This guide is an experimental test edition and provides suggestions for teaching economic ideas for grades one through six. Economic concepts are built into the following themes: home, school, farm, community living, community helpers, foods--then and now; Norway; exploration and discovery; money, banking, and international trade.

LEARNING FOR LIVING IN TODAY'S WORLD. Westchester, Ill.: Benefic, 1973.

This program designed for grades 1-9 aims to present: expanded treatment of social studies disciplines, broader recognition of world communities, economic education at all levels, and understanding of and respect for individual and cultural differences. Teacher's editions and guides are available for all texts. Activity texts are available for grades 3-9.

MAN AND COMMUNITIES PROGRAM. Grand Rapids, Mich.: Fideler, 1970.

This program for grades K-7 is developed around nine concepts: cooperation, rules and government, loyalty, language, education, using natural resources, tools, division of labor, and exchange. The program aims to develop thinking through inquiry and discovery, to develop understandings of significant concepts and generalizations, to develop constructive values and attitudes, and to develop skills.

MAN AND HIS WORLD. New York: Noble and Noble, 1974.

This is a basal social studies series, composed of six titles: "You and Your Family"; "Groups and Communities"; "Cities and Suburbs"; "People and Land"; "Many Americans—One Nation"; "People and Culture." Strong emphasis is placed on charts, graphs, cartoons, and illustrated questions. The organization requires students to respond to a number of questions.

MAN IN A WORLD OF CHANGE. Westchester, Ill.: Benefic, 1971.

This program for grades 1-6 has been developed to prepare children to be effective citizens in our changing world. It aims to help them develop their systems of values, have knowledge to use the social studies disciplines, and to be able to use the social studies processes of comparing, classifying, hypothesizing, interpreting, and generalizing. Data banks of objective information within each unit provide content before the pupils use the social studies processes. Investigation sections in each unit utilize the social studies process skills. An interdisciplinary approach is used. The titles in this series are: "Man and His Families"; "Man and His Communities"; "Man and His Cities"; "Man and Regions of the World"; "Man and United States and Americas"; "Man and His World and Cultures."

OUR FAMILY OF MAN: A CONCEPTUAL APPROACH TO THE SOCIAL SCIENCES. Edited by Perrod Moss and Mary Reed. New York: Harper & Row, 1972.

This series for grades 1-6 provides students with information through an interdisciplinary approach. Each text is divided into three parts, entitled: "Topics for Study," "Information Bank," and "Summaries of Topics." Included in the teacher's edition are: a breakdown of the social science disciplines in each unit; the main idea of the unit; the concept being emphasized; performance objectives; teaching strategies; evaluative criteria; and related materials. The titles in this series are: "Awareness of Ourselves"; "Backgrounds for Understanding"; "Concepts for Comparison"; "Diversity of Ideas"; "Evaluations of Ideals"; "Freedom for Expression."

OUR WORKING WORLD. Chicago: Science Research Associates, 1973.

This social studies program for the elementary grades was designed to provide students with a realistic understanding of their world by involving them in a wide variety of activities. The program develops important concepts in anthropology, economics, geography, history, law, political science, social psychology, sociology, and career education. Problem solving and decision making are stressed as skills needed to get along in today's world. Starting with families in level 1, the program expands to neighborhoods in level 2, cities in level 3, regions of the United States in level 4, the American way of life in level 5, and regions of the world in level 6. Multimedia components include recorded stories for levels 1 and 2, and filmstrips with sound for level 3. Social science satellite kits for levels 4–6 contain readings that relate to text books. Text books contain case studies, photoessays, illustrated stories, maps, charts, and other visual materials.

AN OUTLINE FOR TEACHING CONSERVATION IN ELEMENTARY SCHOOLS. Washington, D.C.: U.S. Department of Agriculture, 1971. 14 p. Available from the Government Printing Office.

This outline suggests an approach to the teaching of environmental conservation as an integral part of all subjects in the elementary school curriculum. General objectives are intended as guides to the preparation of specific behavioral objectives of each teacher. The outline encourages individualized instruction and problem solving. Subjects included are: looking at the environment; change in the natural world; how environments differ; taking care of natural resources; use of natural resources; responsibility of environmental conservation; and making choices in conservation.

SOCIAL SCIENCE: CONCEPTS AND VALUES. New York: Harcourt Brace Jovanovich, 1970.

This program for grades K–6 is built upon a conceptual scheme based on the social science disciplines. Man is presented as a social being; concepts are developed at increasingly sophisticated levels. Instructional strategies are based on direct inquiry. Extra work is provided in each unit to meet needs of students of various abilities.

SOCIAL STUDIES: FOCUS ON ACTIVE LEARNING. New York: Macmillan, 1971.

This elementary program focuses on active learning for students through the emphasis on the use of a variety of media, an organizational structure that accommodates different learning styles, an integrated conceptual structure, and student self-evaluation exercises. The materials treat social sciences in an interdisciplinary way. A wide variety of multimedia learning materials are available.

STUDENT ACTIVITY BOOK FOR THE CHILD'S WORLD OF CHOICES, GRADE 2. Iowa City: Bureau of Business and Economic Research, University of Iowa, 1970. 31 p. TEACHER'S GUIDE TO STUDENT ACTIVITY BOOK. Grade 2, 1970. 71 p.

> Because of the desire to involve students more directly in the learning process, a student activity book and teacher's guide were developed. This guide provides the general framework to be followed in introducing the children to the key economic ideas through the use of activities. It provides a series of discussion questions for each of the activities. (See CHILD'S WORLD OF CHOICES, above).

SUGGESTED GUIDELINES FOR CONSUMER EDUCATION—GRADE K-12. 1970. 63 p. Available from ERIC.

> This curriculum guide, in addition to offering a brief rationale and introduction to consumer education, presents specific suggestions for initiating or developing an individual program. There are generally considered to be four possible methods of implementation: (1) the individual teacher; (2) a team approach; (3) an interdisciplinary structure; or (4) one that involves all relevant agents in the social system. Consideration is given to establishing instructional objectives and creating the necessary climate conducive to teaching and learning. Each teacher must develop his own course content based on the needs and interests of his students, but four interrelated broad topics with introductory concepts are suggested here: (1) the consumer as an individual; (2) the consumer as a member of society; (3) his alternatives in the market place; and (4) his rights and responsibilities.

TABA SOCIAL STUDIES CURRICULUM, HILDA TABA SOCIAL STUDIES MATERIALS. Reading, Mass.: Addison-Wesley, 1969. Developed in association with Contra Costa County, Ga. DEEP project.

> An interdisciplinary approach is used in this program for grades 1-8.

TEACHER'S GUIDE TO ECONOMICS IN GRADES 1-5. Salem, Oreg.: State Department of Public Instruction, 1968. Guides vary from 55-74 pages. Developed by the Oregon DEEP Project.

> These guides are designed to enrich the established social studies curriculum. Basic concepts appropriate for each grade are identified, and simply explained. Teaching activities, resources, and suggestions for evaluating student understanding are included along with a brief overview of "Major Ideas and Sub-ideas of Modern Economics."

UNITS IN ECONOMICS FOR ELEMENTARY GRADES. Minneapolis: Minneapolis Public Schools, 1958.

These units were worked out by the committee on economic education of the Minneapolis Public Schools. These are resource units which include goals, steps in development, and resource materials. These units were updated by ECONOMIC EDUCATION --A SUPPLEMENT TO THE SOCIAL STUDIES GRADE K-2 AND GRADE 3-4. (See above.)

Chapter 16

COURSES OF STUDY—HIGH SCHOOL

ACCENT: THE WORLD OF WORK. Chicago: Follett, 1967.

> This program is designed for students in grades 11 and 12. It
> aims to teach students to learn to handle money and other assets
> wisely. Each booklet has three lessons including discussions, vo-
> cabulary, reading for information, and activities involving the use
> of the information covered. Texts and instructors' books are avail-
> able. Some of the booklet titles are: "You and Your Pay";
> "You and Your Occupation"; "Keeping That Job"; and "Getting
> the Job."

BUSINESS VIEWS THE ECONOMY: ECONOMICS IN ACTION. New York:
Council on Economic Education, 1970. 65 p.

> Highlights of fifteen sessions of an in-service course, presented by
> the Young Presidents' Organization in conjunction with the New
> York City Council on Economic Education, are recorded. The
> fifteen-week program involved fifteen members of the Young
> Presidents' Organization, each speaking to teachers on a subject
> of his own expertise. Questioning and discussions followed.
> Summaries of the sessions are presented.

COMPARATIVE ECONOMIC SYSTEMS: AN INQUIRY APPROACH. New
York: Holt, Rinehart & Winston, 1968. 226 p.

> This is a comparison of the economic systems of the United States,
> where most economic decisions are made in the market, and the
> Soviet Union, where most such decisions are made by the govern-
> ment. The focus is upon three basic questions, namely, what is
> to be produced, how is it to be produced, and for whom is it to
> be produced. There is a teacher's guide.

CONSUMER AND THE AMERICAN ECONOMY: River Forest, Ill.: Laidlaw
Brothers, 1973.

This series is made up of five books designed to involve students in the practical, everyday world of economics. They are written with a concept-oriented, inquiry approach. The books further the student's ability to make intelligent personal decisions as consumers. Readable content, varied illustrations, and special features for involvement encourage problem-solving and application of basic consumer concepts. Titles in the series are: "Consumer and the American Economy"; "Managing Your Money and Credit"; "Learning to Be a Better Buyer"; "Consumer Rights and Protection"; and "Consumer and Current Issues."

CONSUMER EDUCATION: A SENIOR HIGH ELECTIVE COURSE. Glens Falls, N.Y.: City School District, 1970. 60 p.

The objective of this course is to lead the non-college-bound student toward the maturity of consumer judgment necessary in the complex economic market place of today. The scope and sequence section of this guide lists eight units and includes basic objectives and conceptual understandings for each. The units are: consumer purchasing; purchasing food, clothing, furniture and appliances; purchasing and maintaining an automobile; housing; short term consumer credit; budgeting, money management, and investment; security programs; and fraud, quackery, deception, and consumer law.

CONSUMER EDUCATION CURRICULUM MODULES: A SPIRAL PROCESS APPROACH. Washington, D.C.: Government Printing Office, 1974.

These modules focus on skills needed in the process of (1) acquiring information, (2) exploring values, (3) making decisions, and (4) taking action. The processes developed can be applied to any consumer problem. A teacher's guide provides an overview and rationale for the approach. Four manuals provide nationally field-tested pre- and post-assessment measures and modules of instruction. Each module includes consumer competencies, objective activities, and support materials. Materials are designed so that they can be used with groups varying in ages, abilities, and cultural backgrounds. Four modules are now available in this series. The titles are: "Consumer Issues and Action"; "Education and the Consumer"; "The Consumer and Recreation"; "Consumer Problems of the Poor" (see below). Five more titles have been projected in this series.

CONSUMER EDUCATION, MATERIALS FOR AN ELECTIVE COURSE. Albany: New York State Department of Education. 230 p.

An interdisciplinary course which could be taught most effectively using a team-teaching approach.

CONSUMER PROBLEMS OF THE POOR. Expanded Programs of Consumer Education Series. Albany, N.Y.: State Education Department, Bureau of Secondary Curriculum Development, 1972. 58 p. Available from ERIC.

The fourth in a series of modules--expanded programs of consumer education. This material is designed to help the poor make better use of their income and to stimulate those of high income to greater understanding of the problems of their fellow citizens. The modules are prepared for high school students as separate publications to provide flexibility. Students are oriented to the concepts of poverty, its physical, mental, and psychological realities. They are also made aware of the attitudes toward and the factors contributing to poverty as well as attempts to assist the poor.

CURRICULUM GUIDE FOR 8TH GRADE ECONOMICS. Tulsa, Okla.: Tulsa Public School System, 1963. 136 p.

The aim of this course is to relate economics to the problems of people. Students are involved in economic activities which encompass the pupil and his family for the purpose of expanding the pupil's learning beyond the level of factual information, so that he may develop the capacity to think objectively, clearly, and with understanding about economic problems.

A CURRICULUM GUIDE ILLUSTRATING SELECTED SPIRALING ECONOMICS CONCEPTS IN SOCIAL STUDIES, 1967. 94 p. Available from ERIC.

Prepared by a committee of secondary social studies teachers, this publication is designed to show how selected economic concepts can be implemented in the present framework of social studies, grades 7-12, in almost any school system. The same two concepts which serve as the core for all units prepared are (1) limited resources plus unlimited wants make necessary wise allocation of scarce resources, and (2) specialization and exchange play a vital economic role in any nation.

A DATE WITH YOUR FUTURE, MONEY MANAGEMENT FOR THE YOUNG ADULT FOR HOME AND FAMILY LIVING CLASSES. New York: Institute of Life Insurance, 1972. 34 p.

The five chapters with activities and questions following lesson material include: "Shaping Your Future"; "Skills for Your Future"; "Job in Your Future"; "Wedding in Your Future"; "Family in Your Future."

DECISIONS FOR THE SEVENTIES. 8 vols. Washington, D.C.: Chamber of Commerce of the United States of America, 1970.

This reading and discussion course is designed for advanced economic discussion groups. It contains over thirty published articles by distinguished authors on major economic and social problems deemed of outstanding importance in the 1970s. Main elements of the course consist of eight paperback booklets. Each booklet analyzes a major national problem. Each contains articles selected to present significant perspectives and afford an interplay of ideas appropriate for a stimulating discussion program. Titles of the booklets are: "National Goals"; "Environmental and Population Growth"; "Should We Guarantee Income?"; "Unemployment or Inflation"; "Manpower for the Seventies"; "Strikes and the Public"; "Citizen's Stake in Tax Reform"; "The Framework of Decision."

DYNAMIC CONSUMER DECISION-MAKING. New York: J.C. Penney Co., 1972.

This teaching unit focuses on making consumer decisions. The emphasis is on (1) questioning, (2) processing information, and (3) clarifying what is important to the individual consumer. Learning experiences are suggested for varying age groups and for individuals with differing resources. Materials included are: teacher's guide, tape, slides, simulations, transparencies, worksheets, and a flip chart.

ECONOMIC EDUCATION, A SUPPLEMENT FOR THE SECONDARY SCHOOLS. Salt Lake City, Utah: State Department of Public Instruction, 1967. 84 p.

This teacher's guide discusses objectives of economic education, suggests procedures for implementing the economic education course in the secondary schools, and provides materials for teacher preparation and curriculum improvement in thirteen subject areas.

ECONOMIC EDUCATION: ECONOMIC EXPANSION OF THE U.S. SINCE 1865, A SUPPLEMENT TO GRADE 11 U.S. HISTORY. Minneapolis: Minneapolis Public Schools, 1967. 56 p. Developed by the Minneapolis DEEP project.

This guide helps to explain the major forces leading to economic growth in the United States after the Civil War. The impact of each of the following on growth is given historical perspective: consumer demand; savings and capital formation; specialization and trade; technological change; education as investment in human capital; agricultural productivity; and government.

ECONOMIC EDUCATION: THE INDUSTRIAL REVOLUTION, A SUPPLEMENT FOR GRADE 10, WORLD HISTORY. Minneapolis: Minneapolis Public Schools, 1967. 30 p. Developed by the Minneapolis DEEP project.

This guide aims to make the student familiar with particular episodes in the economic development of the European dominated world, particularly Great Britain; and to see this within an analytical framework of economic growth and development.

ECONOMIC EDUCATION FOR WASHINGTON PUBLIC SCHOOLS, GRADES

7, 8, 9. Seattle, Wash.: Superintendent of Public Instruction, 1967. 71 p. Developed by the Seattle DEEP project. Available from the Joint Council of Economic Education.

> These guidelines and activities in economic education represent one part of a series developed through the combined efforts of many teachers from the state of Washington over three years. The paramount purpose of the guide is to help implement a program of integrating economics into the curriculum at all grade levels. The overall objective is to insure that every high school graduate has acquired a critical way of thinking about economic matters and problems through the use of scientific methods. The major economic point to be learned in seventh grade is that every society must have some organized approach to economic decision making. The major theme in eighth grade is the United States today and how it has changed over the years and includes the study of big business, organized labor, government role, competition, industrialization and urbanization, and international trade and investment. In ninth grade, three major emphases appear: the characteristics, growth, and problems of growth in the state of Washington.

ECONOMIC EDUCATION FOR WASHINGTON SCHOOLS: GRADES 10, 11, and 12. Seattle, Wash.: Superintendent of Public Instruction, 1968. 154 p. Developed by the Seattle DEEP project.

> Guidelines and activities for developing economic literacy within the existing curriculum. The guide is set up in chart form. Characteristics and description, economic concepts and teaching suggestions are given for social studies topics in each grade level. The tenth grade course includes economic history of Western Europe, the United States, and the Soviet Union. The eleventh grade course centers on United States history from 1607 to 1945. The twelfth grade has a recapitulation of economic concepts.

ECONOMIC EFFECTS OF EDUCATION: A SUPPLEMENT FOR SECONDARY SOCIAL STUDIES. Minneapolis: Minneapolis Public Schools, 1967. 28 p. Developed by the Minneapolis DEEP project. Available from the Joint Council on Economic Education.

> A resource guide for secondary level courses. Education as an investment is emphasized. How the investment in human capital benefits both student and nation is explained.

ECONOMIC INFLUENCES IN WORLD AFFAIRS. SUPPLEMENTARY MATERIAL FOR WORLD GEOGRAPHY. Austin, Tex.: Austin Independent School District, 1960. 33 p.

> This guide promotes increased emphasis on economic information and principles in the world geography curriculum. Information is presented on eighteen individual nations. Some phases of the

economic situation in each country, representative of economic
situations in several countries, are presented. Broad economic
principles, exemplified by the nations' economies, are discussed.
Questions are posed in order to stimulate an analysis of the nations' economies which would help the student develop general economic understandings.

ECONOMIC MAN. Westchester, Ill.: Benefic, 1972.

This program is intended for use as a year-long supplement to the
social studies curriculum or as a concentrated twenty-two-week
program in economics. There are three units in the program.
Unit 1 concerns a man who is shipwrecked on a deserted tropical
island. He has to make economic decisions about how to spend
his time and how to take advantage of the island's resources.
Later, others are shipwrecked and specialization and division of
labor develop. Unit 2 is built around a simulation game called
Market. The class is divided into retailers and consumer teams.
The unit involves price theory and the determination of a market
clearing price from supply and demand lines. Unit 3 concerns
problems in international trade and introduces graph reading.
Materials include two pupil books with teacher's editions, teacher's
guide, resource readings and the Market simulation game.

ECONOMICS, A SOCIAL STUDIES SUPPLEMENT. Miami, Fla.: Dade County
Board of Public Instruction, 1968. 250 p. Developed by Dade County,
Florida DEEP project.

Teaching units are built around clusters of economic ideas. Objectives are stated in behavioral terms.

ECONOMICS: CHOICE-MAKING; SOCIAL STUDIES TEACHER'S MANUAL,
1968. 264 p. Available from ERIC.

The material in this secondary teacher's manual provides a foundation upon which subsequent courses will build; objectives are for
students to grasp economic principles which serve as fundamental
topics needed to analyze basic facts and institutions of modern
economic life. Focus is upon the basic economic problem, that
is, in all nations a scarcity of resources along with expanding
needs and desires exists; therefore, society must make choices that
are influenced by culture, government, and individual self-interest,
resulting in the various economic systems. Techniques involve
students in gathering, organizing, and classifying data in making
inferences, posing hypotheses, and ultimately formulating generalizations.

ECONOMICS: MODULAR LEARNING UNIT. Glenview, Ill.: Scott, Foresman, 1970. 49 p.

This booklet relates many economic terms and concepts to regional studies. It establishes a pattern that could be used in studying individual communities.

ECONOMICS: PROGRAM AND RESOURCES FOR INSTRUCTION. GRADES 7-12. Rev. ed. Columbus, Ohio: Columbus Public Schools, 1969.

A loose-leaf curriculum guide for grades 7-12 was designed by the local school system. Appendixes on books, free and inexpensive materials, films, filmstrips, transparencies, as well as a glossary are included.

ECONOMICS, SOCIAL STUDIES GRADE 12: A COURSE OF STUDY AND RELATED LEARNING ACTIVITIES. New York: Bureau of Curriculum Development, 1970. 401 p.

This course in economics places a great emphasis on the study of economics from an urban point of view. The course of study goes beyond descriptive learning, giving students a chance to utilize discovery techniques so that they will be equipped to think rationally and logically about economic problems. Stress is placed on concepts and ideas rather than rote learning of facts.

ECONOMICS: STUDENT MATERIALS AND TEACHER'S GUIDE. Athens: Ohio Council on Economic Education, 1966. Readings, 410 p. Teacher's guide, 176 p.

A ninth grade course in economics prepared by the social studies curriculum center of Ohio State University. Student material is expressed in ninth grade vocabulary but the course is appropriate for other grade levels. Economics is presented as a structured discipline.

ECONOMICS FOR EVERYONE. Westchester, Ill.: Benefic, 1971. 160 p.

This text can be used as a basic eight- to ten-week unit or incorporated into existing social studies courses. It provides students with concepts and skills that they can use immediately and continue to use throughout their lives, such as budget planning, wise buying, effects of advertising, over-extended credit, and installment purchases.

ECONOMICS IN SOCIETY. Reading, Mass.: Addison-Wesley, 1974.

This program replaces the program called ECON 12. Economic concepts and their relationships to the other social sciences are stressed, incorporating the basic strategy of problem-solving through inquiry. Six features shape the course content: (1) the course is based on the idea that the study of economic activity and organization is closely tied to the study of society as a whole; (2) a

general systems approach is used which can be applied to studying the economic organization of any society; (3) course emphasis
is on student analysis and decisions about controversial issues; (4)
students are asked to learn only those basic principles of economics which they can apply directly to the problems included in the
course; (5) students' use of abstract reasoning skills is emphasized;
(6) full-length units on Communist and Third World economies are
included.

ECONOMICS IN UNITED STATES HISTORY. Little Rock: Arkansas State
Department of Education, 1971. 181 p.

> Prepared by Little Rock Public Schools, Arkansas State Council on
> Economic Education, and Arkansas State Department of Education.
> This guide features basic economic concepts and ideas, identified
> in the context of narrative history and classroom applications.
> There is a bibliography.

ECONOMICS OF POVERTY AND TEACHER'S MANUAL. Pittsburgh: Pittsburgh Public Schools, 1968. Readings, 62 p. Manual, 25 p. Developed by
the Pittsburgh DEEP project with the cooperation of the Western Pennsylvania
Council on Economic Education. Available from Joint Council on Economic
Education.

> This unit can be used for supplementary reading in economics or
> social studies courses. The problem of poverty is analyzed. Case
> study material is used in discussing antipoverty efforts. The man-
> ual contains lesson plans outlining objectives.

ECONOMICS READINGS FOR STUDENTS OF 8TH GRADE U.S. HISTORY
AND TEACHER'S MANUAL. Pittsburgh: Pittsburgh Public Schools, 1966.
Readings, 87 p. Manual, 75 p. Developed by the Pittsburgh DEEP project
in cooperation with the Western Pennsylvania Council on Economic Education.
Available from Joint Council on Economic Education.

> This material has been designed to fit in with and supplement the
> existing course of study and accompanying textbook in use in the
> Pittsburgh Public School System. Economic growth is the main
> theme with emphasis on economic concepts as analytical tools to
> help understand historical events. The manual explains the eco-
> nomic concepts developed and suggests use with students of varying
> abilities and background. Lesson plans include clearly stated ob-
> jectives. Sketches suitable for transparencies are included, as are
> appropriate test questions and background information helpful to
> the teacher.

ECONOMICS READINGS FOR STUDENTS OF 9TH GRADE SOCIAL SCIENCE
AND TEACHER'S MANUAL. Pittsburgh: Pittsburgh Public Schools, 1967.
Readings, 104 p. Manual, 85 p.

These readings review and build on concepts introduced in the
eighth grade. Scarcity, opportunity, cost, economic growth, and
productive resources are examined. Students are given more tools
with which to analyze current social economic problems and are
introduced to a logical approach to economic reasoning.

ECONOMICS STUDENT MATERIALS. Athens: College of Business Administration, Ohio University, 1966. 176 p.

This course of study was set up to give the student a clearer understanding of his involvement with economics. There are eighteen
units in areas such as: definition of scarcity, factors of production,
stimulating efficiency, dividing goods and services, definition of
flows, measure of nation's income, definition of economic growth,
GNP, and so forth.

ECONOMIC THEMES IN THE U.S. HISTORY. Riverside, Calif.: Office of
Superintendent of Schools, 1962. 15 p.

Material is based on the lecture series part of an in-service teaching program designed to encourage eighth and eleventh grade
teachers to promote economic understandings as they teach U.S.
history. Case studies show economics materials incorporated in
American history courses. Economic growth, the role of business,
and the economic role of government are examined.

EXPANDED PROGRAMS IN CONSUMER EDUCATION. Albany, N.Y.: State
Education Department, Bureau of Secondary Curriculum Development, 1974.

Each module in this series is a separate publication and can be
used as a unit or with others in the series. Each module poses a
series of questions and includes suggested pupil and teacher activ-
ities and sources for information. Module titles: "Travel and the
Consumer"; "Education and the Consumer"; "Consumer Issues and
Action"; "Consumer and Recreation"; "Consumer and His Health
Dollar"; "Consumer Problems of the Poor"; "Consumer Looks at His
Automobile Insurance"; "Credit and the Consumer"; "Law and the
Consumer"; "Coping with the Problems of a Technological Age."

FLUCTUATIONS IN THE AMERICAN ECONOMY. New York: Joint Council
on Economic Education, 1972. 38 p.

This program is designed to develop an understanding of the nature
of booms, panics, recessions, depressions, inflation, and deflation,
and an understanding of the impact these phenomena have on the
individual citizen. The volume aims to enable the student to acquire the basic knowledge needed to view objectively and partici-
pate in decision making.

GOVERNMENT AND THE ECONOMY: A RESOURCE UNIT FOR GRADES
7, 8 AND 9. New York: Joint Council of Economic Education, 1974. 26 p.

This unit suggests a large number of activities, initiatory, developmental, and culminating, from which teachers can select those best suited for their own classroom use. Many are based on entries in the Kazanjian Foundation Awards program for the teaching of economics. A list of materials for student use and ideas for evaluating results are included.

GRADE 12: ECONOMICS, A COURSE OF STUDY AND RELATED LEARNING ACTIVITIES. Brooklyn: Bureau of Curriculum Development, 1970. 401 p.

This course of study includes a detailed overview of the major concepts covered within the discipline of economics. A large number of classroom activities and many pupil materials are listed.

GROWTH OF THE AMERICAN ECONOMY. New York: Joint Council on Economic Education, 1972. 38 p.

This unit is designed for use in courses which follow a chronological curriculum in American history, specifically the part which deals with the rise of industry. A teacher's guide and filmstrip are available. The basic requirements an economic system must meet to produce efficiently and develop steadily are presented; it is shown how our economy met these requirements from the American Revolution to the present. Problems of economic growth are discussed.

HOLT SOCIAL STUDIES CURRICULUM. Edited by Edwin Fenton. 4 vols. New York: Holt, Rinehart & Winston, 1968, 1973.

The four volumes in this series for ninth and tenth grade are: "Comparative Political Systems"; "Comparative Economic Systems"; "The Shaping of Western Society"; "Studies in the Non-Western World." An inquiry approach is used in this series. The student is encouraged to ask questions, compare contradictory data, distinguish between fact and opinion to determine the validity of an argument, and to make up his own mind on an issue. A comparison of the contemporary governments and the economic systems of the United States and the Soviet Union is made. Changes from ancient to modern times in the area of politics, economics, social organization, and patterns of thought are discussed. Four non-Western countries, South Africa, China, India, and Brazil are examined.

INSTRUCTOR'S HANDBOOK TO THE PACKAGE ECONOMICS COURSE. Portland: Oregon Council on Economic Education, 1969. 71 p.

This handbook was developed for use in school districts which wished to give their teachers additional in-service training in economics. This course supplements curriculum guides to economics and is concerned with giving teachers a better understanding of economic principles.

IN TODAY'S WORLD. 5 vols. Mankato, Minn.: Creative Education, 1965-67.

> In this group of books, designed for use in grades 7-9, the story of civilization unfolds in concise readable prose. Using an interdisciplinary approach, the authors present man in relation to himself and to his social and economic environments. Titles: "Transportation" by Etta Ress; "Cities and Metropolitan Areas" by Samuel Arbital; "Communications: Signals to Satellites" by Etta Ress.

Jackstadt, Steve. ADVENTURES OF PRIMERO DINERO. New York: Follett, 1972. Unp.

> This book was written for high school students in comic strip form and traces the adventures of Primero Dinero through a shipwreck, being washed up on a tropical island, and subsequently trying with his fellow castaways to build a sound economy on this deserted island.

LIFE ON PARADISE ISLAND. Glenview, Ill.: Scott, Foresman, 1970. 144 p.

> Designed for junior high school, this is a fictional story of economic "growing up" of the primitive Jubilant tribe on imaginary Paradise Island. As the story advances, the islanders discover the economic principles of barter, specialization, labor, and wages. Money is invented, laws, taxation, and public services follow, and finally a representative government is established. There is a teacher's manual.

MAKING THE MOST OF YOUR MONEY: LESSONS IN CONSUMER EDUCATION FOR ADULTS. New York: Institute of Life Insurance, 1967. 47 p.

> Five stories are presented about people using money in typical situations such as buying a car, shopping, or using credit. Questions are listed after each story to assist in developing discussion.

MANPOWER AND ECONOMIC EDUCATION: A PERSONAL AND SOCIAL APPROACH TO CAREER EDUCATION. Denver: Love Publishing Co., 1973. 329 p.

> This book, intended for adoption in the secondary school curriculum, contains a series of seventy-two lessons within the broad area units which explain both the economic and human aspects of employment to help young people make sound career decisions. This instruction in the "world of work" seeks to help students understand the American economic system, how various jobs fit into this system, and includes the changing nature of work, impact of technology, the manpower market, career opportunities, rational decision making and career planning, and the value of education as an investment. The student comes to realize how work influ-

ences his life style, choice of clothing and friends, hobbies. and recreational activities, and even how his choice of work influences his ideas about the kind of person he is.

MANPOWER AND ECONOMIC EDUCATION: OPPORTUNITIES IN AMERICAN ECONOMIC LIFE. Rev. ed. Athens: Ohio University Center for Economic Education, 1970. 329 p. Available from Joint Council for Economic Education.

This year-long high school economic education course is written from the viewpoint of the individual as a worker/income-earner. Its primary purpose is to provide the schools with a means for improving the preparation of young people for effective participation in the changing economy. The educational objectives are: (1) to develop an understanding of the economic process and the role of work; and (2) to explain how students can enhance their future employability, productivity, earning, and work satisfaction by investing in the development of their own knowledge, skills motivation, and behavior patterns.

MANPOWER EDUCATION IN A GROWING ECONOMY. Athens: Ohio University Center for Economic Education, 1968. 63 p.

This is a description of the curriculum project, "Manpower Development: Opportunities in American Economic Life," out of which the manpower and economic education program evolved. There is an evaluation of the changes in understanding and attitudes resulting from the experimental teaching of the course in three Ohio school systems.

MINNEAPOLIS TRADES WITH JAPAN, A SUPPLEMENT TO GRADE 7 GEOGRAPHY. Minneapolis: Minneapolis Public Schools, 1967. 43 p. Developed by the Minneapolis DEEP project.

The mechanics and theory of international trade are examined together with the development problems of eastern hemisphere countries and the growth of Japan.

MODERN PROBLEMS ECONOMIC UNITS: A PROGRAM FOR GRADE 12. 1969. 86 p. Available from ERIC.

The introductory material includes the identification of main areas of modern economics, basic objectives, and techniques for evaluating objectives. The guide covers six units: (1) importance and nature of economics; (2) the common problem and the need for an economic system; (3) modified market economy of the United States; (4) economic growth and stability; (5) distribution of income; and (6) consumer economics. The material for each unit is set out in three columns--concepts, activities, and instructional resources.

ONE-WEEK ADVANCED TEACHING UNIT ON CONSUMER CREDIT. Washington, D.C.: National Consumer Finance Association, 1970.

This is a kit of materials for the teaching of consumer credit to high school students or adults. Among the teacher's materials are: a manual, FINANCE FACTS YEAR BOOK; Little Giant film; teacher's guide; Association Distribution Centers list; educational catalog; film; filmstrip; and poster flyers. The student materials include: consumer credit pre-study inventory; basic principles in family money and credit management; family budget slideguide; finance facts newsletter; radio script.

POLICIES FOR PROTECTION: HOW HEALTH INSURANCE, LIFE INSURANCE WORKS. New York: Institute of Life Insurance, 1967. 35 p.

This explanation of the benefits of insurance policies was designed to use with students in general business, business law, consumer economics, and other basic business courses. There is a teacher's manual available.

POLITICAL AND ECONOMIC BEHAVIOR OF MAN: A COURSE OF STUDY. 1970. 258 p. Available from ERIC.

This curriculum guide is designed to assist teachers in using such innovative techniques in the new social studies as concept teaching and inquiry with below-average students. It is divided into two nonsequential semesters. Each of eleven units emphasizes a single concept in economics: (1) consumption, consumer purchasing, credit deception, budget; (2) economic systems; (3) scarcity; (4) distribution; (5) resources; and (6) interdependence.

PRIVATE INVESTMENT AND ECONOMIC GROWTH. New York: American Petroleum Institute, n.d. 24 p.

This study unit includes a teacher's guide, student manual, and filmstrip. It was designed to emphasize and explain one of the important determinants of economic growth: private investment.

READINGS IN ECONOMICS FOR 11TH GRADE STUDENTS OF UNITED STATES HISTORY, A UNIT ON THE GREAT DEPRESSION AND TEACHER'S MANUAL. Pittsburgh: Pittsburgh Public Schools, 1968. Readings, 32 p. Manual, 17 p.

A case study of how the 1930s Depression affected Pittsburgh. Readings reflect the successive efforts by the private sector, city, state, and federal governments to help the jobless. Many tables and graphs are included for analyzing the results of these efforts to stabilize Pittsburgh's depressed economy. The teacher's manual defines the economic concepts involved, and suggests classroom procedures and lesson plans.

Courses of Study—High School

READINGS IN ECONOMICS FOR 10TH GRADE STUDENTS OF WORLD CUL-
TURES AND TEACHER'S MANUAL. Pittsburgh: Pittsburgh Public Schools,
1967. Readings, 35 p. Manual, 18 p.

> Prepared as an introduction to the economics of world trade, these
> readings describe problems related to world trade and some solu-
> tions. Tables listing American imports and exports from colonial
> times to present day are included. Analytical tools to analyze
> world trade problems are explained. Readings define current
> issues related to balance of payments, tariffs, and international
> monetary systems, and stresses interdependence between nations.

READINGS IN ECONOMICS FOR 12TH GRADE STUDENTS OF AMERICAN
DEMOCRACY AND TEACHER'S MANUAL. Pittsburgh: Pittsburgh Public
Schools, 1968. Readings, 199 p. Manual, 82 p.

> This twelve-week course segment covers economic principles as
> applied to economic problems. It focuses on the development,
> operation, and problems of a market economy, but also contains
> readings about comparative economic systems including the USSR.
> It is designed to help students develop a rational approach to
> problem solving and also a healthy skepticism in their own think-
> ing. The teacher's manual outlines daily assignments, objectives,
> and suggested procedures.

REAL WORLD OF ECONOMICS. 11 vols. Minneapolis: Lerner Publications
Co., 1970.

> This series was designed for use in the fifth through tenth grades.
> It explores man's role in the world's changing economic structure;
> complex economic institutions and relationships are explained.
> The texts are supplemented by photographs, charts, and graphs.
> Strategic economic theories and their applications are presented
> and facets of the complex economic systems are viewed as they
> are interrelated with community life and other disciplines.

SOCIAL STUDIES: INTRODUCTION TO ECONOMICS. Miami, Fla.: Division of Instruction, Dade County Public Schools, 1971. 47 p. Available from
ERIC.

> The course for grades 10-12 outlined in this guide provides a study
> of the American system of private enterprise and the economic
> principles upon which it is based. Course goals are, among
> others, to enable the student to: (1) discover that American
> economy as evidenced through the free enterprise system exists
> for the individual; (2) integrate the relationship between the func-
> tions of money and banking into the American economy; (3) ana-
> lyze types of investments that can improve one's financial posi-
> tion; (4) justify the importance of supply and demand; (5) analyze
> the economics of international trade; and (6) formulate hypotheses
> as to the ideal economic model or policy to which the United
> States should subscribe.

SOCIAL STUDIES GRADE 12 ECONOMICS COURSE OF STUDY AND RELATED
LEARNING ACTIVITIES. Brooklyn: Board of Education, City of New York,
1970. 701 p.

This course of study presents an extensive variety of teaching/
learning activities. Many of the readings, pictures, charts, cartoons, and tables are selected from current and authoritative
sources, such as government reports and newspapers. These items
are used as a basis for student questions and a variety of student
activities. There are seven selected themes in the course. They
are: (1) economics and economic problems; (2) organizing production to satisfy economic choices; (3) income distribution in our
market economy; (4) how we try to maintain a growing and stable
economy; (5) economics of the metropolitan region; (6) comparative
economic systems; and (7) international economics.

SOCIAL STUDIES, TENTATIVE SYLLABUS, GRADE 12: ADVANCED ECO-
NOMICS. New York: Bureau of Secondary Curriculum Development, State
Education Department, 1966. 42 p.

This one-semester twelfth grade course, advanced economics, is
intended to give students an opportunity to examine economics
topics in some depth, applying the analytic techniques of the
discipline.

SOCIAL STUDIES, YOU AND THE WORKING WORLD. Curriculum Bulletin
1966-67 series, no. 8. New York: Board of Education, 1966. 36 p.

This is a resource guide for career guidance instruction covering
the economics area of the social studies. It consists of five units:
(1) you as a buyer; (2) you as a producer; (3) you as a business
man; (4) you as a professional; and (5) you as a student.

STRATEGIES AND MATERIALS FOR TOPIC III AMERICAN ECONOMIC LIFE
FROM 11TH GRADE SOCIAL STUDIES SYLLABUS. Geneseo, N.Y.: Genesee
Region Council on Economic Education and Center on Economic Education,
State University College of Arts and Science, 1971.

This is a set of readings and activities to provide suggestions for
the teaching of the economic content contained in the New York
state syllabus for an eleventh grade American studies course. It
should supplement the history text. Activities suggested are intended to develop specific economic concepts within the context
of American history.

SUGGESTED PROCEDURES AND RESOURCES FOR A MINIMUM COURSE IN
ECONOMICS. Curriculum Development Series, no. 4. Harrisburg, Pa.:
Department of Public Instruction, 1962. 39 p. Available from the Joint
Council on Economic Education.

This illustrated guide suggests background readings and content outlines for teaching of a six-unit thirty-six hour mandated senior high school course in economics. There is also a description of eight other possible units.

TEACHER'S GUIDE TO ECONOMICS IN GRADE 8. Salem, Oreg.: Board of Education, 1968. 134 p. Available from Joint Council on Economic Education.

This guide is one of a series intended to present a carefully designed plan to teach a progression of economic concepts in the elementary and secondary grades. Basic concepts, or "big ideas" appropriate to the grade are given. These are expanded upon and accompanied by teaching activities.

TEACHER'S GUIDE TO ECONOMICS IN THE BUSINESS EDUCATION CURRICULUM. New York: Joint Council on Economic Education, 1963. 104 p.

This guide was developed by the participants of a National Workshop on Economics for business education teachers. It presents suggestions for including economic education in business education courses.

TEACHING A COURSE IN PERSONAL ECONOMICS. New York: Joint Council on Economic Education, 1971. 77 p.

This course content focuses on the individual's decision-making process and participation in economic life in the roles of worker, consumer, and citizen. Emphasis is placed on the activities of earning, spending, borrowing, saving, investing, and influencing collective decisions.

TEACHING CONSUMER EDUCATION: A RESOURCE KIT. Editors Park, Md.: Kiplinger Washington Editors, 1970.

This kit was developed by the Changing Times Educational Service. It includes a teaching guide and five units on earning, spending, borrowing, saving, and budgeting.

TEACHING ECONOMICS. Albany: New York State Education Department, 1962. 303 p. Bibliography.

This handbook deals with economic content that cuts across all secondary school social studies curriculums. Ten topics have been selected from the viewpoint of importance and teachability. Special attention is given to the study of economic activities in the local community and the state. The handbook aims to give the teacher help in planning activities to develop economic understanding. It is not a course of study. The topics that are developed are: American economic system; resources and economic growth; economics of business enterprise; economics of agriculture;

economics of labor management relations; family and personal economics; economic stabilization; public finance; the money, credit, and banking system; and the United States and international economics.

TEACHING ECONOMICS IN AMERICAN HISTORY: A TEACHING MANUAL FOR SECONDARY SCHOOLS. New York: Joint Council on Economic Education, 1973. 100 p.

This book is designed to aid teachers in extending the economic content of American history courses. Twenty-one topics are presented in chronological fashion that can be used to incorporate economic facts, concepts, principles, and problems into the study of American history.

TEACHING PERSONAL ECONOMICS IN THE BUSINESS EDUCATION CURRICULUM. New York: Joint Council on Economic Education, 1971. 116 p.

This guide for secondary teachers, an interdisciplinary approach integrating economic concepts into business courses, stresses education about business, analyzing individual and aggregate consumer behavior, and interrelationships between the two. Part 1 focuses upon the consumer's earning, spending, borrowing, saving, investing, and decision making. Part 2 consists primarily of a discussion of economics and the consumer, emphasizing interrelationships of individual consumers to the total economy and the economic analysis of the concepts of freedom of choice, opportunity costs, income, private and public consumer interests, budgets, savings, and investing.

TEACHING PERSONAL ECONOMICS IN THE HOME ECONOMICS CURRICULUM. New York: Joint Council on Economic Education, 1971. 102 p.

The guide for secondary teachers, a new interdisciplinary approach integrating macroeconomic and microeconomic concepts with home economics courses, is divided into two major parts. Part 1 stresses consumer behavior in four units on clothing, housing, foods, and family. The fifth unit, comprised of case studies, presents an opportunity for students to learn economic principles by applying them to specific situations. Part 2, "Economics and the Consumer," emphasizes interrelationships of individual consumers to the total economy and economic analysis of the concepts of freedom of choice, opportunity costs, income, private and public consumer interests, budget, savings, and investing.

TEACHING PERSONAL ECONOMICS IN THE SOCIAL STUDIES CURRICULUM. New York: Joint Council on Economic Education, 1971. 96 p.

The purposes of this guide are to: (1) define the nature and scope of personal economics; (2) identify basic ideas and concepts;

(3) describe a process of personal economics decision making; (4) provide a "personal economics grid" that relates the major areas of personal economic activity to the decision-making process and to the effects on the economy as a whole; and (5) suggest a method of teaching personal economics understandings and provide specific curriculum applications. Areas of the social studies curriculum chosen for emphasis are: civics, government, American and world history, economics, and other social sciences.

TODAY'S ECONOMICS. Columbus, Ohio: American Education Publications, 1967. 63 p.

The book contains seventeen economic problems presented in case studies followed by expert points of view and sample questions. The cases introduce students to techniques of economic analysis.

TRADITION AND CHANGE IN FOUR SOCIETIES: AN INQUIRY APPROACH. New York: Holt, Rinehart & Winston, 1974.

The four societies and corresponding concepts emphasized in this course are: China (political change), India (economic development), Brazil (race relations), and West Africa (urbanization). A variety of materials and activities helps the students to better understand these particular countries and to explore the human issues and values involved in social change no matter where the locale.

UNDERSTANDING OF ECONOMICS. Washington, D.C.: Chamber of Commerce of the United States of America, 1970.

This is a discussion group program. It contains a series of ten booklets, a leader's guide, charts relating to the booklet material and an Eco-tape set of ten recorded interviews featuring national leaders. The titles of the booklets are: "Why Economics?"; "Why Prices?"; "Productive Resources"; "Money and Finance"; "National Income"; "Business Ups and Downs"; "Government and Economy"; "International Economics"; "Science, Technology and the Economy"; and "Power of Choice."

THE USE OF AN ADVERSARY APPROACH IN TEACHING ECONOMICS. Cincinnati, Ohio: South-Western Publishing Co., 1970. 86 p.

The purpose of this monograph is to present a paradigm for the secondary teacher on how to employ debate as a teaching tool. The paradigm is applied to the propositions of government policy that commonly emanate from the subject matter of an economics course.

WHAT EVERYONE SHOULD KNOW ABOUT THE NATURE OF ECONOMICS, A SCRIPTOGRAPHIC STUDY UNIT. Greenfield, Mass.: Channing L. Bete Co., 1967. 15 p.

A brief, simple explanation, illustrated with cartoons, describing what economics is, how one learns some basic economics, what the scientific method is, microeconomics and macroeconomics, five great divisions of economics, and things a student of economics must face.

WORLD HISTORY THROUGH INQUIRY SERIES. Edited by Bryon Massialas and Jack Zevin. 8 vols. Chicago: Rand, McNally, 1970.

This series offers a variety of topics applicable to global education. Designed as a world history course, its format makes it easily adaptable to other social studies courses as well. The program seeks to teach students to think systematically and to generalize from given data, including photographs, maps, graphs, slides, charts, documents, fictional excerpts, paintings, and essays. Relevant units include those on cultural exchange and social structure. The titles in this series are: "Looking into History"; "Political Systems"; "Social Structure"; "Man and His Environment"; "Religious-Philosophical Systems"; "Cultural Exchange"; "Two Societies in Persepective"; "World Order."

YOUR GUIDE FOR TEACHING MONEY MANAGEMENT. Chicago: Household Finance Corp., 1970. 30 p.

This guide was designed to help teachers build a strong program in personal and family economic education. It can be used with groups of different ages, income, and ability levels.

Chapter 17
TESTS OF ECONOMIC UNDERSTANDING

JUNIOR HIGH SCHOOL TEST OF ECONOMICS. New York: Joint Council on Economic Education, 1974.

> An evaluative instrument developed by the Joint Council on Economic Education, suitable for measuring student knowledge and understanding of economics. The thirty-eight-page interpretive manual provides a rationale for the forty questions as well as normative data and suggestions for use of the test.

PRIMARY TEST OF ECONOMIC UNDERSTANDING. Prepared by Donald G. Davison and John H. Kilgore. New York: Joint Council on Economic Education, 1971.

> An outline of five major economic generalizations with related understandings, concepts, and subconcepts which provide the conceptual framework of the test is included in the examiner's thirty-two-page manual. Sixty-four yes-no questions make up this evaluation instrument, which aims to measure the student's growth and to assess the effectiveness of existing materials in the primary grades.

TEST OF ECONOMIC UNDERSTANDING. Prepared by a Committee for Measurement of Economic Understanding of the Joint Council on Economic Education. Chicago: Science Research Associates, 1963.

> Fifty multiple-choice questions are designed to measure the understanding of economics of students in secondary school and college. It aims to evaluate student understanding of basic economic concepts deemed essential for good citizenship by the National Task Force on Economic Education.

TEST OF ELEMENTARY ECONOMICS. Grades 4-6. New York: Joint Council on Economic Education, 1971.

> This experimental evaluation instrument to measure learning of

economic concepts at the intermediate level was developed by the Economic Education Enrichment Program in West Springfield, Massachusetts. It includes forty multiple-choice questions. The twenty-six-page interpretive manual contains a rationale for each question.

TEST OF UNDERSTANDING IN PERSONAL ECONOMICS. New York: Joint Council on Economic Education, 1971.

This evaluative instrument consists of fifty multiple-choice questions. It was prepared for use in social studies, business, and home economics classes in grades nine and twelve. The twenty-eight-page manual gives an explanation of the importance of the questions and explains the concepts on which the questions focus.

Chapter 18

TEACHER'S MATERIALS

ABA FILM GUIDE. Washington, D.C.: American Bankers Association, 1969.

Films useful for elementary, junior and senior high school students, adults, and bank personnel are included in this guide. Subjects covered include: bank services, economy, money management, automation, stocks and bonds, and systems of banking.

American Bankers Association, Banking Education Committee. LIST OF MA-TERIALS ON MONEY AND BANKING FOR SECONDARY SCHOOL TEACHERS. Washington, D.C.: 1970.

A well annotated selective list of materials available to teachers.

Anderson, Randall. CURRENT TRENDS IN SECONDARY SCHOOL SOCIAL STUDIES. Lincoln, Nebr.: Professional Education Publications, 1972. 114 p.

The author reflects futuristic thinking in social studies curriculum which incorporates the study of major interdisciplinary themes involving human and social conditions. The development of a program around selected contemporary themes would place emphasis upon the interdisciplinary nature of various issues confronting society and make social studies more relevant for American youth.

Andreano, Ralph L., et al. STUDENT ECONOMIST'S HANDBOOK: A GUIDE TO SOURCES. Cambridge, Mass.: Schenkman, 1967. 169 p.

A guide to sources of materials in economics including: periodical indexes, bibliographies, government documents, and periodical literature.

AUDIOVISUAL MATERIALS FOR TEACHING ECONOMICS. New York: Audiovisual Materials Evaluation Committee of Joint Council on Economic Education, 1972. 56 p.

An annotated bibliography of selected audiovisual materials in economic education, K-12. Included is a discussion of the evalua-

tion process used by the committee, an overview of "the state of
the art" in the field of audiovisual materials production, and a
listing of publishers and distributors.

Bahr, Gladys, ed. TWO DECADES OF PARTNERSHIP IN ECONOMIC EDU-
CATION. New York: National Business Association, 1969. 79 p.

This is a collection of reports on the Joint Council on Economic
Education and the National Business Association, with articles on
economic concepts, economic education in high school, business
education, teaching economic concepts in high school, and the
world of work.

Boocock, Sarane S., and Schild, E.C., eds. SIMULATION GAMES IN
LEARNING. Beverly Hills, Calif.: Sage Publishing Co., 1968. 279 p.

The development of simulation games as a learning device is traced.
Some games are described and reports on their testing is given.

Calderwood, James D., et al. ECONOMICS IN THE CURRICULUM: DE-
VELOPMENTAL ECONOMIC EDUCATIONAL PROGRAM. Huntington, N.Y.:
Robert E. Krieger Publishing Co., 1973. 141 p.

This is a basic reference for in-service programs. It is a teacher's
guide to economic ideas and concepts, and grade placement of
economic concepts. The central ideas of economics are explained
and practical suggestions are made for fitting them into the K-12
curriculum.

Committee for Economic Development. ECONOMIC LITERACY FOR AMERI-
CANS: A PROGRAM FOR SCHOOLS AND FOR CITIZENS; A STATEMENT
ON NATIONAL POLICY BY THE RESEARCH AND POLICY COMMITTEE.
New York: 1962. 55 p.

This statement firmly puts forth a realistic plan for rapid improve-
ment in economic education. It disagrees in some instances with
the National Task Force on Economic Education report, ECO-
NOMIC EDUCATION IN THE SCHOOLS. (See National Task
Force on Economic Education. ECOMOMIC EDUCATION IN THE
SCHOOLS, below).

DEEP 1969: PERSPECTIVES ON A 5-YEAR EXPERIMENT IN CURRICULUM
CHANGE. New York: Joint Council on Economic Education, 1969. 112 p.

This report analyzes the five-year history of the Developmental
Economic Education Program (DEEP). It explains the significance
of DEEP, the approach to it, and the reasons behind it. The
authors have written from a variety of perspectives explaining how
and why certain objectives were realized and others were not.

Developmental Economic Education Program (DEEP). HANDBOOK FOR CUR-
RICULUM CHANGE: GUIDELINES. New York: Joint Council on Economic
Education, 1969. 32 p.

This handbook will provide resources, for those with leadership
roles in local schools, that will help make curriculum change a
more orderly process. Step-by-step guidelines introduce economic
understanding suitable for the curriculum of any school.

_____. TEACHER'S GUIDE TO DEVELOPMENTAL ECONOMIC EDUCATION.
2 pts. New York: Joint Council on Economic Education, 1964. Pt. 1,
46 p. Pt. 2, 95 p.

Some basic concepts in economics are explained. Important ideas
that should be part of each high school graduate's development
are identified. Also includes a series of conceptual statements
expressed in simple terms and accompanied by examples which
will convey the fundamentals of each economic idea.

ECONOMIC EDUCATION EXPERIENCES OF ENTERPRISING TEACHERS. 10
vols. Vols. 1-3, edited by Jere Clark and Percy L. Guyton. 1963-66.
Vols. 4-10, edited by George G. Dawson. New York: Joint Council on
Economic Education and Calvin Kazanjian Foundation, 1967-73.

Each volume contains selected articles submitted as entries in the
Kazanjian Award Program for the teaching of economics. In
these articles, teachers disclose educational strategies in precise
step-by-step detail, indicating exactly how they conveyed an
economic fact, problem, or concept to their students. The articles
are grouped by education level ranging from primary to college.

ECONOMICS IN SOCIAL STUDIES TEXT BOOKS. 4 vols. New York:
Joint Council on Economic Education, 1973.

These four books evaluate the economics and the teaching strategies in social studies textbooks in elementary grades, junior high
school, high school, and in United States and world history textbooks in eleventh and twelfth grades. A study to evaluate the
treatment of economics in social studies text materials, grades
1-12, was conducted by the Joint Council, 1971-73. The reports will aid textbook selection committees in what to look for
to promote better economic education, and help make teachers
aware of strengths and weaknesses in the area of economics.

ERIC Clearing House for Social Studies/Social Science Education. SOCIAL
STUDIES AND SOCIAL SCIENCE EDUCATION AND ERIC BIBLIOGRAPHY.
New York: Macmillan, 1973. 598 p.

Educational Resources Information Center (ERIC) is a national information system designed to meet needs of the educational community by

disseminating significant educational research and resources that
are not available through major publishing channels. The function of this center is to acquire, select, index, and abstract documents and journal articles in particular subject areas.

Huff, Darrell, and Geis, Irving. HOW TO LIE WITH STATISTICS. New
York: W.W. Norton, 1954. 141 p.

This is an introduction to the art and science of statistics. It
has many attractive drawings that effectively alert the students to
some of the tricky aspects of charts, tables, and other statistical
devices.

Joint Council on Economic Education. DEVELOPMENTAL ECONOMIC EDU-
CATION PROGRAM: HANDBOOK FOR CURRICULUM CHANGE GUIDE-
LINES. New York: 1969. 39 p.

This pamphlet blueprints a step-by-step process of curriculum
change. It reflects a philosophy of change and is meant to do
two things: (1) to specify the kinds of decisions that must be
made to achieve meaningful change; and (2) to provide acceptable
tools to carry out the tasks.

_____. HANDBOOK FOR CURRICULUM CHANGE: APPENDIX 1-6. New
York: 1971.

This loose-leaf file includes over one hundred concrete examples
for achieving curriculum change. There are reports of individual
DEEP projects, examples of organizing techniques, examples of
implementation of teacher in-service education and materials development, evaluation materials for measuring the effectiveness of
a program, and a list of agencies and names of individuals who
can provide manpower, materials and funds to help schools carry
out curriculum change.

_____. STUDY MATERIALS FOR ECONOMIC EDUCATION IN THE SCHOOLS.
REPORTS OF MATERIALS EVALUATION COMMITTEES TO THE JOINT COUN-
CIL ON ECONOMIC EDUCATION. New York: 1969. 70 p.

An annotated bibliography of selected supplementary materials in
economic education. It includes written and audiovisual materials
reviewed and recommended for classroom use.

Leamer, Laurence E., and Dawson, George G. SUGGESTIONS FOR A BASIC
ECONOMIC LIBRARY. 5th ed. New York: Joint Council on Economic Education, 1973. 72 p.

A step-by-step purchasing guide that includes a bibliography of
280 titles divided into ten categories. Five successive priorities

are established to assist the purchaser, who can start with $50 in basic purchases and over a period of time develop a good basic library.

Lewis, Darrell R., and Orvis, Charles. RESEARCH IN ECONOMIC EDUCA-TION: A REVIEW, BIBLIOGRAPHY AND ABSTRACTS. New York: Joint Council on Economic Education, 1971. 114 p.

This is a review of current trends in economic education research with a summary of problems and prospects for future research.

Lewis, Darrell R., et al. EDUCATIONAL GAMES AND SIMULATIONS IN ECONOMICS. 2d ed. New York: Joint Council on Economic Education, 1974. 148 p.

A list of 130 games for use in elementary and secondary class-rooms is included. There are also articles on constructing, se-lecting, and using simulation games and an annotated bibliography of articles and references related to the use of games.

Nappi, Andrew T. LEARNING ECONOMICS THROUGH CHILDREN'S STO-RIES. New York: Joint Council on Economic Education, 1973. 56 p.

A bibliography of children's books, K-6, which can be used to supplement elementary school reading and social studies programs. Annotations show how the stories reflect economic concepts, and reading levels are indicated.

National Commission on Economics and the Consumer. ECONOMICS AND THE CONSUMER. New York: Joint Council on Economic Education, 1966. 40 p.

Principles of economics through the experiences of the student and his family are detailed. The minimum economic understandings needed for high school graduates to make wise consumer decisions are identified.

National Task Force on Economic Education. ECONOMIC EDUCATION IN THE SCHOOLS. New York: Committee for Economic Development, 1961. 78 p.

This is the report that started the movement to improve the teach-ing of economics throughout our educational system. It explains what economics is and argues for economics by analysis rather than by absorption of miscellaneous and unrelated data. Economic understandings essential for citizenship and reasonably attainable in the schools are spelled out.

Sayre, J. Woodrow. PAPERBOUND BOOKS IN ECONOMICS: AN ANNO-TATED BIBLIOGRAPHY. 3d ed. Albany: New York State Council on Economic Education, 1968.   69 p.

> This frequently revised bibliography of selected materials is for use in
> schools but is also useful in identifying items of interest to libraries.*

Senesh, Lawrence.   NEW PATHS IN SOCIAL SCIENCE CURRICULUM DESIGN.
Chicago: Science Research Associates, 1972.   64 p.

> The author provides the underlying philosophy of an interdisciplinary,
> problem-solving, social science program--Our Working World.   He
> describes how and why a social studies curriculum is developed, and
> deals with the application of the fundamental ideas of the social sci-
> ences to elementary classroom learning situations.

Smith, Harlan, ed.   STUDY GUIDE FOR SELECTED 60-SESSION SERIES OF
AMERICAN ECONOMY TV FILMS.   Prepared under the direction of Minnesota
Council on Economic Education.   New York: Joint Council on Economic Edu-
cation, 1964.   305 p.

> A study guide to a series of films produced for television about the
> American economy.   For each film a statement has been prepared
> telling why it is useful.   Key ideas are outlined, notes are prepared
> for the teachers, and suggestions are made for testing economic
> understandings.

Uhr, Carl G.   ECONOMICS IN BRIEF.   New York: Random House, 1968.
149 p.

> This book is written for teachers who need background if they are to
> teach economics.   Its aim is to present the central ideas of eco-
> nomics in clear perspectives.   An overview of major economic
> areas including the nature of economics, the economics system,
> national income, GNP, and growth is provided.

Youngers, John C., and Aceti, John.   SIMULATION GAMES AND ACTIVI-
TIES FOR SOCIAL STUDIES.   Dansville, N.Y.:   Instructor Publishers, 1969.
48 p.

> Over one hundred classroom-tested simulation games and tradition-
> al activities are suggested that will involve children in repeated
> problem-solving situations.   Concepts of family, community, pro-
> ducers, consumers, exchange, and so forth, are developed.

Chapter 19

GAMES AND SIMULATIONS

AID COMMITTEE GAME. Newton, Mass.: Oxfam-America. 3-5 hrs. JH.

This game is actually a series of decision-making situations drawn from twelve different countries of Africa and South America. After reading a brief overview of each country, including data on such aspects as its economic condition, size and distribution of population, primary products and trading partners, the students must decide their priorities in allocating limited funds to specific development projects.

BALDICER. Richmond, Va.: John Knox Press. 2-4 hrs. Grades 6-12.

This game simulates the problems of providing food for the world's populations. Students are encouraged to think about solutions in an economically interdependent world. Students are "food co-ordinators" for a hypothetical country and through negotiation, trading, and buying, try to sustain their population explosions. The players learn the effects of the population explosion, unequal distribution of resources and technology, inflation, and competition among nations.

BANKING. Chicago: Science Research Associates. 2-5 hrs. Grades 10-12.

This game involves the financial activities and decisions of commercial banks.

BLACKS AND WHITES. Anaheim, Calif.: Dynamic Design Industries. 1-2 hrs. 4-20 players. Grades 10-12.

The participants of this game deal with welfare, housing, and other issues of the ghetto.

BLIGHT. St. Paul, Minn.: Instructional Simulations. 3-8 hrs. 20-40 players. Grades 10-12.

The players attempt to solve problems relating to change and renewal in a community.

BUDGET. Lakeside, Calif.: Interact. 2-4 hrs. 40 players. Grades 10-12.
The participants in this game try to reach a consensus on a budget
for the country.

BUDGETS AND TAXES. Middleton, Conn.: Education Ventures. 4-6
hrs. 6-20 players. Grades 10-12.
Participants play roles of public officials submitting annual budget
requests and citizens affected by public services and taxes.

BUSINESS STRATEGY. Baltimore: Avalon Hill, 1973. Grade 9-adult.
The participant becomes involved in analyzing the stock market,
learning to take advantage of competitors' circumstances, and
operating his own factories and warehouses at peak efficiency.

COLLECTIVE BARGAINING. Chicago: Science Research Associates. 2-5
hrs. Grades 10-12.
The atmosphere and conditions that prevail during negotiations of
a new labor contract are simulated.

COMPETITION OR SUBSIDY? Cincinnati, Ohio: South-Western Publishing
Co. 1 hr. Up to 42 players. Grades 10-12.
The participants are exposed to conditions of a free competitive
market and government involvement through subsidies.

CREDIT GAMES. San Rafael, Calif.: Leswing Communications. Up to 8
players. Grades 7-12.
This is a board game. The players obtain all needs and wants
through the use of credit. Players should learn about using the
tools of credit.

DEVELOPMENT. Chicago: Science Research Associates. 2-4 hrs. Grades
7-12.
DEVELOPMENT simulates relations between the developing nations
of the world and the two major powers that compete for their
loyalties through the granting of foreign aid.

DIRTY WATER. Westwood, Mass.: Damon/Educational Division. 3 players.
Grades 6-10.
The participants play roles of water pollution control officials trying
to work out pollution problems.

DISUNIA. Lakeside, Calif.: Interact. Grades 7-9.

This game makes students cope with problems of the kind Americans faced from 1781 to 1789, through similar experiences on a new planet in the year 2087.

ECONOMIC SYSTEM. Racine, Wis.: Western Publishing Co. 2-6 hrs. 7-13 players.

ECONOMIC SYSTEM simulates basic features common to a wide variety of economic systems. Each player takes one of these economic roles: worker, farmer, or manufacturer. Farmers and manufacturers control the farms and the factories; workers supply labor to run the factories and to provide additional labor for the farms. Each player attempts to achieve a high number of satisfaction points through obtaining and consuming manufactured goods and foods.

ENTERPRISE. Lakeside, Calif.: Interact. 2-4 hrs. 20-30 players. Grades 10-12.

The players interact with each other in their roles as bankers, businessmen, brokers, consumers, welfare poor, lobbyists, and politicians.

GHETTO. Racine, Wis.: Academic Games Associates. 2-4 hrs. Grades 7-adult.

This game simulates the conditions, pressures, and choices of the urban poor. Students experience the discouragement, frustrations, and occasional luck involved in trying to improve one's lot. They learn how poor education and poor living conditions can perpetuate themselves.

GOLDMINERS AND MERCHANTS. Athens: Georgia Environmental Curriculum Studies Project. Grades 2-4.

A game designed to supplement THE GOLD MINING CAMP, through structured role play in a simulated market economy. Buying and selling of goods by students leads to an understanding of selected economic concepts: profit-loss-savings, scarcity-surplus, and supply-demand.

THE GOLD MINING CAMP. Athens: Georgia Environmental Curriculum Studies Project. Grades 2-4.

This game simulates economic problems of the 1850s gold mining camp. Economic concepts such as supply and demand and profits are presented.

GUNS AND BUTTER. La Jolla, Calif.: Simile II. 1-1 1/2 hrs. Grades 10-12.

The participants are leaders of nations trying to increase their country's real wealth while making it secure from attack by others. They may trade, form common markets, and establish alliances.

INFLATION. Minneapolis: Paul S. Amidon. Grades 10-12.

This simulation game was designed to study the process of political and economic decision making. Five major groups represented by students attempt to influence the federal government to gain economic advantages as the government works to control inflation.

LAND USE GAME. Middleton, Conn.: Education Ventures. 1-2 hrs. Any number of players. Grades 10-12.

Participants decide where to locate roads, recreation areas, and so forth, to meet human needs and protect the environment.

MARKETPLACE. New York: Joint Council on Economic Education. 12 sessions of 50 mins. ea. 20-50 players. Grades 10-12.

Teams of students play households, businesses, manufacturers, retailers, or banks. Basic economic concepts are translated into a series of transactions that simulate a microeconomic world. Students develop a better understanding of most economic concepts.

MICRO-COMMUNITY. San Jose, Calif.: Classroom Dynamics Publishing Co. 20-40 players. Grades 10-12.

Participants face the problems of earning money, paying rent, going into business, inflation, and paying for welfare.

MR. BANKER. Minneapolis: Federal Reserve Bank. 2-4 hrs. 6-30 players. Grades 7-12.

This simulation acquaints students with money and the credit system of our nation, and how it affects and is affected by changes in economic conditions including business cycles.

THE MONEY GAME. San Raphael, Calif.: Leswing Communications. Up to 6 players. Grades 4-6.

Counting, arithmetic practice, and purchasing judgment are used in this card game about using money to purchase needs and wants.

MULBERRY. Minneapolis: Paul S. Amidon. 2-4 hrs. 20-35 players. Grades 7-9.

Participants play roles of citizens, officials, and professional planners in an urban renewal project.

NEW TOWN. Convent Station, N.J.: Harwell Associates. Up to 3 hrs. 10-20 players. Grades 10-12.

The development of a new town is the object of this game. Participants become involved in economic and political activities.

OLD SAN FRANCISCO GAME. San Raphael, Calif.: Leswing Communications. 6 players. Grades 6-10.

This is a board game. It teaches the concept of trading goods for services. Players learn that services are sometimes available on a limited basis only.

PANIC. Lakeside, Calif.: Interact. 2-3 hrs. Grades 7-12.

Players become economic pressure groups during the period from 1920 to 1940. Mock congressional committees try to solve the economic crisis.

PINK PEBBLES. Middleton, Conn.: Education Ventures. 12-36 players. Grades 5-12.

This is a board game designed to help players experience basic economic concepts, from subsistence to specialization to market fundamentals.

POWDERHORN. Culver City, Calif.: Social Studies School Service. 1-2 hrs. Grades 5-9.

The players are frontiersmen who swap rifles, traps, and pelts.

PRESSURE. Lakeside, Calif.: Interact. 2-4 hrs. 6-36 players. Grades 7-?.

The players in this game, citizens in a community beset by typical problems facing local governments such as zoning, try to cope with these problems.

PROMOTION. Chicago: Science Research Associates. 1-2 hrs. Grades 7-12.

Interacting developments of city growth and railroad expansion in nineteenth-century America are simulated in this game.

RECONSTRUCTION. Chicago: Science Research Associates. 1-2 hrs. Grades 7-12.

Relations between planters, freedmen, and self-sufficient farmers amid the economic disruption in the South after the Civil War are simulated.

ROARING CAMP. La Jolla, Calif.: Simile II. Grades 4-7.

The purpose of this simulation is to help students to learn about life in a mining community in the western United States in the nineteenth century. Mining, filing claims, measurement and description of land, writing checks, and balancing a checking account are activities involved.

STAR POWER. La Jolla, Calif.: Simile II. 1-3 hrs. Grades 7-adult.

A highly involving game about the world's unequal distribution of wealth and power in which individual players have a chance to progress from one economic level to another by acquiring wealth through trade. At one point, the rich are given the right to make the rules for the game and invariably act to keep them-selves in the privileged position. The postgame discussion should focus on the world's unequal distribution of wealth and power.

THE STOCK MARKET GAME. Baltimore: Avalon Hill. Grade 5-adult.

In this simulation of the stock market crash of 1929, players buy and sell stocks exactly as in real life. An investor's guide ex-plains the stock market in layman's terms.

STRIKE. Lakeside, Calif.: Interact. Grades 7-12.

This is a simulation of the problems of two nineteenth-century company towns, one with a steel mill, one with a coal mine. Students play roles of owners, managers, foremen, workers, immi-grants, black migrants, labor union organizers, Socialists, and an-archists.

STRIKE OR SETTLE. Cambridge, Mass.: Games Central. 24-36 players. Grades 7-12.

Labor and management bargain on wages, union security, senior-ity, vacations, and contract duration.

TRACTS. St. Paul, Minn.: Instructional Simulations. 2-4 hrs. 14-40 players. Grades 7-12.

Players become private land developers, public housing officials, industrialists, and city planners facing problems of what to do with land in the core city.

TRADING POST GAME.   San Raphael, Calif.:   Leswing Communications. 6 players.   Grades 4-6.

This board game teaches the concept of bartering.   Players must obtain needed goods by going through a trading post.

TRANSIT.   St. Paul, Minn.:   Instructional Simulations.   4-10 hrs.   20-40 players.   Grades 10-12.

Participants are local officials dealing with problems of mass transit, freeway development, parking, and safety.

Chapter 20
PERIODICALS

ACCI NEWSLETTER. American Council on Consumer Interests, 238 Stanley Hall, University of Missouri, Columbia, Mo. 65201. 9 times a year.

AMERICAN FEDERATIONIST. American Federation of Labor and Congress of Industrial Organizations, 815 Sixteenth Street, N.W., Washington, D.C. 20006. Monthly.

BALANCE SHEET. South-Western Publishing Co., 5101 Madison Road, Cincinnati, Ohio 45227. Monthly.

BUSINESS WEEK. McGraw-Hill, 330 West Forty-second Street, New York, N.Y. 10036. Weekly.

CHANGING TIMES. Kiplinger Washington Editors, 1729 H Street, N.W., Washington, D.C. 20006. Monthly.

CHILDHOOD EDUCATION. Association of Childhood Education International, 3615 Wisconsin Avenue, N.W., Washington, D.C. 20016. 6 times a year.

CLEARING HOUSE. Fairleigh Dickinson University, Rutherford, N.J. 07666. Monthly, September-May.

CONSUMER AFFAIRS JOURNAL. American Council on Consumer Interests, 238 Stanley Hall, University of Missouri, Columbia, Mo. 65201. Twice a year.

CONSUMER NEWS. Office of Consumer Affairs, Superintendent of Documents, U.S. Government Printing Office, Washington, D.C. 20402. Twice a month.

CONSUMER PRICE INDEX. U.S. Department of Labor, Bureau of Labor Statistics, Washington, D.C. 30212. Monthly.

Periodicals

CONSUMER REPORTS. Consumers Union, Orangeburg, N.Y. 10962. Monthly.

CURRENT EVENTS. American Education Publications, 1240 Fairwood Avenue, Columbus, Ohio 43216. Weekly during the school year.

EDUCATIONAL FORUM. Kappa Delta Pi, Box A, West Lafayette, Ind. 47906. Quarterly.

EDUCATIONAL LEADERSHIP. National Education Association, 1201 Sixteenth Street, N.W., Washington, D.C. 20036. Monthly.

EDUCATIONAL TECHNOLOGY. 456 Aylvan Avenue, Englewood Cliffs, N.J. 07632. Monthly.

ELEMENTARY SCHOOL JOURNAL. University of Chicago Press, 5750 Ellis Avenue, Chicago, Ill. 60838. Monthly.

EVERYBODY'S MONEY. Credit Union National Association, P.O. Box 431, Madison, Wis. 53701. Quarterly.

FDA CONSUMER. Superintendent of Documents, U.S. Government Printing Office, Washington, D.C. 20402. 10 issues annually.

FINANCE FACTS. National Consumer Finance Association, 1000 Sixteenth Street, N.W., Washington, D.C. 20034. Monthly.

FORTUNE. Putney Westerfield, Time-Life Building, New York, N.Y. 10021. Monthly.

HARVARD EDUCATION REVIEW. Graduate School of Education, Harvard University, Lawrence Hall, Cambridge, Mass. 02138. Quarterly.

HIGH SCHOOL JOURNAL. School of Education, University of North Carolina, Chapel Hill, N.C. 27514. 8 times a year.

INSTRUCTOR. Instructor Publications, Dansville, N.Y. 14437. Monthly.

ISSUES TODAY. Middletown, Conn. 06457. 18 issues a year.

JOURNAL OF ECONOMIC EDUCATION. Joint Council on Economic Education, 1212 Avenue of the Americas, New York, N.Y. 10036. Semiannual.

MONTHLY LABOR REVIEW. U.S. Department of Labor, U.S. Government Printing Office, Washington, D.C. 20402. Monthly.

NASSP BULLETIN. National Association of Secondary School Principals, 1201 Sixteenth Street, N.W., Washington, D.C. 20036.

NATION'S SCHOOLS. McGraw-Hill Publications, 1050 Merchandise Mart, Chicago, Ill. 61654. Monthly.

NEWSWEEK. Newsweek, 444 Madison Avenue, New York, N.Y. 10022. Weekly.

SOCIAL EDUCATION. National Association for Social Studies, 1211 16th Street, N.W., Washington, D.C. 20036. Monthly, 9 times a year.

TIME. Time, Time-Life Building, New York, N.Y. 10021. Weekly.

URBAN WORLD. American Education Publications, 1250 Fairwood Avenue, Columbus, Ohio 43216. 18 issues each school year.

U.S. NEWS AND WORLD REPORT. U.S. News and World Report, 2300 N Street, N.W., Washington, D.C. 20037. Weekly.

Chapter 21

PAMPHLET SERIES

American Economy Series. New York: McGraw-Hill.

American Primers. Chicago: University of Chicago Press.

American Problem Series. New York: Holt, Rinehart & Winston.

Area Studies in Economic Progress. Minneapolis: Curriculum Resources.

Basic Economic Series. Chicago: Industrial Relations Center, University of Chicago.

CASE Economic Literacy Series. Washington, D.C.: Council for the Advancement of Secondary Education.

Economic Forces in American History Series. Glenview, Ill.: Scott, Foresman.

Economic Issues in American Democracy. Bedford Hills, N.Y.: Teaching Resources Films in cooperation with Joint Council on Economic Education.

Economic Topics Series. Bedford Hills, N.Y.: Teaching Resources Films in cooperation with Joint Council on Economic Education.

Exploring Basic Economics Series. New York: Good Reading Rack Service.

Forces in American Growth Series. New York: Harcourt, Brace & World.

Headline Series. New York: Foreign Policy Association.

Money Management Library. Chicago: Household Finance Corp.

Primer of Economics Series. Iowa City: Bureau of Business and Economic Research.

Pamphlet Series

Public Affairs Pamphlets. New York: Public Affairs Committee.

Publications of the Bureau of Labor Statistics. Washington, D.C.: U.S. Department of Labor.

Series for Economic Education. Philadelphia: Federal Reserve Bank.

Studies in Economic Issues Series. Glenview, Ill.: Scott, Foresman.

U.S. Department of Commerce Series. Washington, D.C.: Government Printing Office.

Chapter 22

PUBLISHERS, PRODUCERS, AND SUPPLIERS

Addresses for materials produced by city school systems have not been included in this list because these materials, if available, can be purchased through ERIC.

Abelard-Schuman
Six West Fifty-seventh Street
New York, N.Y. 10019

Abingdon Press
201 Eighth Avenue
Nashville, Tenn. 37203

Academic Games Associates
Racine, Wis.

Academic Press
111 Fifth Avenue
New York, N.Y. 10003

Addison-Wesley
Reading, Mass.

AEVAC
500 Fifth Avenue
New York, N.Y. 10036

AIDS Audio Visual Instructional Devices
4720 Bell Boulevard
Bayside, N.Y. 11361

AIMS Institutional Media Service
P.O. Box 1010
Hollywood, Calif. 90028

Allied Educational Council
Galien, Mich.

Allyn & Bacon
470 Atlantic Avenue
Boston, Mass. 02210

American Association of School Administrators
1801 North Moore Street
Arlington, Va. 22209

American Bankers Association
1120 Connecticut Avenue, N.W.
Washington, D.C. 20036

American Book Co.
55 Fifth Avenue
New York, N.Y. 10003

American Education Publications
1230 Fairwood Avenue
Columbus, Ohio 43216

American Federation of Labor and Congress of Industrial Organizations
815 Sixteenth Street, N.W.
Washington, D.C. 20013

American Petroleum Institute
1271 Avenue of the Americas
New York, N.Y. 10020

American Stock Exchange
86 Trinity Place
New York, N.Y. 10006

Paul S. Amidon
5408 Chicago Avenue S.
Minneapolis, Minn. 55417

Appleton-Century-Crofts
440 Park Avenue
New York, N.Y. 10016

Argus Communications
7440 Natchez Avenue
Niles, Ill. 60648

Association Sterling Films
866 Third Avenue
New York, N.Y. 10022

Audio-Visual Center
Indiana University
Bloomington, Ind. 47401

Audio Visual Narrative Arts
Box 398
Pleasantville, N.Y. 10570

Avalon Hill Co.
5417 Harford Road
Baltimore, Md. 21214

AVI Associates
825 Third Avenue
New York, N.Y. 10022

Avid Corp.
10 Tripps Lane
East Providence, R.I. 02914

Bailey Film Associates
11559 Santa Monica Boulevard
Los Angeles, Calif. 90025

Barclays Bank
PanAm Building, Seventh Floor
200 Park Avenue
New York, N.Y. 10017

Arthur Barr Productions
P.O. Box 7C
Pasadena, Calif. 91104

Benefic Press
10300 West Roosevelt Road
Westchester, Ill. 60153

BFA Educational Media
2211 Michigan Avenue
Santa Monica, Calif. 90404

Board of Governors of the Federal
Reserve System
Washington, D.C. 20551

Stephen Bosustow Productions
11428 Santa Monica Boulevard
West Los Angeles, Calif. 90025

Brookings Institute
1775 Massachusetts Avenue, N.W.
Washington, D.C. 20036

Bruce Publishing Co.
400 North Broadway
Milwaukee, Wis. 53201

Bureau of Business and Economic Research
State University of Iowa
College of Business Administration
Iowa City, Iowa 52240

Charles Cahill and Associates
(See AIMS Instructional Media Service)

Cambridge University Press
32 East Fifty-seventh Street
New York, N.Y. 10022

Canfield Press
850 Montgomery Street
San Francisco, Calif. 94133

Carousel Films
1501 Broadway
New York, N.Y. 10036

Center for Economic Education
State University College
Oneonta, N.Y. 13820

Center for Information on America
Washington, Conn. 06793

Centron Educational Films
1621 West Ninth Street
Lawrence, Kans. 66044

Chamber of Commerce of the United
States of America
1615 H Street, N.W.
Washington, D.C. 20006

Chandler Publishing Co.
124 Spear Street
San Francisco, Calif. 94105

Changing Times
1729 H Street, N.W.
Washington, D.C. 20006

Channing Bete Co.
Greenfield, Mass. 01301

Children's Press
1224 West Van Buren
Chicago, Ill. 60607

Chilton Book Co.
401 Walnut Street
Philadelphia, Pa. 19106

Churchill-Wexler Productions Films
662 North Robertson Boulevard
Los Angeles, Calif. 90069

Civic Education Service
1725 K Street, N.W., Suite 1009
Washington, D.C. 20006

Classroom Dynamics Publishing Co.
231 O'Connor Drive
San Jose, Calif. 95128

Collier Books
688 Third Avenue
New York, N.Y. 10022

Collier-Macmillan
Riverside, N.J. 08075

Columbia Broadcasting System
485 Madison Avenue
New York, N.Y. 10022

Committee for Economic Development
477 Madison Avenue
New York, N.Y. 10022

Conference on Economic Progress
1001 Connecticut Avenue, N.W.
Washington, D.C. 20036

Congressional Quarterly Service
1735 K Street, N.W.
Washington, D.C. 20006

Consumer's Union of the U.S.A.
Mt. Vernon, N.Y. 10550

David Cook Publishing Co.
850 North Grove Avenue
Elgin, Ill. 60120

Coronet Instructional Films
65 East South Water Street
Chicago, Ill. 60601

Council for the Advancement of
Secondary Education
1201 Sixteenth Street, N.W.
Washington, D.C. 20036

Coward McCann & Geoghegan
200 Madison Avenue
New York, N.Y. 10016

Creative Educational Society
515 North Front Street
Mankato, Minn. 56001

Creative Studies
P.O. Box 830
7404 Belvan Avenue
San Bernardino, Calif. 92402

Credit Union National Association
Box 431
Madison, Wis. 53701

Publishers, Producers, Suppliers

Criterion Books
Six West Fifty-seventh Street
New York, N.Y. 10019

Thomas Y. Crowell Co.
201 Park Avenue
New York, N.Y. 10002

Crowell-Collier Educational Corp.
866 Third Avenue
New York, N.Y. 10022

Crown Publishers
419 Park Avenue S.
New York, N.Y. 10016

Current Affairs Films
24 Danbury Road
Wilton, Conn. 06897

Curriculum Resources
1515 West Lake Street
Minneapolis, Minn. 55401

Damon Educational Division
80 Eilson Way
Westwood, Mass. 02090

John Day Co.
257 Park Avenue S.
New York, N.Y. 10010

Delacorte Press Books
750 Third Avenue
New York, N.Y. 10017

Denoyer-Geppert Audio Visuals
5235 Ravenswood Avenue
Chicago, Ill. 60640

Dodd, Mead & Co.
79 Madison Avenue
New York, N.Y. 10016

Doubleday & Company
Garden City, N.Y. 11530

Doubleday Multimedia
Box 11607
1371 Reynolds Avenue
Santa Ana, Calif. 92705

Dow Jones Book Co.
Box 300
Princeton, N.J. 08540

E.P. Dutton & Company
201 Park Avenue S.
New York, N.Y. 10003

Dynamic Design Industries
1433 North Central Park
Anaheim, Calif. 92802

Ealing Corp.
2225 Massachusetts Avenue
Cambridge, Mass. 02140

Education Ventures
209 Court Street
Middleton, Conn. 06457

Educational Activities
P.O. Box 392
Freeport, N.Y. 11520

Educational Audio Visual
Pleasantville, N.Y. 10570

Educational Dimensions Corp.
Box 126
Stamford, Conn. 06904

Educational Media Services
211 East Forty-third Street
New York, N.Y. 10017

Educational Projections Corp.
3070 Lake Terrace
Glenview, Ill. 60025

Herbert M. Elkins Co.
10031 Commerce Avenue
Tujunga, Calif. 91042

Encyclopaedia Britannica Films
425 North Michigan Avenue
Chicago, Ill. 60611

ERIC Document Reproductions
ERIC Document Reproduction Service
Post Office Drawer 0
Bethesda, Md. 20014

ERS Audio Visual Division
Educational Reading Service
320 Route 17
Mahwah, N.J. 07430

Eye Gate House
146 Archer Avenue
Jamaica, N.Y. 11436

Fairchild Visual Department PV
Seven East Twelfth Street
New York, N.Y. 10003

Farm Credit Administration
South Agriculture Building
Washington, D.C. 20578

Federal Reserve Bank of Chicago
Research Department
P.O. Box 834
Chicago, Ill. 60690

Federal Reserve Bank of Kansas City
Research Department
Kansas City, Mo. 64406

Federal Reserve Bank of Minneapolis
250 Marquette Avenue
Minneapolis, Minn. 35480

Federal Reserve Bank of New York
Public Information Department
33 Liberty Street
New York, N.Y. 10045

Federal Reserve Bank of Philadelphia
Public Services Department
Philadelphia, Pa. 19101

Federal Reserve Bank of Richmond
Richmond, Va. 23213

Federal Reserve Bank of San Francisco
400 Sansome Street
San Francisco, Calif. 94120

Fideler Publishing Co.
31 Ottawa N.W.
Grand Rapids, Mich. 49502

Field Educational Publications
2400 Hanover Streer
Palo Alto, Calif. 94304

Field Enterprises Educational Corp.
Merchandise Mart Plaza
Chicago, Ill. 60654

Film Associates
1014 Santa Monica Boulevard
Los Angeles, Calif. 90025

Films
1144 Wilmette Avenue
Wilmette, Ill. 60091

Filmstrip House
432 Park Avenue S.
New York, N.Y. 10016

First National Bank of Chicago
Chicago, Ill. 60607

First National City Bank
399 Park Avenue
New York, N.Y. 10022

Follett Educational Corp.
1010 West Washington Boulevard
Chicago, Ill. 60607

Foreign Policy Association
345 West Forty-sixth Street
New York, N.Y. 10017

Free Press of Glencoe
60 Fifth Avenue
New York, N.Y. 10022

Games Central
55 Wheeler Street
Cambridge, Mass. 12138

General Motors Corp.
Detroit, Mich. 48202

Georgia Environmental Curriculum
Project
University of Georgia
Athens, Ga. 30601

Ginn & Co.
Statler Office Building
Boston, Mass. 02117

Globe Publishing Co.
175 Fifth Avenue
New York, N.Y. 10010

Good Reading Rack Service
505 Eighth Avenue
New York, N.Y. 10018

Government Printing Office
Superintendent of Documents
Washington, D.C. 20402

Graphic Research
557 West Douglas Street
Wichita, Kans. 67201

Grolier Educational Corp.
575 Lexington Avenue
New York, N.Y. 10022

Grossman Publications
44 West Fifty-sixth Street
New York, N.Y. 10019

Guidance Associates
23 Washington Avenue
Pleasantville, N.Y. 10570

Handel Film Corp.
8730 Sunset Boulevard
West Hollywood, Calif. 90069

Harcourt Brace Jovanovich
757 Third Avenue
New York, N.Y. 10017

Harper & Row Publishing Co.
49 East Thirty-third Street
New York, N.Y. 10016

Harper's Magazine Press
Two Park Avenue
New York, N.Y. 10016

Harwell Associates
Box 95
Convent Station, N.J. 07961

Hawthorn Books
70 Fifth Avenue
New York, N.Y. 10011

D.C. Heath & Co.
285 Columbus Avenue
Boston, Mass. 02138

Holt, Rinehart & Winston
383 Madison Avenue
New York, N.Y. 10017

Houghton Mifflin Co.
Education Division
110 Tremont Street
Boston, Mass. 02107

Household Finance Corp.
Money Management Institute
Prudential Plaza
Chicago, Ill. 60601

Hudson Photographic Industries
Educational Products Division
Two South Buckholt Street
Irvington-on-Hudson, N.Y. 10533

Imperial Film Co.
Educational Development Corp.
202 Lake Miriam Drive
Lakeland, Fla. 33801

Indiana University
Audio Visual Center
Bloomington, Ind. 47401

Industrial Relations Center
University of Chicago
1225 East Sixtieth Street
Chicago, Ill. 60637

Institute of Industrial Relations
University of California
Los Angeles, Calif. 90024

Institute of Life Insurance
Health Insurance Institute
277 Park Avenue
New York, N.Y. 10017

Instructional Materials Laboratory
Ohio State University
Columbus, Ohio 43216

Instructional Simulations
2147 University Avenue
St. Paul, Minn. 55104

Instructor Publishers
P.O. Box 6108
Duluth, Minn. 55806

Interact
Box 262
Lakeside, Calif. 92040

International Communication Films
1371 Reynolds Avenue
Santa Ana, Calif. 92705

International Film Bureau
332 South Michigan Avenue
Chicago, Ill. 60614

Interstate
19-27 North Jackson Street
Danville, Ill. 61832

Intext Educational Publishers
Oak Street and Pawnee Avenue
Scranton, Pa. 18515

Invest in America Council
121 South Broad Street
Philadelphia, Pa. 19107

Richard D. Irwin Co.
1818 Ridge Road
Homewood, Ill. 60430

Jam Handy Organization
2843 East Grand Boulevard
Detroit, Mich. 48233

Johns Hopkins Press for Resources
for the Future
1755 Massachusetts Avenue, N.W.
Washington, D.C. 20036

Joint Council for Economic Education
1212 Avenue of the Americas
New York, N.Y. 10036

King Screen Productions
320 Aurora Avenue N.
Seattle, Wash. 98109

Kiplinger Washington Editors
Editors Park, Md.

Alfred A. Knopf
201 East Fifieth Street
New York, N.Y. 10022

Robert E. Krieger Publishing Co.
P.O. Box 542
Huntington, N.Y. 11743

Laidlaw Brothers
River Forest, Ill. 60305

League of Women Voters of the United
States
1026 Seventeenth Street
Washington, D.C. 20006

Learning Corporation of America
711 Fifth Avenue
New York, N.Y. 10022

Learning Tree Filmstrips
Thorne Films
934 Pearl Street, Suite F
P.O. Box 1590
Boulder, Colo. 80302

Lerner Publications Co.
241 First Avenue
Minneapolis, Minn. 55401

Lippincott Co.
East Washington Square
Philadelphia, Pa. 19105

Listening Library
One Park Avenue
Old Greenwich, Conn. 06870

Little, Brown and Co.
34 Beacon Street
Boston, Mass. 02106

Littlefield Adam and Co.
81 Adams Drive
Totowa, N.J. 07512

Lothrop, Lee & Shepard Co.
105 Madison Avenue
New York, N.Y. 10016

McGraw-Hill
1221 Avenue of the Americas
New York, N.Y. 10020

Machinery and Allied Products Institute
and Council for Technological
Advancement
1200 Eighteenth Street, N.W.
Washington, D.C. 20036

David McKay Co.
750 Third Avenue
New York, N.Y. 10036

Macmillan Co.
Riverside, N.J. 08075

Harold Mantell
505 Eighth Avenue
New York, N.Y. 10018

Media Materials
Department MC one
409 West Cold Spring Lane
Baltimore, Md. 21210

Charles E. Merrill Publishing Co.
1300 Alum Creek Drive
Columbus, Ohio 43216

Julian Messner
One West Thirty-ninth Street
New York, N.Y. 10016

Miller Book Co.
409 Pasqual Drive
Alhambra, Calif. 91801

Miller Brody Productions
342 Madison Avenue
New York, N.Y. 10017

Modern Learning Aids
1212 Avenue of the Americas
New York, N.Y. 10036

Modern Talking Picture Service
1212 Avenue of the Americas
New York, N.Y. 10036

William Morrow & Co.
105 Madison Avenue
New York, N.Y. 10016

Multi Media Productions
Box 5097
Stanford, Calif. 94305

National Association of Manufacturers
277 Park Avenue
New York, N.Y. 10017

National Consumer Finance Association
701 Solar Building
1000 Sixteenth Street, N.W.
Washington, D.C. 20036

National Council for the Social Studies
National Education Association
1201 Sixteenth Street, N.W.
Washington, D.C. 20036

National Council of Churches of Christ
in the U.S.A.
475 Riverside Drive
New York, N.Y. 10027

National Educational Program
900 East Center Street
Searcy, Ariz. 72143

National Educational Television
Audio Visual Center Indiana University
Bloomington, Ind. 47401

National Education Association
1201 Sixteenth Street
Washington, D.C. 20036

National Foundation for Consumer Credit
1411 K Street, N.W.
Washington, D.C. 20005

National Planning Association
1606 New Hampshire Avenue, N.W.
Washington, D.C. 20009

Natural History Press
501 Franklin Avenue
Garden City, N.Y. 11530

New American Library
120 Woodbine Street
Bergenfield, N.J. 07621

New York Stock Exchange
11 Wall Street
New York, N.Y. 10036

New York Times Co.
229 West Forty-third Street
New York, N.Y. 10036

Noble and Noble Publishers
750 Third Avenue
New York, N.Y. 10017

W.W. Norton and Co.
55 Fifth Avenue
New York, N.Y. 10003

Oceana Publications
Dobbs Ferry, N.Y. 10522

Ohio State University
Instructional Materials Laboratory
1885 Neil Avenue
Columbus, Ohio 43210

Oxfam-America
474 Center Street
Newton, Mass. 02158

Pantheon Books
437 Madison Avenue
New York, N.Y. 10016

Parents' Magazine Press
52 Vanderbilt Avenue
New York, N.Y. 10017

Pathescope Educational Films
71 Weyman Avenue
New Rochelle, N.Y. 10802

Pathways of Sound
102 Mt. Auburn Street
Cambridge, Mass. 02138

Pegasus Films
45 West Thirty-eighth Street
New York, N.Y. 10018

Penguin Books
330 Lipped Mill Road
Baltimore, Md. 21211

Edward Perry
Eight Surry Road
Norwood, Mass. 02062

Pitman Publishing Corp.
Two East Forty-third Street
New York, N.Y. 10017

Population Reference Bureau
1755 Massachusetts Avenue, N.W.
Washington, D.C. 20036

Praeger Publishers
111 Fourth Avenue
New York, N.Y. 10003

Prentice-Hall
Englewood Cliffs, N.J. 07632

Public Affairs Committee
381 Park Avenue S.
New York, N.Y. 10016

Public Affairs Press
2153 Florida Avenue, N.W.
Washington, D.C. 20036

George P. Putnam & Sons
22 Madison Avenue
New York, N.Y. 10016

Pyramid Films
Box 1048
Santa Monica, Calif. 90406

Q-ED Productions
P.O. Box 1608
Burbank, Calif. 91505

Rand McNally & Co.
Box 7600
Chicago, Ill. 60680

Random House
457 Madison Avenue
New York, N.Y. 10022

Random House Educational Media
Department 3-2
201 East Fiftieth Street
New York, N.Y. 10022

Riley and Lee
114 West Illinois Street
Chicago, Ill. 60610

Ronald Press Co.
79 Madison Avenue
New York, N.Y. 10016

Sage Publishing Co.
275 South Beverly Drive
Beverly Hills, Calif. 90212

Schenkman Publishing Co.
Three Revere Street
Cambridge, Mass. 02138

Schloat Productions
150 White Plains Road
Tarrytown, N.Y. 10591

Scholastic Book Services
904 Sylvan Avenue
Englewood Cliffs, N.J. 07632

Science Research Associates
259 East Erie Street
Chicago, Ill. 60611

Scott Education Division
235 Lower Westfield Road
Holyoke, Mass. 01040

Scott, Foresman & Co.
1900 East Lake Avenue
Glenview, Ill. 60025

Seabury Press
815 Second Avenue
New York, N.Y. 10017

Simile II
Box 1023
1150 Silverado
La Jolla, Calif. 92137

Simon & Schuster
630 Fifth Avenue
New York, N.Y. 10020

Singer/SVE
Society for Visual Education
1345 Diversey Parkway
Chicago, Ill. 61614

South-Western Publishing Co.
5101 Madison Road
Cincinnati, Ohio 45227

Sterling Educational Films
241 East Thirty-fourth Street
New York, N.Y. 10016

Superintendent of Documents
Government Printing Office
Washington, D.C. 20402

John Sutherland Productions
8425 West Third Street
Los Angeles, Calif. 90048

Teaching Resources Films
Station Plaza
Bedford Hills, N.Y. 10507

Tweedy Transparencies
208 Hollywood Avenue
East Orange, N.J. 07018

United Nations Television
United Nations
New York, N.Y. 10017

Publishers, Producers, Suppliers

U.S. Bureau of the Census
U.S. Department of Commerce
Washington, D.C. 20230

U.S. Department of Commerce
Office of Business Economics
Washington, D.C. 20402

U.S. Department of Labor
Bureau of Labor Statistics
Washington, D.C. 20212

University of Chicago Press
5750 Ellis Avenue
Chicago, Ill. 60637

Urban Media Materials
212 Mineola Avenue
Roslyn Heights, N.Y. 11577

Valient I M C
237 Washington Avenue
Hackensack, N.J. 07602

Van Nostrand Co.
120 Alexander Street
Princeton, N.J. 08540

VMI Visual Materials
2549 Middlefield Road
Redwood City, Calif. 94063

Wadsworth Publishing Co.
Ten David Drive
Belmont, Calif. 94002

Henry Z. Walck
750 Third Avenue
New York, N.Y. 10017

Ward's Natural Science Establishment
P.O. Box 1712
Rochester, N.Y. 14603

Washington Tapes
5540 Connecticut Avenue N.W.
Washington, D.C. 20015

Franklin Watts
575 Lexington Avenue
New York, N.Y. 10022

Western Publishing Co.
850 Third Avenue
New York, N.Y. 10022

Westinghouse Learning Press
100 Park Avenue
New York, N.Y. 10017

Albert Whitmena & Co.
560 West Lake Street
Chicago, Ill. 60606

John Wiley & Sons
605 Third Avenue
New York, N.Y. 10016

H.W. Wilson Co.
950 University Avenue
Bronx, N.Y. 10452

H. Wilson Corp.
555 West Taft Drive
South Holland, Ill. 60473

World Bank
1818 H Street, N.W.
Washington, D.C. 20433

World Publishing Co.
2231 West 110th Street
Cleveland, Ohio 44102

Wyden, Peter H.
750 Third Avenue
New York, N.Y. 10017

Yale University Press
92 A Yale Station
New Haven, Conn. 06511

AUTHOR INDEX

Included in this index are all authors, editors, compilers, and contributors whose works are cited in this bibliography. Those who have contributed in any way to audiovisual works cited in the text are also included. This index is alphabetized letter by letter. References are to page numbers.

A

Abbott, Lawrence 99
Aceti, John 200
Alexander, Albert 79, 99
Alvarez, Joseph 71
American Bankers Association, Banking Education Committee 145, 195
American Federationist 41
American Federation of Labor and Congress of Industrial Organizations 117, 131
Ames, Gerald 1
Ammer, Dean S. 99
Anderson, Randall 195
Anderson, Sherwood 108
Andreano, Ralph [L.] 7, 195
Arbital, Samuel 183
Arnold, Oren 145
Ashell, Bernard 41
Attiyeh, Richard 99
Axon, Gordon V. 145

B

Babian, Haig 146
Bach, George L. 100
Bahr, Gladys 196
Barach, Arnold B. 61, 117

Barbash, Jack 131
Bardach, John 69
Barr, Jene 146
Barron, J.F. 79
Bell, Carolyn Shaw 41
Berger, Gilda 131
Berkowitz, Monroe 117
Berle, Adolf A. 61
Bernstein, Peter L. 37, 94, 146
Birch, David L. 41
Bish, Robert L. 41
Bixby, William 69
Black, Robert P. 146, 152
Blaustein, Arthur 42
Bloom, Clark C. 61
Boardman, Fon W. 107
Bohlman, E.M. 23
Bohlman, H.W. 23
Boocock, Sarane S. 196
Boucher, Bertrand P. 131
Breetveld, Jim 42
Brindze, Ruth 146
Brown, Douglas M. 42
Brown, James E. 100
Brown, Lester 118
Buckingham, Walter 7
Buehr, Walter 7, 146
Bullock, Paul 7, 132
Burke, William 69

227

Author Index

Burns, Scott 147

C

Cahn, Rhoda 132
Cahn, William 132
Calderwood, James D. 100, 118, 196
Calhoun, Donald W. 100
Campbell, Elizabeth 147
Cerami, Charles A. 119
Chalmers, James A. 100
Chamberlain, John 8
Chamber of Commerce of the United
  States of America 8, 42, 61, 79,
  93, 119, 147
Chandler, Alfred D., Jr. 8
Chang, Perry P. 119
Cheyney, William J. 147
Chilton, Shirley 8, 9, 132
Chinitz, Benjamin 42
Cipolla, Carlo M. 107
Clark, Jere 197
Cobb, Vicki 147
Cochran, Thomas C. 9
Cochrane, Willard W. 1
Colby, Carroll B. 132
Coles, Robert 43
Colm, Gerhard 79
Committee for Economic Development
  1, 37, 43, 44, 93, 119-20, 196
Committee for Measurement of Economic
  Understanding of the Joint Council
  on Economic Education 193
Congressional Quarterly Service 94
Cooke, David C. 147
Council for the Advancement of Secon-
  dary Education 62
Council of Economic Advisers 94
Credit Unions National Association 24

D

Dale, Edwin L., Jr. 81
Dalton, George 120
Daugherty, Marion 37, 101
Davies, Delwyn 69
Davis, Daniel S. 132
Davis, Kenneth S. 44
Davis, Lance E. 107
Davison, Donald G. 193

Dawson, George [G.] 166, 197,
  198
DeCamp, Catherine Crook 24
Developmental Economic Education
  Program (DEEP) 197
Diebold, John 14
Doherty, Robert E. 132
Dorfman, Robert 9
Douglas, Paul H. 80
Dowd, Douglas F. 107
Downs, Anthony 44
Drucker, Peter 11
Duesenberry, James S. 148
Duffy, Helene 51
Dumont, Rene 2
Dutton, William S. 9

E

Ehrlich, Paul 44
Ellis, Harry B. 120
Elting, Mary 108
Engle, Elizabeth W. 9
ERIC (Educational Resources Informa-
  tion Center) Clearing House for
  Social Studies/Social Science
  Education 197

F

Fanning, Leonard M. 133
Federal Reserve Bank of Chicago 148
Federal Reserve Bank of Minneapolis
  120, 148
Federal Reserve Bank of New York
  148
Federal Reserve Bank of Philadelphia
  9, 38, 45, 94, 149
Federal Reserve Bank of Richmond
  149
Federal Reserve Bank of San Francisco
  120
Feeney, Georgiana 45
Fels, Rendigs 45
Fenton, D.X. 70
Fenton, Edwin 182
Fielder, William 45
First National Bank of Chicago 121
Fisher, Tadd 46
Floherty, John J. 149

Author Index

Author Index

V

Venn, Grant 85
Victor, R.F. 112

W

Waage, Thomas O. 153
Wade, William W. 154
Wagner, Lewis E. 10, 13, 39, 85
Wakin, Edward 137
Ward, Barbara 125
Warmke, Roman F. 27
Wass, Philmore 112
Weiner, Sandra 137
Weiss, Leonard W. 13
Weitzman, David 104
Welfing, Weldon 154

Werstein, Irving 112, 137
Whittlesey, Charles 154
Wilcox, Clair 125
Winn, Marie 137, 154
Wolf, Harold A. 100
Woock, Roger R. 42
World Bank 52
Wyler, Rose 1

Y

Youngers, John C. 200

Z

Zevin, Jack 191
Zimmerman, Erich W. 72

TITLE INDEX

Index entries refer to page numbers. The titles listed in the index are alpha-betized letter by letter and in some cases the titles have been shortened. Audiovisual materials are listed in a separate index.

A

ABA Film Guide 195
Accent: The World of Work 173
Adam Smith 111
Adjustments to Depression and War, 1930-45 111
Adventure in Big Business 9
Adventures of Primero Dinero 183
Advertising: Ancient Market Place to Television 24
Affluent Society, The 62
After the Crash 111
Age of the Economist, The 108
All Aboard 108
Alliance Born of Danger 119
America and the World Economy 121
American Battle for Abundance, the Story of Mass Production 108
American Capitalism: An Introduction 81
American Capitalism: Its Promise and Accomplishment 108
American Capitalism: The Concept of Countervailing Power 62
American Cities 109
American Economic Life 83
American Economic Republic, The 61
American Economy, The 101

American Economy: Analysis, Issues and Principles 103
American Labor Today 135
American Labor Unions 135
America's Place in the World Economy 62
Assisting Development in Low-Income Countries 119
Audiovisual Materials for Teaching Economics 195
Automation 9
Automation: Implications for the Future 11
Automation: Its Impact on Business and People 7
Automation, Capital Equipment and Economic Progress 7

B

Balance of Payments Crisis 117
BAM. Social Studies Supplement 161
Barter, Bills and Banks 153
Basic Economic Principles 103
Basic Economics (Appleton-Century-Crofts) 104
Basic Economics (Doubleday) 101
Basic Economics: Theory and Cases 99
Basic History of American Business 9

233

Title Index

E

Early Childhood Consumer Education 164
Earning Money 136
Eco-Catastrophe 44
Economic Analysis and Policy 47
Economic Development 38, 80
Economic Development and Social Change 120
Economic Development of Central America 120
Economic Education: A Guide to New York Schools, Grades K-11 164
Economic Education: A Supplement to the Social Studies, K-2d Grade 164-65
Economic Education: A Supplement to the Social Studies, 3rd and 4th Grade 165
Economic Education: Economic Expansion of the U.S. since 1865, a Supplement to Grade 11 U.S. History 176
Economic Education: The Industrial Revolution, a Supplement for Grade 10, World History 176
Economic Education, a Supplement for the Secondary Schools 176
Economic Education Experiences of Enterprising Teachers 197
Economic Education for Arkansas Elementary Schools, Teaching Guide, Grades 1-6 165
Economic Education for Washington Public Schools, Grades 7, 8, 9 177
Economic Education for Washington Schools 177
Economic Education for Washington Schools, Kindergarten through Grade Six 165
Economic Education in the Schools 199
Economic Education Supplements, Grades 3, 4, 5, and 6 165
Economic Effects of Education 177
Economic Future of City and Suburb, The 41

Economic Growth, Evolution or Revolution 123
Economic Growth in the United States 37
Economic Growth in the United States --Its History, Problems and Prospects 39
Economic Growth of the United States 1790-1860 38
Economic History of World Population, The 107
Economic Influences in World Affairs 177
Economic Literacy for Americans 196
Economic Man 178
Economic Principles 100
Economic Principles and Urban Problems 41
Economic Problem, The 102
Economic Process, The 101
Economic Process, The: Inquiry and Challenge 81
Economic Report of the President 94
Economics (Franklin Watts) 79
Economics (Harper & Row) 102
Economics: An Analytical Approach 101
Economics--An Introduction to Analysis and Policy 100
Economics: An Introductory Analysis 104
Economics: An Introductory View 84
Economics: Choice-Making 178
Economics: Ideas and Men 107
Economics: Modular Learning Unit 178
Economics: Principles and Applications 102
Economics: Principles and Practices 100
Economics: Principles, Problems and Policies 103
Economics: Program and Resources for Instruction 179
Economics: Student Materials and Teacher's Guide 179
Economics and Our Community 166
Economics and the Consumer 25, 199
Economics and the Modern World 99

Title Index

Title Index

Title Index

AUDIOVISUALS INDEX

This index includes films, filmstrips, pictures, kits, cassettes, charts, tapes, games and simulations. For those who have contributed to this index, see the author index. In some cases the titles have been shortened. The references are to page numbers.

Audiovisuals Index

SUBJECT INDEX

This index is alphabetized letter by letter. Underlined page numbers refer to main areas within that subject.

A

Abortion, economics and 83
Absenteeism (labor) 144
Accounting 14, 150
Advertising
  consumer and 24, 27, 28, 31,
    32, 35, 179
  false 29, 30, 33
  need for regulation of 29
  prices and 15
  value of 30
Aerospace
  budget cuts in programs for 101
  industries 69
Africa
  agriculture in 3
  economy of 123-24, 125, 127,
    182
  labor in 140-41
  urbanization in 190
Aged, poverty of 57
Agricultural cooperatives 3
Agricultural laborers. See Migrant
    laborers; Tenant farmers
Agriculture 1-6, 189
  audiovisual materials about 3-6
  in economic growth 176
  free enterprise and 11
  history of 107, 110, 114

industrialization and urbanization
    and 3, 6
New Deal and 108
policies for 13
politics in 6
poverty and 49
reform in 120
role of government in 1-2
technical assistance in 2, 42
technology in 4, 5, 6, 13, 47
in West Africa 3
See also Animal husbandry; Farmers;
    Fertilizers and manures; Food
    production; Plant breeding;
    types of farming and products
Air pollution. See Pollution and pol-
    lution control
Alaska
  agriculture in 3
  labor in 137
Alliance for Progress 122
Allocation of resources and goods 12,
    44, 62, 67, 82, 85-86, 175
  in China 65
  commerce and 129
  in the Common Market 127
  games and simulations concerning
    201
Allowances 35
American Federation of Labor 41

Subject Index

Japanese 18
organization of 14, 66, 89, 101,
102
role of in the economy 182
Russian 129
in the Southern states 6
specialization in 21, 54, 86, 88,
128, 139, 140, 141, 162,
167, 175, 176, 178, 183
urban improvement programs and
56
See also Assembly-line methods;
Big business; Cartels; Industrial Revolution; Mass production; Monopolies; Product
development; Production; Research, industrial; Standardization of parts; names of
industries
Business cycles 10, 14, 16, 40, 83,
86, 87, 91, 101, 104, 115
games and simulations concerning
204
Business ethics 12
Business forecasting 9

C

California, economy of 69
Canals 114
Capital 67, 81, 84, 85, 91, 148,
149-50
accumulation of 159
allocation of 82
in economic growth 116
employment and 7
flow of 124, 127
formation of 40, 123, 159, 176
movement of out of agriculture 1
savings and 21
Capital goods 162
Capital investments
poverty and 49
productivity of 7
Capitalism 62, 63, 64, 65, 66, 81-
82, 104, 167
foundations of 40
history of 107, 108
See also Free enterprise; Market
economy; United States,
economy of

Carnegie, Andrew 134
Cartels 13. See also Monopolies
Cattle raising. See Animal husbandry;
Livestock farming
Central American Common Market 120
Checks and check writing 152-53
Chicanos. See Mexican Americans
Child labor 109, 132
Children, of migrant laborers 109,
133
Chile, commerce of 126
China
compared with the Indian economy
80
economic development in 119
economy of 125, 182
political change in 190
trade with 120-21, 123
See also Communism, economics of
Cities. See Ghettoes; Urban areas
City life
compared to suburban life 56
interrelationships with farm life 4
See also Ghettoes; Urban areas
City planning. See Urban renewal and
planning
Civil rights, relationship to poverty 46
Civil War, industrial growth and 107.
See also Reconstruction, games
and simulations concerning
Clark, William A. 111
Climate in agriculture 4
food types and 5
Clothing
environmental conditions and 75
purchasing of 28, 32, 35, 174, 189
Clothing industry 3, 15, 16, 17, 18
Coinage. See Money
Collective bargaining 131, 135, 136,
139
games and simulations concerning
202, 206
Colonization
impact on less developed areas 120
as a stimulant to trade 115
Commerce 2-3, 15, 58, 86, 88, 102,
104, 118, 119, 120, 124, 128,
129-30, 132, 161, 168, 177,
178, 181, 185

Subject Index

Subject Index

Food 47
distribution and preservation of 51
environmental conditions and 75
government distribution of 52
new products 47
population and 48, 50, 51, 54, 55
purchasing of 26, 28, 32, 34, 174, 189
shortages of 56, 76, 118
storage of 2
See also Hunger; Nutrition
Food for Peace Act 2
Food production 1-6, 24
audiovisual materials about 3-6, 15, 17
games and simulations concerning 201
in India 129, 168
in Southeast Asia 5
technical assistance in 42
See also Ocean resources
Ford, Henry 134
Foreign aid 118, 122, 123, 129
games and simulations concerning 202
See also Economic assistance; Military assistance; Technical assistance
Foreign exchange 88, 100
Foreign investment. See Investment, foreign
Forests, conservation of 71, 73, 75, 76. See also Lumber Industry
Fraud, consumer 26, 28, 29, 30, 174. See also Counterfeits and counterfeiting
Free enterprise 9, 11, 79, 81-82, 90, 162, 186-87
under communism 20
profit in 10
role of consumer in 26
See also Capitalism; Market economy
Free silver movement 6
Free trade and protection 123, 126, 128, 130
Fruit and vegetable growing 3, 5, 6
in Southeast Asia 5

wholesale trade 20
Fuel. See Power resources
Fulton, Robert 133

G

Games and simulations, economic. See Economic education, games and simulations concerning
Garment industry. See Clothing industry
Gas, natural. See Power resources
Geography, economic 40, 66, 75, 87, 177-78
of Japan 67, 121
of Russia 162
Geography, political 14
Geography, urban 109
Ghettoes 41, 46, 54-55
games and simulations concerning 201, 203
See also Blacks; Poor; Urban areas
Global village concept 54
Gold 121, 128, 146, 147
Government 93-97, 101, 177, 182, 190
in agricultural policy 1-2, 6
as an ally of industry 63
audiovisual aids about 96-97
automation and 11
bank regulation and 145
in capitalistic economies 11, 63, 65, 66, 67, 87, 90
commerce and 128
consumer protection and 23, 24, 25, 29
cost of 102
credit regulation and 23
economic growth and 176
environmental quality and 46
as a foil to economic power 62
food programs of 52
goods and services of 50, 54, 58, 88, 89, 90, 91, 184
in income distribution 16
in industrial policy 16
insurance regulation and 23
manpower training by the 44
monopolies and 12
price competition and 64

Subject Index

Subject Index

Public service employment. See Employment, in public service
Public welfare. See Social services
Publishers and publishing
  of economic material 215-25
  vanity 26
Puerto-Ricans, education of 43
Purchasing
  inflation and 51
  by retailers 19
Purchasing power 59, 147
  wages and 8

Q

Quacks and Quackery. See Medical
  services, fraud in

R

Race
  attitudes of agricultural laborers on
    6
  economics of 104
  in employment exclusion 48
Railroads 18, 108
  in the economic system 66
  games and simulations concerning
    205
Randolph, A. Philip 132
Raw materials. See Natural resources
Real estate
  fraud in 26
  as an investment 23
Reconstruction, games and simulations
  concerning 205-6
Recreation 58, 73, 174, 182
  development of resources for 3
Recycling operations 35
Refrigeration 15
Research, industrial 11, 13, 91
  in economic growth and development 115, 116
  See also Automation; Technology
Retailers, purchasing by 19
Revenue-sharing 94
Rice growing 5
Riots, costs of 101
Roads and highways
  effect of on farm life 4

rise of toll 114
Robert, Nicholas-Louis 133
Roosevelt, Franklin Delano. See New
  Deal
Russia
  economy of 79, 124, 125, 127,
    129, 162, 173, 177, 182, 186
  influence in Arab countries 127
  relations with the U.S. 118
  trade with 123
  See also Communism, economics of

S

Salary. See Wages
Salesman, fraudulent 26
Saving and investment 23, 25, 30, 31,
    32, 33, 39, 63, 86, 87, 90,
    145, 146, 148, 150, 153, 157,
    159, 174, 187, 188, 189, 190
  capital funds and 21
  economic growth and 176, 185
  economic influence on 90
  fraud in 26
  games and simulations concerning
    203
  See also Banks and banking; Bonds;
    Capital investments; Credit
    unions; Mutual funds; Stock
    market
Schools, urban 49. See also Education
Science. See Technology
Sea. See Ocean resources
Security, national, games and simulations concerning 204
Security, personal 47, 81, 83, 86,
    112, 131, 142
Service occupations and industries 46,
    136, 142, 144
  public 50, 54, 58, 88, 89, 90, 91,
    183
  See also Urban areas, services to
Sheep raising 3
Shipping industry 113
Shopping. See Consumer economics
Sierra Club 70
Silver question. See Free silver movement
Skilled labor
  in economic development 115

Subject Index

loss of business in 57
population in 42
problems of 100
services to 50, 54, 58, 90, 91,
136, 138-39
taxation of 56, 57
transportation in 42, 46, 53, 54,
57, 58
See also City life; Ghettoes;
Government, municipal
Urbanization 177
in Africa 190
agriculture and 3
problems of 41
Urban renewal and planning 42, 46,
53, 57, 59, 71, 75, 101
games and simulations concerning
204-5

V

Vegetable industry. See Fruit and
vegetable growing
Vietnamese War
economic stability and 38
inflation and 55

W

Wage-price controls 43, 52, 56,
96, 101
Wages 10, 85, 133, 173, 183
of agricultural laborers 6
determination of 7-8
in tariff determination 117
Wall Street. See Stock market
War, commerce and 123. See also
names of wars
War industries, economics of 103
Warranties and guarantees 25, 34
fraud in 26, 29

Water 69
conservation of 71, 72, 75, 76
desalination of 69, 70
in economic development 115
shortages 50
See also Drought; Irrigation; Pol-
lution and pollution control
Water transportation 15, 114, 126.
See also Canals; Shipping
industry
Watson, Thomas J. 134
Watt, James 133
Wealth 62, 83, 84, 94, 112
games and simulations concerning
206
maintenance of in the U.S. 50
redistribution of 44
West (The), in American development
111, 114
Westinghouse, George 134
Wheat growing 5, 20
Whitney, Eli 133
Wholesale trade 20
Wildlife, conservation of 70, 71
Wilkinson, David 133
Women, employment of 48, 141
Wool. See Sheep raising
Work. See Labor
Working class
employment of 17
poverty among 57
Working conditions. See Conditions of
labor
World Bank. See International Bank
for Reconstruction and De-
velopment
World War II
economics of 111
unemployment after 58

Y

Youth, employment of 48